THE ROW TO RECOVERY

To my wife, Debs, the light of my life.
To Mum and Dad, thank you.

THE ROW TO RECOVERY

SAM PETERS

ROW2RECOVERY™
BEYOND INJURY, ACHIEVING THE EXTRAORDINARY

Published by Vision Sports Publishing in 2012

Vision Sports Publishing
19-23 High Street
Kingston upon Thames
Surrey
KT1 1LL

www.visionsp.co.uk

ISBN: 978-1-907637-82-7

Edited by: Jim Drewett
Copy editing: Justyn Barnes and Alex Morton
Design: Neal Cobourne

Cover photography: Brian Finke/Talisker Whisky Atlantic Challenge

Typeset by Palimpsest Book Production Limited, Falkirk, Stirlingshire
Printed and bound in the UK by TJ International, Padstow, Cornwall

A CIP Catalogue record for this book is available
from the British Library

CONTENTS

ACKNOWLEDGEMENTS

There are so many people to thank, not just for their help in delivering this book, but also for their help in delivering the wider Row2Recovery campaign. We have all been on an amazing journey and it is almost impossible to know where to begin.

Firstly, to all of you who have supported the charity by donating your time, money, professional expertise and contacts to this magnificent cause. We simply could not have done it without you.

To Ed and Alex for having the idea in the first place, to the rest of the crew who were willing to undertake such a daunting challenge while appreciating it was part of a wider cause.

Thank you to the charities who have bought into the vision, in particular Help for Heroes, ABF The Soldiers' Charity and The Soldiers, Seamen, Airmen and Families Association (SSAFA). Good luck with all your future work.

THE ROW TO RECOVERY

To all the sponsors, especially BP, News International and Talisker, as well as all those who provided clothing and equipment and support in kind. Companies such as Gill, Oakley, Salamanca, McKinney Rogers, PricewaterhouseCoopers to name just a few.

To the patrons and trustees of the charity, thank you for your calm guidance and the benefit of your experience. To all those who sat on the executive committee, thank you and well done. To all those who volunteered to help put on events such as the One Million Metre Row, the London dinner and the Hong Kong dinner, thank you.

A huge thank you of course to all the families, loved ones and friends of the crew who put aside their own concerns about the risks involved and wholeheartedly supported the venture. We couldn't have done it without you.

To my own newspaper, the *Mail on Sunday*, and my sports editor Malcolm Vallerius, a sincere thanks for your understanding while I've been working on this project and for seeing the bigger picture. I only hope I can repay you in the future.

Thank you to all the media who supported the cause from such an early stage, especially Caroline Froggatt and Geraint Vincent at ITN, Adam Lusher at the *Sunday Telegraph*, Patrick Kidd at *The Times* and Mike Hamilton at the *Sunday Mirror*.

To Jim, Toby, Henry, Alex and Justyn, and everyone at Vision Sports Publishing, thank you for 'getting it' straightaway. Your time and patience in guiding me through my first book is hugely appreciated. I think we have all learned a great deal from each other over the past few months.

To Steve King and his team at Blaze Concepts and to Tony Reid and the Marine Camera Solutions team, thank you.

To the race organisers and crew of Aurora, thanks for getting there in the end! Thank you Graham for your determination and expertise.

A special thank you to my old friend James Grant who got into this for all the right reasons and stayed involved through thick and thin. Who'd have thought a converted church in west London could have been the R2R hub?

ACKNOWLEDGEMENTS

To all those people who came out to welcome the crew into Port St Charles, especially the Barbados Council for the Disabled, thank you. To Virgin Atlantic who provided flights for the crew and some of their families, thank you.

To my own family and friends, thank you for all your words of encouragement and for putting up with my absence. I'm sure you coped!

To everyone at Selly Oak Hospital, Headley Court, surgeons, doctors and medical staff who support our wounded and help re-build their lives.

Lastly, but by no means least, thank you to all of our Armed Forces and their families for what they do every single day on our behalf.

FOREWORD BY
BARONESS TANNI
GREY-THOMPSON DBE

Some people are defined by their jobs, the letters behind their names, their popularity. The Row2Recovery guys can be defined by their courage, determination and motivation. They took on the most amazing challenge, and with the planning and organisation skills they had honed in their years of service, completed that challenge and confronted attitudes to disability at the same time.

These men have been in far tougher situations, whether in the field of battle or battling injury and disability in rehabilitation units, and often rehabilitation is a battle, with many injured servicemen facing years of rehabilitation of their bodies and minds, sometimes with only their families and loved ones to support them. Row2Recovery provides help for families in those circumstances and an outlet for their fears.

THE ROW TO RECOVERY

More than anything they have achieved, Row2Recovery have sent a powerful message that disability need not hold you back; disabled people can achieve the extraordinary.

Tanni Grey-Thompson DBE
October 2012

PROLOGUE

'What's that noise?'

'It's nothing, it's fine. Stop worrying. Bloody hell, you're always worrying.'

'No, there is definitely a noise. Shut up. Listen.'

The two men, both heavily bearded and emaciated, are huddled in the cramped, stuffy cabin of an ocean rowing boat in the middle of the Atlantic being tossed around like a cork on a lake, listening intently. Every few seconds huge waves crash down on the 29-foot-long boat and its six-man crew, only half of whom can fit into its two tiny cabins at one time.

After 42 days at sea, things look bleak. With two-thirds of the Atlantic crossing completed, any thoughts of winning the 2012 Talisker Whisky Atlantic Challenge vanished 16 days ago when their water desalinator, crucial for their survival at sea, packed up.

THE ROW TO RECOVERY

Unable to make drinking water from seawater, they have been forced to ration the emergency bottled water they have on board and eventually lay down a parachute anchor to stop the boat altogether and wait for the race organisers to resupply them.

After four days static on the ocean waves, continually pounded by the monstrous seas, the resupply vessel has finally arrived. But they need to wait until daylight as it's too rough to attempt to transfer 350 litres of bottled water in a rubber dinghy at night. The crew are down to drinking two litres of water a day despite the searing temperatures. They've been warned they face long-term kidney damage if they maintain this routine.

With the support boat close by, the crew dare to hope they are over the worst when skipper Ed Janvrin hears a bumping noise outside the cabin. It's coming from underneath the boat and it doesn't sound good.

Will Dixon looks at Ed and scratches nervously at the stump of what was once his left leg. Three years earlier, almost to the day, Will's life had changed forever when the vehicle he was travelling in drove across an Improvised Explosive Device (IED) while on patrol in the notorious Sangin district of Helmand Province in southern Afghanistan. The force of the resulting explosion shattered the young lieutenant's femur and both his heels. He underwent emergency surgery in Camp Bastion Field Hospital where surgeons removed his left leg below the knee.

Will phoned home when he came around from surgery. 'I've picked up a bit of an injury,' he told his mum, Jilly.

Ironically, considering his current predicament, among wounded soldiers his injury is known as a 'deck slap' and has become increasingly common in recent years as insurgents have seeded Afghanistan with their hellish inventions.

Will cried as he was flown off the battlefield. Not because of the searing pain that was tearing away at his leg, but at the thought of leaving his men behind to carry on the tour without him. In Will's own mind, if in no one else's, he had failed. He didn't want to fail again.

PROLOGUE

Even by the standards of Atlantic crossings, what the crew of this boat are trying to achieve is both exceptional and extraordinary. For the vast majority of human beings the challenge of rowing the Atlantic would be considered beyond them. But the members of this crew have all already faced – and conquered – even tougher tests of courage and mental and physical strength. This is not about personal goals or individual challenges, there is something bigger and more important at stake. This is the Row2Recovery, the attempt by six ex-soldiers, four of whom have suffered and overcome catastrophic injuries, to row the Atlantic and raise money and awareness for the plight of service personnel wounded in action in Iraq and Afghanistan. This is the Row2Recovery, which by now has captured the public imagination and has millions of ITV news viewers glued to their TV screens as the drama of the crossing unfolds day by day.

'Smash'. Another wave hits the side of the boat, and both Will and Ed are lifted from their prone positions before being deposited back with a thud.

'Whoooaaaahhh!' come the shouts from up on deck. 'That one was huge!'

Next to Will, Ed continues to press his ear to the side of the rear cabin. As captain of the boat and the man largely responsible for dreaming up a task many believed was impossible, Ed is a man on a mission.

'Listen,' he repeats to Will. 'I can definitely hear something. I'm not making this up.'

They wait for the roar of the waves to gradually subside, before it inevitably gathers again, and listen intently for any sign of the abnormal.

Thud.

'There it is again,' says Ed.

Thud.

'And again'.

Ed stares at Will, the skin on his weather-beaten face stretched taught across his cheekbones through a combination of stress and dehydration, and attempts a frown.

'That's wrong. I don't like the sound of that one little bit. It's the fucking rudder.'

There are several pieces of 'mission critical' kit on board and, along with the water desalinator, the rudder is one of them. No rudder would mean no steering. No steering would mean the boat, and the six men on board, would have no hope of completing the crossing. They'd be left at the mercy of the seas and forced to finally admit defeat, or worse, as capsize would almost certainly follow as they floundered in the massive mid-Atlantic swell.

'No I'm sure it's not,' replies Will, more in hope than expectation. Prior experience has taught him to fear the worst on this trip, just as it had when he led his men on patrol in Afghanistan. He's been trained to identify the absence of normality. His mind is telling him there's a problem, but his heart is refusing to accept it.

Enormous waves continue to pound relentlessly over the side of their little boat. The parachute anchor, or 'para anchor' as it is known, has been holding the vessel in position 500 nautical miles east of the Caribbean for the past four days, and is straining at the end of the 40-metre rope attaching it to the front of the boat. It feels as if the full force of the Atlantic Ocean is trying to bully the little boat into submission.

So near and yet so far. They've already rowed almost 2,100 nautical miles – around 2,400 land miles – across the Atlantic. Ever since the desalinator broke they've reduced their personal water intake to potentially dangerous levels in an effort to ensure they can complete the crossing without having to be assisted by a nearby commercial vessel (which would pose a huge risk of them being sunk).

They've been monitoring their urine output all that time, conscious that the two litres of water they've been consuming each day is well below what is considered safe in the relentlessly hot conditions. Their urine has taken on an unhealthy brown hue.

Condensation drips off the roof of the rear cabin and onto Ed and Will's exposed backs and legs, tanned bronze but covered in painful salt rashes. They've become used to their skin sticking uncomfortably to the flattened plastic matting that has acted as bedding for this interminable crossing. They chose to accept this mission, but more than once they've questioned their own sanity for doing so. Both men have cuts and grazes all over their heads and bodies – as do all the crew – an inevitable consequence of life aboard a 29-foot by six-foot rowing boat attempting to cross the Atlantic.

Technical problems have dogged the team's attempt to row the 2,560 nautical miles across the Atlantic Ocean from day one of their voyage. They have all learned that if they think something is broken, then it almost certainly is. Automatic steering systems, foot plates, rowing seats, bilge pumps and of course the desalinator have all failed at various points, leaving the crew in a near-permanent state of 'constructive paranoia' as their dream of reaching Barbados grows seemingly ever more distant. Now, it seems, it's the rudder's turn.

One of the few things that hasn't broken on board – apart from the men themselves – has been the communication and camera equipment, installed at a hefty cost before departure, which has proved essential in recording the crossing and feeding that content back for a support team in London to distribute to the world's media. At least this means that they can keep the media and an increasingly concerned public back home informed of their struggle on the high seas.

'What's going on down there?' comes a voice from above deck. 'What are you two ladies getting your knickers in a twist for?' A tanned, salt-flecked face appears at the cabin's hatch.

It's Alex Mackenzie, an outwardly jovial but highly driven former Parachute Regiment captain from the west coast of Scotland who had been awarded a Mention in Despatches for saving the lives of his comrades, and two *Sunday Times* journalists, in a vicious Taliban ambush in Helmand Province five years earlier.

Alex is in charge of communications with the outside world. Just like Ed, he suffered no outward physical injuries as the result of his tour. He often wonders how that was possible, such was the ferocity of some of the fighting he experienced. But just like so many soldiers who have returned from the front line outwardly unscathed over the centuries, both men wear their scars on the inside as they struggle to come to terms with the slower pace of civilian life and the lack of direction it provides. Both men often yearn for a return to the heightened sensory state they've only ever experienced in combat. 'It's where you feel most alive,' Ed once said. 'It's strangely addictive.'

'Ed reckons the rudder's broken,' Will shouts, trying to make his voice heard above the crashing din of the 25-foot-high waves that continue to batter the creaking boat.

'No chance. There's nothing left on board to break!' Alex says, trying to lighten the mood.

As he utters the word 'break', there's another almighty thump, followed immediately by a crack, as the rudder, so essential to their hopes of plotting a safe route to their destination at Port St Charles on Barbados's sheltered west coast, finally gives way. There is a collective groan inside the cabin.

'Fuck,' says Ed.

The skipper puts his head hesitantly out of the aft hatch and, just before another wave hits him squarely in the face, he's able to see the damage that has been inflicted as a result of the pounding the ocean has given the boat. The top part of the boat's steering mechanism has completely snapped in two, while an ominous looking crack has appeared straight down the middle of rudder itself.

Will's heart sinks as his skipper turns around and confirms the news he feared. The rudder is broken, and so too seemingly are the crew's hopes of completing the crossing.

They have come so far, achieved so much, but here and now they have to confront the reality that their dream is almost certainly over.

Will feels physically sick. Not from the constant rolling of the ocean but from the growing sense that he is about to suffer another terminal mission failure. The idea of returning home to be

PROLOGUE

greeted with pats on the back and well-intentioned words of commiseration on another plucky failure does not bear thinking about. For much of the crossing he's repeated the phrase, 'Morale is high'. Right now, it isn't. A gloom descends over the boat.

Squeezed into the forward cabin, or the 'Barbados Suite' as it has been tagged, lies Rory Mackenzie. A strapping South African-born former company medic, Rory's right leg was blown off when a massive IED sliced through his Warrior armoured vehicle while on patrol in the Iraqi city of Basra in 2007. The power of the blast killed the young soldier who'd been sleeping in Rory's usual seat opposite him.

Rory spent months battling chronic infections and searing pain in the small stump he'd been left with that made using a prosthetic limb more difficult for him than for most. The pain eventually gave way to anger, resentment and frustration. Gradually, as the anger subsided, Rory discovered that participating in extreme sports was the only effective form of rehabilitation, not just for his physical wounds, but also his psychological ones.

For now, all he can think of is getting to Barbados and seeing his girlfriend, Lara. Early in the crossing it appeared he would be confined to the role of passenger as small pieces of shrapnel, residual from the blast that had taken his leg, worked their way to the surface of his stump, causing angry welts to form beneath the surface of his skin. Initially he put the pain down to the lack of 'padding' afforded by what was left of his buttock – much of the tissue and muscle had been torn or burned away in the blast, leaving the bone uncomfortably close to the skin. The pain had been enough to stop him rowing.

In agony barely three weeks before, he had spent much of Christmas Day bent over double with a mirror thrust underneath what was left of his buttock extracting particles of copper shrapnel from his backside. After weeks of pain, he'd finally decided the only way to avoid becoming a passenger was to extract the foreign objects, unwanted internal reminders of the blast that had maimed him forever. High as a kite on a combination of painkillers and armed with a grotesque-looking pair of arterial forceps, Rory had dug the offending items out from beneath his skin and resumed his position as a fully functioning member of the crew.

Up on deck, Alex sits with the other two crew members, Carl Anstey and Neil Heritage, contemplating their predicament. They are all soaked to the skin as they have been for most of the previous 42 days – they soon established the most comfortable way to row and reduce the chafing caused by the salty seawater was to do so naked – and spirits on board have never been lower. All three know the potential impact a broken rudder could have on their mission.

Neil, the first double amputee ever to attempt the crossing, lost both his legs above the knee when a suicide bomber blew himself up next to him and his friend and colleague, Mick Brennan, as they were loading equipment into the back of their bomb disposal vehicle in Fallujah, Iraq, in 2005. He had argued most vociferously against going on the para anchor and is unsurprised by the damage that has been caused to the boat's infrastructure as a result of the constant pounding from the sea.

Neil's lack of legs has made it extremely difficult for him to move around the boat, leaving him confined to the space in and around his cabin and rowing position for the majority of the crossing. He's suffered from seasickness for the entire crossing but has not let on to his crew mates about this. Complaining isn't Neil's style.

He's also coped the best with the chronic lack of water, even managing to save a little at the end of each shift to put back into a communal container.

Carl Anstey, who was severely wounded when a Rocket Propelled Grenade (RPG) launcher misfired near Musa Qala in Afghanistan in 2009, remains grimly determined. The former sniper is as mentally strong as anyone on board, his slight frame and baby face belying the fierce warrior spirit and teak toughness that lies beneath.

He retains faith. The tight-knit crew have already achieved so much, surely they can overcome one more hurdle before rowing triumphantly to Barbados. Carl figures that if he keeps telling himself that then perhaps it will prove true.

Ed reappears at the cabin door and pokes his head out. Outwardly he seems calm, but inside he's on edge, his mind racing, desperately seeking solutions at every turn.

He's commanded men in some of the most inhospitable and dangerous places on earth, leading soldiers into battle when every sinew of his body was warning him of the danger they faced. He's taken over the running of Sangin district centre, perhaps the deadliest town on earth, and mentored a battalion of the Afghan National Army in one of the most testing environments known to man.

But completing this mission means as much to Ed as completing those missions he'd been set in Afghanistan and Iraq. This is about proving what is possible, going beyond injury, inspiring a generation of young men who have been maimed and wounded, both mentally and physically, by the horrors of war. This is about showing the families of severely wounded servicemen and women that their battle-damaged sons and daughters have a future they can all look forward to and be proud of. On a personal level, for Ed and Alex, it is also about reclaiming the responsibility and sense of purpose they've both yearned for in the intervening years since they'd both left the Army.

At home in the UK, the crew's anxious families, many of them also traumatised by the experiences their loved ones, wounded or not, have been through in recent years, wait for news. Initially, many of them had resisted this latest venture into the unknown, resenting being put through yet another ordeal. Over time that resistance has turned into fervent support. Right now, the only emotion is worry.

'We've got a serious problem here,' Ed tells his friends. 'I think this could be terminal.'

As the rudder flaps loosely, pathetically, at the side of the boat, the entire Row2Recovery campaign is on the verge of being sunk.

CHAPTER 1:
THE IDEA

'Hurry up you slacker,' Alex called back to Ed, his lungs burning as the two cyclists egged each other on their way to the top of Box Hill in Surrey.

The showers had passed and it was a glorious April spring day. Both men's sweat-drenched T-shirts were speckled with mud as they forced their way up the track on a tough climb normally only undertaken by the keenest of cyclists.

The two men, both in their early thirties, have been close friends since Sandhurst Military Academy, where they were trained to lead men into war against the backdrop of the 9/11 terrorist atrocities, which occurred three days after their course started. They hadn't realised at the time they were summoned off the drill square and into the classroom by the Company Sergeant Major to watch the horrifying events in New York unfold on television, but that moment, just as it would for hundreds of thousands of others around the world, was to trigger off a chain of events that would define their futures.

Nine years later the two men had left the Army, both veterans of tours to Iraq and more recently Afghanistan. Both men had witnessed scenes that few civilians in the western world will, thank God, ever witness. Both men had lost friends and both men had seen combat at its rawest. Both men had changed forever.

That morning their cycle ride had started as normal. They'd begun at a gentle pace after leaving Ed's house in Surbiton, that most unremarkable of leafy south-west London suburbs, en route to the South Downs. Both of them were feeling the effects of one too many beers the night before, but they were in high spirits as they slowly worked up a sweat on their way through the Surrey countryside. Their route, coincidentally, took them past a turn-off signposted 'DMRC Headley Court' on the outskirts of Leatherhead. The pair nodded solemnly to one another as they passed the turning. The Defence Medical Rehabilitation Centre at Headley Court was a place they knew something of – their friend and fellow Sandhurst graduate, Tony Harris, was an in-patient there – but it retained a certain mystical quality for those servicemen and women who had been fortunate enough to escape serious injury in the line of active service. It was a place they would come to understand far better over the course of the next two years.

The sedate pace of the ride inevitably quickened. It was always going to. The competitive juices still coursed through Alex and Ed's veins. Even a Sunday morning cycle had to have an element of competition. They'd both achieved so much in their military careers, where they'd thrived on the adrenaline that had flooded their systems every time they had led their men into battle. Both men, if they were honest, missed the buzz. They missed leading men. Whereas once they wore military fatigues and carried SA80 assault rifles, now their day jobs saw them wearing suits and carrying laptops. Once they lived on the edge, now their days were dominated by emails, iPhone diaries and back-to-back meetings.

Their story is as old as mankind: for as long as young men have been sent to fight wars they have returned forever altered in mind, body or both. If they are lucky enough to return at all. Ed and Alex were just two more survivors, trying to make sense of what they'd been through and what lay ahead. Both shared a burning desire to achieve, to succeed, to contribute. Both shared a common belief in service and both were fit as butchers' dogs.

As Alex pushed hard on the pedals, the familiar lactic acid burn built in his thighs. Over years spent pushing his body to its limit, he'd learned to enjoy the pain. Ed, his cheeks flushed with exertion and his lungs craving oxygen, worked hard to keep pace with his old mate as they careered along the same roads that would thwart Great Britain's cyclists Bradley Wiggins and Mark Cavendish in their quest for Olympic team gold two years later.

As they approached the top of Box Hill for a second time, Alex could sense his friend closing behind him.

'Fuck you, Ed. You're not beating me this time,' he grinned as his doggedly determined mate cranked through the gears of his Italian racing bike.

'I fucking am,' Ed shouted back.

The pair raced over the brow of the hill, Ed gaining with every push before they both skidded simultaneously to a halt at the top, just in front of a metal cattle gate.

They gasped for breath, bent double over their handlebars desperately trying to force oxygen back into their lungs.

'Prick,' Alex muttered.

'Dickhead,' Ed replied.

'You always have to turn it into a competition don't you?' Ed said with a knowing smile.

'Me?' Alex responded incredulously.

'Yes, you. You always turn it into a race.'

Alex didn't dignify him with a response. The fact was they were as competitive and determined as each other. If a race could be had, they would have it. If a fight was offered, they'd accept. If a challenge was laid down, they couldn't resist.

'I'm going to row the Atlantic,' Ed said out of the blue.

Silence.

'Shut up.'

'No really, I am.'

Alex knew straightaway Ed was serious. Over the past few years his friend had completed an Ironman (two-mile swim, 112-mile cycle, 26.2-mile run), run the Marathon des Sables (seven full marathons in seven days across the Sahara Desert) and completed the notoriously gruelling Gurkha 'doko' induction race in Nepal, which involves running three miles up a near vertical slope carrying a basket filled with 35 kilos of rocks.

But rowing the Atlantic?

'I want in,' Alex said, deadly serious. He hadn't had time to consider the implications but he knew he had to be part of it. A keen endurance athlete himself, he missed the adventure and the sense of stepping into the unknown that a career in the Parachute Regiment had provided him on a near day-to-day basis. He was always on the lookout for adrenaline extremes. Not recklessly, but he craved them in the same way his lungs had craved oxygen moments earlier.

'Sorry mate,' Ed replied. 'I've already got a partner.'

Alex was visibly crestfallen.

'Oh, right.'

Two weeks before Ed had seen an advert for a transatlantic rowing race while flicking through a magazine. 'More people have been into space than have rowed an ocean. More people have climbed Everest than rowed an ocean. Do you have what it takes?'

It hadn't taken Ed long – seconds in fact – to answer the question in his mind. He had immediately bought Ben Fogle and James Cracknell's book *The Crossing* and read about the celebrity rowers' attempt to cross the Atlantic in 2006. His next big challenge, apart from telling his wife Helen, was to find someone else to go with him. His initial approach had been to another

THE IDEA

friend, Rhodri Darch. He'd arranged to meet with Rhodri, another ex-Army connection, a couple of days later and, six pints of beer into a night out, he had popped the question.

'Mate, I'm going to row the Atlantic, do you want to join me?'
'Er, maybe. When?'
'Next year, around Christmas. It'll take about 50 days.'
'Jesus, 50 days over Christmas. Really? Well, I suppose. Okay.'

At the time Ed suspected it was the beer talking, but held on to Rhodri's 'okay' a little too readily. After all, a deal was a deal. But deep down he knew Rhodri's heart, and more importantly his mind, wasn't really in it. He'd tried to initiate a couple of planning meetings, but they'd never got off the ground, so when Alex showed such an appetite to take the row on, Ed saw his opportunity to go back to Rhodri and offer him a way out.

Initially Ed's decision to take on the Atlantic challenge had been born out of the need to challenge himself. But as he and Alex began to plan their great adventure, inspired by the story of their friend at Headley Court, Tony Harris, the idea of using the row for a far greater purpose began to gain momentum.

Tony had been part of the same September 2001 Sandhurst intake as Alex and Ed. A larger-than-life personality who loved nothing more than a beer and a smoke at the end of a tough day, the trio had immediately hit it off as they forged their fledgling careers as infantry officers.

In so many ways Tony's story is typical. A fit, strong, confident, affable young man who had enjoyed a successful military career with the Royal Regiment of Fusiliers before his life, and that of his family, was turned upside down when his vehicle drove over a roadside bomb while on patrol on the outskirts of Sangin in Afghanistan in May 2009.

The devastating impact of the blast shattered both of Tony's heels and forced his elbow bone through the skin of his arm. After surgery in Helmand's Camp Bastion Hospital, he was flown to Birmingham's Selly Oak Hospital, where a metal plate was inserted into his left heel. From there he was moved to Headley Court. The relief of not losing his legs soon turned into a long and painful battle to save his left foot from amputation.

But infections, the scourge of all IED survivors, constantly plagued him. One day, two months after being injured, his foot, in his words, 'literally exploded' because of the build-up of pus caused by bacteria.

Tony underwent 20 operations all told, involving skin, tissue and muscle grafts, but they all failed. Surgeons even resorted to applying leeches to his foot in an effort to rid him of infection.

Tony's story hit close to home for Alex and Ed. The three men had remained firm friends, despite joining different regiments after Sandhurst, writing to each other whenever possible and always seeking each other out for a night 'on the lash' when they found themselves in London on leave.

Tony's injury, and the journey he'd been on with his wife, Elizabeth, and their children, Felix and Emily, very quickly moved to the forefront of Alex and Ed's minds once they'd agreed to do the row.

Ed: *Tony's situation was a big motivator for us. I'd been to visit him a few times and was frustrated I couldn't do more for him. He was just one soldier, but he represented a struggle that literally hundreds of young men and women were going through at that very moment.*

I remember sitting in my office at work one day thinking, 'There's probably a bloke, right now, in the dust, wondering if he's still got a leg'. I couldn't get that thought out of my head. I missed the lads and I missed being part of something really significant. I missed the passion I had for soldiering.

I wanted to do something to help. I'd developed a real hunger for endurance sports. They were highly addictive. I enjoyed the challenge of setting myself a task that seemed implausible but working a way through to achieve it. I'd completed an Ironman the year before but hadn't raised any money. I wanted this to be different. I saw it as a real opportunity to fundraise, to do something for good and put something back into society. I thought it would be great to raise a few thousand pounds.

It is a fact that survival rates among wounded soldiers are getting better all the time. A survey by the Royal College of Surgeons found that during the Second World War wounded soldiers had between a one in two and one in three chance of dying. Today that figure is closer to one in 10.

Ed: *The sheer number of soldiers surviving catastrophic injuries, which would have seen them die in previous conflicts, is both reassuring but also concerning. On the one hand medical advances and immediate casualty care have improved so much, meaning guys are surviving longer, with worse injuries. But the net result of that is that many more severely wounded men and women will need care for many, many years to come. They have earned the right to be treated with dignity and respect and it seemed obvious to Alex and I that we should raise money to support them and their families.*

After he was injured I went to visit Tony at Selly Oak and Headley Court and tried to keep in touch. I tried to be around. I didn't do half as much as I wanted to do. I wanted to help Liz with the kids and help around the house and stuff. But she seemed to have quite good support from her family.

They had to decide whether to take Tony's leg off, finally made their minds up to do it, and it turned out to be a great decision. It's given them their life back because it was hell for a year. Just little things like not being able to go on holiday or look forward to things. They couldn't plan because everything revolved around this piece of meat that was dying and wouldn't get better, just infected. He was constantly in hospital and it was really depressing stuff. It put a lot of pressure on their relationship.

There were some really sad moments seeing him in hospital when he was just a broken man, very pale, in his wheelchair. There were glimpses of the old Tony and I remember seeing him cutting about in his chair getting cigarettes and stuff. But he was definitely not his old self. Getting rid of that leg has given him a new lease of life.

What Liz and the kids had to go through really struck me. I knew from my tour that the families took a beating but I wasn't back in the UK when these things happened. Now it was much more vivid. I was seeing it for real. The families are so often the forgotten ones in all this but in many ways they are in a tougher position than the guys going on tour. We have our jobs to do and we crack on. The families can't control anything. They just have to sit and wait. When they do receive news that their loved one has been killed or seriously wounded so often the burden of responsibility falls on them. They become the primary carers. Often, they are left to pick up the pieces.

Tony's experience was critical to Ed and Alex's decision to turn their Atlantic row into a fundraising campaign. The would-be transatlantic rowers realised they needed a focus, and what better motivation than the knowledge that so much needed doing to help their stricken comrades and their families? The seeds of the Row2Recovery had been sown.

On the practical front, the first thing the pair did was plough £26,000 of their own money into buying a second-hand, two-man ocean-going rowing boat. Then they began to plan their mission with military precision. Hours and hours were spent poring over plans and detailing a mission statement and an overall strategy document as well as pooling any contacts they could potentially bring in to help with the administrative, financial, marketing, PR, sponsorship and fundraising sides of things.

Alex: *We sat down in my new flat on a plastic chair and a wooden box and had a long debate about what the mission for the campaign should be. What were we looking to achieve? The mission discussion alone probably went on for two or three weeks and it was agreed that the fundamental underlying principle of what we were going to do was that we wanted to raise a significant amount of money for the wounded and their families.*

THE IDEA

That's about the only thing that has never changed throughout the Row2Recovery campaign. We knew what we wanted to do, we just had no idea how we were going to do it.

Ed: *We very quickly decided we wanted to do it for a cause and that there was only one cause we believed in more strongly than every single other thing out there. We had to do it for the wounded and their families. Therefore when we asked ourselves, 'What is our mission?' it was no longer to cross the Atlantic. Our mission was to support the cause.*

The two friends were brutally honest with each other and several times their discussions led to blazing rows over the direction each thought the mission should take. It was testament to the enduring strength of their friendship that those arguments were always quickly forgotten and never taken personally.

Ed: *It was great to feel passionate about something again. Neither of us had felt that for a while.*

Through their network of military, business and family contacts, the pair began to work on the finer details of their plan. They secured a meeting with Jamie Lowther-Pinkerton, Prince Harry's private secretary and an advisor to the 'Walking with the Wounded' campaign, which went on to see four wounded soldiers successfully trek 200 miles to the North Pole in early 2011. It was another pivotal moment.

Alex: *Jamie asked us if we'd thought about getting wounded guys on board. I asked if he was talking about having them in a separate boat or whether he meant one guy coming with each of us. He said, 'No, just get a bigger boat'. I thought, 'Shit, we've just paid the best part of £26,000 for the other one'. But pretty rapidly I realised the idea could transform the entire campaign.*
At the time we didn't actually know many wounded guys apart

from Tony. We asked Tony straight out if he wanted to come with us and his response was, `That's a shit idea, no'. That's Tony, he's pretty straightforward and sensible.

But Tony's lack of enthusiasm for taking an active part in the row didn't diminish Alex and Ed's determination to put together a crew of wounded servicemen to join them in their attempt to cross the Atlantic. They had no idea what the appetite would be within the wounded community for such a monumental challenge, but they were intent on finding out.

Tony remained a key part of the Row2Recovery campaign, and was able to provide valuable links into the wounded community.

Ed: *So much happened in those initial few months of getting the campaign up and running. We formed a charity and started approaching sponsors, and we received some very good advice from senior people that not only should we seriously think about doing it with wounded soldiers but we should set ourselves a £1 million fundraising target.*

We also began to look at the possibility of getting a US crew of wounded servicemen involved to go head to head with. These were all big ideas that came from us going out and consulting widely. That was another great lesson because it's amazing how powerful it can be to have an external voice of reason. Someone saying, 'Half a million quid . . . no, go for a million'. It gave us confidence in what we were doing.

The sheer scale of what they were trying to achieve led some people they encountered to be sceptical. Many people make bold statements, but far fewer actually deliver on them.

Ed: *When it came to fundraising there was a bit of scepticism about the £1 million target. Certainly when we met with some of the charities there was a bit of doubt as to how serious we were. For Alex and I that only reinforced our determination. A couple of times I came* *off the phone or walked out of a meeting absolutely fuming. We were given short shrift several times, some of the experts seemed to belittle our goals rather than encourage our ambition, but it only served to re-energise and motivate us more.*

The pair started to explore which charities they should support, and met with Bryn Parry, the founder of Help for Heroes, as well as representatives from ABF The Soldiers' Charity and the Soldier's Seamen, Airmen and Families Association Forces Help (often referred to simply as 'SSAFA'). They decided to split any money raised between those three charities, leaving it up to them how they dispersed the funds.

Thanks mainly to their relentless determination, the two founders began to see the charity take shape. Alex helped put together a PR and media team led by an old friend from university, Sam Peters, who had forged a career as a sports journalist, while Ed led the fundraising effort in tandem with another trusted friend, ex-Gurkha captain Tom Rose, and his wife-to-be, Diana. Between the team, they also settled on a name for the campaign: 'Row2Recovery'.

Alex: *Ed and I would joke about it, but at the beginning of the campaign we were briefing people like the Chief of the Defence staff, General Sir David Richards. If someone had told me when I was in the Army that I would be briefing General Richards I would have thought, 'Shit!' But now Ed and I just thought, 'Cool'. We didn't think it was a nightmare. Chief executive of BP? Cool. Managing director of News International? No bother.*

We had a jokey saying, 'We only speak to Prime Ministers and Generals' and it seemed to work. We got to decision-makers within big organisations and if they said 'no' to begin with we made bloody sure we kept banging down their door until they said 'yes'.

Thanks to the efforts of its co-founders, the Row2Recovery campaign soon found support from within the current and ex-military communities. General Sir David Richards agreed to throw his support behind the campaign by agreeing to be a patron, as did General Sir Rob Fry, former head of the Royal Marines, former chief executive of Rolls-Royce, Sir John Rose, and Ed's dad, Lord Robin Janvrin, who as a former private secretary to the Queen was ideally placed to raise awareness in the corridors of power.

A group of highly respected current and former businessmen formed the Trustees board to oversee the prudent management of funds, while an executive board was formed to deliver on the day-to-day running of the charity.

While Alex and Ed had initially focused heavily on fundraising through their own military and corporate connections, they were soon to realise the extraordinary depth of support the cause had among the wider British public. As soon as they began to ask around for help, the volunteer support flooded in. An initial supporter meeting in central London in November 2010 saw Ed and Alex present to more than 30 business professionals all eager to support in some way. Almost all of them went on to play significant roles in the development of the charity.

Alex: *We knew there was a groundswell of support for the cause of wounded soldiers, but it was only when we started to speak to people outside the military that we really began to understand just how powerful that was. At various stages we had up to 60 volunteers working tirelessly on our behalf.*

Crucially, two heavyweight sponsors were found in the guise of BP and News International, who both agreed to part with significant five-figure sums in return for branding on the boat and on the website, which was designed by creative agency Jobe London, before being handed over to former Royal Marine Steve King.

Steve had been critically injured in southern Afghanistan in 2007 when he was shot five times on his way back from a patrol deep in enemy territory. Two rounds entered his left upper thigh, shattering his femur, three rounds entered the right side of his abdomen and he suffered broken ribs, a lacerated liver and a severed radial nerve. Surgeons were unable to extract one round, which remains in situ to this day adjacent to Steve's spine. 'I'll keep that one,' he had joked at the time.

Steve spent several years rehabilitating from his injuries and was helped enormously by the time he spent in Headley Court. He was eventually medically discharged from the Royal Marines in 2008. Within six months of being discharged, he had set up Blaze Concepts, a Somerset based web-design company. Steve didn't hesitate for a second in offering his services to Row2Recovery free of charge 'for as long as it takes'. It was a fantastic gesture from a man who perfectly symbolised the message the charity was trying to put across: That no matter how badly wounded you may be, your future can still be bright. Just as importantly, he became a critical member of the team.

Ed: *Having Steve play such an integral role in the team fitted perfectly with the charity. Yes, he was wounded, but was he in anyway less capable than anyone else in his field of expertise? Far from it. In many ways he was, and is, more able.*

With the infrastructure of the charity in place, Ed and Alex were in a position to begin recruiting the crew. The initial idea was to find two wounded crew members to partner them so they asked several service charities to send invitations out to their training day via their databases. Posters were put up at Headley Court and Selly Oak Hospital inviting would-be applicants to get in touch. The pair also set to work speaking to friends and contacts within the military in an effort to spread the word as widely as possible.

The team also spent time producing some promotional and marketing material, including a slick video produced by a friend, James Levelle, which they subsequently posted on YouTube. The central question of the two-minute film was, 'If you've survived a war, can you survive an Atlantic crossing?'

THE ROW TO RECOVERY

Alex: *We had Tony putting posters up at Headley Court and he put messages out through service charities like Band of Brothers and Battle Back and we asked Help for Heroes to do the same. We asked the charities we were supporting to help us and word of mouth started to take effect.*

Ed: *We pushed the word out and then collected all the replies and started recruiting. But the nature of the event and the fact it was going to take so long, with so much preparation time, meant there were actually very few wounded lads who got in touch. The initial response was actually a little disheartening. Maybe 12 guys replied in total.*

One of the names that immediately leapt off the list of applicants was that of Neil Heritage, a double amputee who had become something of a poster boy for the Help for Heroes charity since its foundation in 2007. As the first British soldier of modern times to survive a double traumatic amputation on the battlefield, along with his friend, Mick, who also lost both his legs in the same blast, Neil had paved the way for countless more double amputees injured after him. By 2011 there was a far greater likelihood of surviving that injury, but at the time Neil and Mick's prognosis had been bleak.

As enemy tactics in Iraq and Afghanistan evolved over time and moved towards toward counter-insurgency 'guerrilla' warfare, more reliant on IEDs and suicide bombers than traditional infantry tactics, more and more British soldiers had begun returning home with multiple amputations, severe brain trauma and other complicated blast injuries. Advancements in battlefield medical care also ensured that more young men and women were living with injuries that had previously been considered 'unsurvivable'.

At the time of Neil's injury, three years into the so-called 'War on Terror', there was very little formal infrastructure in place for wounded service personnel and their families in terms of compensation, while the provision of prosthetic legs was chaotic and desperately underfunded. Neil and his family suffered, usually in silence, as a result.

Men like Paralympic athlete Oscar Pistorius have brought double-amputee athletes into the public consciousness, while the Paralympic movement has provided opportunities which were never previously there. In 2004, when his body was torn apart by the impact of a suicide bomber detonating a massive bomb just metres from him, there were few role models for Neil to look up to. His refusal to accept a life in a wheelchair forced the medical profession to realise that double above-knee amputees were capable of achieving so much more than that had previously been believed.

By 2010, Neil had, through sheer bloody-minded determination and quiet, understated courage, unwittingly built up a reputation within the wounded community as a trailblazer, constantly proving experts wrong by achieving extraordinary mobility despite his loss of limbs, and giving hope to his fellow survivors.

Truly, Neil Heritage was ahead of his time.

'Imagine what a story it would be if we could get Neil to row as part of our crew,' Alex said to Ed when he had first seen his name. 'Can you imagine that? A double amputee rowing the Atlantic Ocean. Imagine how powerful that would be.'

My Story:
Neil Heritage

Age: 32
Regiment: Royal Signals (11 EOD Regiment)
Army career span: 1997–2008
Rank: Corporal
Combat experience: Bosnia 1999, Northern Ireland twice 2002 and 2003, Iraq twice Jan–Jul 2004 and Oct–Nov 2004
Injury: Double bilateral above knee amputee

I lost my legs in Iraq on 7th November, 2004. We were clearing the road that led into Fallujah, making sure there were no IEDS and disposing of any we found. The Black Watch guys we were working alongside had blocked the road so there were no vehicles moving around us while we worked. After the clearance had been completed, we started to pack away our equipment. Me and my colleague, Mick, were stood at the back entrance of a Warrior armoured vehicle packing our stuff away. I was so focused on the job in hand that I didn't even notice the road had been reopened. I didn't see the suicide bomber coming. He drove straight up to where we were standing and detonated. There was about a quarter of a ton of high explosives in the bomb – artillery shells and things like that. Warriors weigh about 28 tonnes and it threw it off its axle. It was a massive explosion.

I was conscious for around half an hour afterwards. I'd been thrown into the back of the Warrior by the force of the blast and Mick had been thrown in the other direction. I was on fire and frantically looking around for my rifle because a firefight was going on outside as some of the Black Watch lads engaged another suspect vehicle.

I tried to jump out of the back door, not realising my legs had already gone, and landed hard on the dusty ground. That was the moment people ran over to me, put the fire out and started treating me.

It wasn't obvious to me what had happened so I asked one of the guys who told me it was a suicide bomber. I remember looking at what was left of my legs and thinking, 'I'm fucking dead here'. I knew it wasn't going to be long until I was gone.

The guys driving the Warriors transporting me and Mick saved us big time. They carried out well-advanced first aid and had lines into us straightaway pumping fluids in and keeping our blood pressure up. They got tourniquets on in no time.

Everyone was doing their best but having the Black Watch doctor on the ground massively turned things around. He must have been there within five or six minutes and having that level of skill so immediately available undoubtedly made the difference.

I could hear Mick. I didn't know what his injuries were, but he was shouting and really out of control. The Warrior door had shielded us but there was about two feet of clearance between the foot of the door and the ground and we'd both lost our legs. Mick suffered a severe brain injury as well when he was flung away from the explosion. The armoured door saved our lives, unquestionably. With a blast that size, if we hadn't been stood behind it there would have been absolutely nothing left of us. I don't think there was anything left of my legs.

I remember quite clearly talking to my friend Si De Gruchy and these lads injecting morphine into me. I remember everything from that half hour. Si kept telling me I was fine. 'You're going to hospital and Mick's going as well, you'll see him in hospital'. He was trying to play it down but I knew it was serious.

People say I was really calm. I guess I was terrified. But I don't remember being in pain, I was in total shock.

My Story: **Neil Heritage**

An American helicopter came, kitted out like a hospital inside, and I was flown straight into Baghdad. I was touch and go for the first day or so. Then, in the middle of the night, not even 24 hours after being injured, I was flown to an American hospital in Germany.

Ian Heritage (Neil's dad): *It was around lunchtime and I was getting ready for work when the doorbell rang. There were two people there. One elderly gentleman around 60 and a woman aged around 40. They insisted on speaking to me. They wouldn't even tell me where they were from.*

I said, 'What do you want?'
'We're from the Army.'
I immediately thought, 'He's dead'.
They wouldn't say anything until they'd got into the house. Walking down the passage the gentleman said, 'He's alive but he's seriously wounded'.

Slowly they told us what had happened.
I asked them what the injuries were and was told it was a 'lower trauma'. I didn't know what they meant.
The man said, 'He's lost his legs'.

You go into shock then. Everything goes numb. I don't even remember what he said to me after that.
We were told: 'We'll get you to Germany but don't be surprised if he doesn't make it.' The pressure was right on to get to Neil in Germany as fast as possible. We flew out from Heathrow on the Monday evening.

We were put on a plane to Frankfurt. An Army officer who wasn't in uniform picked us up and drove us to the hospital. For the entire journey we didn't know if he was alive or not. I think if he'd died they'd have told us but . . . .
We were taken to an intensive care room and saw Neil and his mate, Mick, with pretty much the same injuries. When I first saw that he was alive I just broke down. I couldn't stop crying. I don't know if it was relief or what. It was upsetting. On the one hand I was glad to

have him but there was part of me thinking, 'What sort of life is he going to have?'

Neil could hear us, he knew we were there, but he could only respond by squeezing your hand. We met Mick's family who'd been flown out from the Darlington area. Mick's dad was a miner. We were together, just trying to get through each day.

Eventually after three days they decided they were fit enough to fly home so the RAF came out and flew him and Mick and another badly wounded Scottish soldier back. We all flew back to Birmingham in an RAF jet set up for intensive care.

There were three ambulances waiting for them and we had a police escort through Birmingham to Selly Oak Hospital and he went straight into intensive care. They really got on with it there and started cleaning him up. He hadn't been shaved or washed, but within two or three hours of him getting to Selly Oak he was still unconscious, but he actually looked a lot better.

Claire Heritage (Neil's ex-wife): When I first saw Neil I felt numb. I wanted to give him a kiss and hold his hand because I thought it would be the last time I saw him. Even then they didn't know if he would survive. He had a really bad infection and even though they were pumping him full of antibiotics it just wasn't getting any better. It was touch and go.

It was horrible seeing him. He was burnt and really swollen. Each one of his fingers was about four centimetres wide. He was unrecognisable. If I'd have been walking around that ward looking for Neil I would have walked straight past.

They lightened his sedation so he could respond by squeezing our hands. He squeezed each one of his family's hands but he wouldn't respond to me. I was absolutely devastated. The nurse came in and told him off but he wouldn't do it.

I was pretty horrible to him. I told him if he didn't wake up and survive then I'd kill him myself. I told him he was going to be a dad and that he had to get better. His heart monitor went nuts.

I just wanted him to wake up and give me a cuddle. I didn't care if *he had no arms, no legs, no ears whatever. I just wanted him to wake up and be okay.*

Claire was by my bed. They deliberately brought me out of the coma by reducing my sedation and just to add to the confusion Claire was like, 'I'm pregnant'. That was the first thing I heard. I was so confused.

I know Mick has no recollection of being blown up or losing his legs whereas I remembered it all. I was under masses of medication. I was having two or three operations a day to flush out all the infections from my legs. I think I was awake for five or six days in Selly Oak until they actually sealed my legs up.

Claire Heritage: *Just to add to Neil's confusion it was the Hindu festival of Dewali, the Festival of Light, at the time. There were fireworks going off right outside his window for days.*

He was having hallucinations and panicking. He couldn't settle at all. It was horrible. Every time there was a bang from a firework he would jump and be startled. He thought we were over in Iraq and he was panicking and telling everyone they needed to get his family out of there.

In the end he had to be heavily sedated again. He was in such a state. He was crying and shouting military terms. It wasn't nice. We were asked to leave because it wasn't really helping having us around.

I'd been on tours to Northern Ireland and Bosnia before I first deployed to Iraq in 2003 as part of the 11 Explosive Ordinance Disposal Regiment. We were bomb disposal specialists.

Our job was to respond to any suspicious devices or packages the infantry out on the ground saw. We'd get the call to attend a device and we'd go out and do what needed to be done. We were a four-man team, close-knit, and we all knew our roles. It was a good team to be part of.

We encountered a wide range of devices on that first tour. The biggest threat came from what are called Remote Controlled

THE ROW TO RECOVERY

Improvised Explosive Devices (RCIEDs). To put it in layman's terms, the enemy press a button and it goes bang. You'd need someone physically watching to make the device go off. My whole job was to create an electronic bubble to block any signals used to trigger devices. The life of the Ammunition Technical Officer (ATO), the person responsible for physically disarming the device, depended on me getting it right.

The sheer volume of devices we encountered in Iraq took us a bit by surprise. In Northern Ireland there might have been one RCIED every three or four years and it would be a really big event but out in Iraq there were often several each day.

It was a bit of a game of cat and mouse. The insurgents would develop something and we would come up with a way of defeating it. We were constantly playing catch-up. There was no mutual respect at all. They were making bombs that killed people indiscriminately. There was definitely a level of technical skill to what they did, and whether that was coming from a central source I don't know, but individuals had it and it was our job to overcome it. As a team, we were on top of our game.

We learned a lot on that first tour. We dealt with a wide range of situations and scenarios. Anything from large-scale public disorder to massive bombs packed in the boots of cars. It was pretty relentless but it was what I'd signed up to do.

When you've done your tour you get four weeks off so I went home and chilled out for a bit. About two weeks after I'd started back at work I got the news one Monday morning that I was going to be redeployed.

I got home in the evening and Claire was like, 'You're going again aren't you?'

'Yep.'

I'd been told I would be deploying again on the Wednesday!

After that first tour I'd got a promotion and a new office-based job. It was supposed to be for the next three years so, thinking I wouldn't be deploying for a while, we decided to try to buy a flat and I cancelled my personal injury insurance to help pay for it. It was something like £15 a month but when you're buying a flat you try to save every penny. Then I got redeployed pretty much straight after that, and I didn't renew my insurance.

I didn't actually know what I was going to be doing when I redeployed. The original plan was for us to go and take over the depot in Basra and the Basra team that was already out there were going to move north with the Black Watch. As it turned out it was my team, Mick Brennan, Dave Humphreys and the ATO, Si De Gruchy, who got sent north.

We drove from Basra to Baghdad. It took about three days in a massive convoy with a load of Americans. It was slow going. I remember there was this mad lightning storm which was actually hitting the vehicles and the lights were exploding on the vehicles in front. It was really eerie.

We arrived late at night at a place called Camp Dogwood. There were some old blown-up buildings there and not much else. We were aware we were going into a hot situation. The press had really hammed it up, calling the area we were going into 'the Triangle of Death'. It was quite a large area and there had obviously been a lot of activity there.

There were tons and tons of mortars and artillery shells which were just out and about in certain areas. Our priority was to make the area as safe as possible.

Claire Heritage: *When Neil was away it was really hard. You feel like your entire life is on hold. My phone was never out of my hand. I always hung on to it so he could phone me. You worry constantly. Where is he? How is he?*

I never settled the whole time Neil was away that second time. I found out I was pregnant and went to a fireworks display on 6th November. I don't know if it was a mixture of hormones or sadness that he wasn't there but I cried all the way through the display. I had a really awful feeling. I didn't sleep at all that night.

The next day I was in a restaurant having lunch with my mum.

No one else knew I was pregnant at the time, not even Neil. I was excited about telling him but at the same time I had a bad feeling. It was odd that he hadn't called but Mum was reassuring me saying he was bound to phone soon.

When I looked up there was a man in a suit standing by our table. He asked my name and then said, 'Can you come with me please because I need to talk to you?'

I burst into tears and said, 'He's dead isn't he?'

We went outside and got in his car and he told me what had happened. He told me it wasn't looking very good and Neil had lost his legs. I was physically sick.

Once I was a bit more with it after a few weeks at Selly Oak, the realisation of what had happened began to sink in. People I spoke to early on said walking again was not an option. The limb centre councillor just said matter-of-factly, 'Get used to your wheelchair'. It was her job so I assumed she knew what she was talking about. I was gutted. It definitely set me back mentally. For several days I lay there thinking, 'That's it, I won't walk again'.

Claire Heritage: *I remember that woman like it was yesterday. She sat on Neil's bed and was talking to him about the wheelchair. She basically said to him, 'You need to get used to this because you're never going to walk again. You're going to be in this for the rest of your life.'*

I'd never seen Neil look so sad in my entire life. I was angry. She just wrote him off. Neil was very quiet. He got in his wheelchair and went off for a little while on his own. He was really upset.

I know he had a chat with his dad when he cried and asked, 'What kind of dad am I going to be?' He was really, really sad. His dad came and told me Neil was worried about what would happen between us and that he needed reassurance.

I always knew he'd be a good dad. No matter what had happened I knew he'd be an amazing dad.

It was really hard to see Neil broken. Before he was injured he was

My Story: **Neil Heritage**

6ft 3in and towered over everyone. He was always a pillar of strength. Among our circle of friends there were around 10 who he'd grown up with and he was always the one everyone went to. He was always sensible but fun. Now he just looked broken.

Ian Heritage: *To begin with I couldn't get my head around what his prospects were. I'd never met anyone who'd lost limbs before.*

We didn't know where he was going to live and, knowing nothing about prosthetic limbs, assumed he'd be in a wheelchair for the rest of his life. I wondered about his career, how he'd make money, how he'd look after his kids.

He'd never let you push his wheelchair, he'd always insist on doing it himself, but I remember being in the grounds of Selly Oak, just the two of us about two weeks after he'd regained consciousness. It was early December. He said: 'I've really buggered it up, haven't I Dad? I won't be able to look after the baby.'

I'd got my head around it a bit by then and said, 'You will, all kinds of disabled people have children. They will just love you for who you are'. But he wasn't having any of it. He broke down. He thought he'd failed and let everyone down.

Whereas nowadays, with the advancement of medical treatment, it's almost routine for guys to survive as double or even triple amputees, back then me and Mick were pretty unusual. In effect, we were guinea pigs.

I started getting pretty interested in other double amputees and survivors. There was a guy from the Royal Military Police who'd lost both his legs when an IRA bomb had detonated under his car. That was in the 1980s. He survived but wasn't using prosthetics.

I wanted to find someone with the same injuries who used prosthetics. There were people who'd survived traumatic incidents and subsequently had their legs amputated but there definitely weren't many who'd had their legs blown off and survived. There was certainly no one walking around doing it. There were a couple of guys, survivors of the 1979 Warren Point ambush in Co Tyrone who are double amputees. But it is nothing like now. It was really difficult to try to find someone, especially someone walking on prosthetics.

The first guy to really give me hope was the prosthetist, Andy Sharpe, at the limb centre in Birmingham. Andy told me: 'It is possible, it does happen, I've seen people walking with no legs. It may take a while but we'll get there.'

Everyone at the limb centre talked to me about the importance of being patient and determined. But overall their attitude was, 'You can do this, it can happen'.

But in those days prosthetic limb technology was nowhere near as advanced as it is today. They had these legs which aren't fitted to you which they use for people who have had amputations. They had me up on those walking between the bars in early December and that was horrendous, really bad. It was incredibly painful. Just walking a few steps would leave me absolutely soaked in sweat. The pain in the stumps was excruciating.

Claire Heritage: *The first time we went to the Selly Oak limb-fitting centre they had these horrendous-looking legs. You wouldn't believe what he had to start on compared to what he has now. They were very, very short and he had to hold himself on the bars and then sink into these little leg things. They were all strapped around his waist and tied around his back like a corset. They had these big brown leather straps. They were awful.*

Neil was in absolute agony. He took one step and you could see he was crying but no tears were coming out. Andy, his prosthetic bloke, told him to stop but Neil wouldn't. He took another step and Andy said, 'Come on mate, you really have to stop.' Most people don't even get to lift one leg up the first time. Neil managed about four or five steps. His determination was incredible.

I sat on the bed watching him. I was crying but trying not to let him see. It was horrible. He was so skinny and frail. It was like it wasn't Neil. He was so skinny, drugged up, half his size.

My Story: **Neil Heritage**

I went home on 24th December, 2004, seven weeks after I was injured. There were mixed emotions. It was more difficult for everyone else than it was for me because I was in the mindset of being lucky just to be alive whereas everyone else was pretty down about what had happened. Everyone did their best under the circumstances but it wasn't easy.

I had to be really careful not to bang my stumps. The wounds had pretty much healed when I left hospital so that wasn't an issue, but if I just touched them on something it would be absolute agony. But on the whole I was thankful. I reminded myself it could have been worse. I figured I was better off than if I'd been paralysed from the waist down.

Ian Heritage: *Neil came back in a wheelchair for Christmas with his first pair of artificial legs. We went out to Poole Park one day to practise on them and within one step he fell over. I thought, 'He's never going to do this. He'll never walk again'. It took us ages to get him up and standing on those legs. I just thought, 'It's never going to happen'.*

He was conscious of people looking at him. I think that hurt. People just stared. I never said anything but people did stare. I just felt for Neil because if I could see them looking he could see them. Once, when he was at Selly Oak he went down to King's Norton where there's a little row of shops. When we turned up at the hairdresser's we couldn't get in because there was a bloody step there. We had to juggle the wheelchair across it while this woman just stood there gawping at him. She just stood and stared. I didn't say anything.

One of the first skills I mastered was learning how to pick myself up and get back upright again. I spent a lot of time getting up off the floor.

When I was on my own I could cope with it fine but when I was in a crowd of people they'd all come over and try to offer help, but actually you're pretty embarrassed, humiliated even, and no one can actually help you. Because of the way the legs were I had to get back up on them on my own. I hated the attention, people looking.

For the first 18 months I would expect to fall over every time I left the front door. Either that or something would go wrong. I was always scared that if I broke my arm or wrist then it would only add to my problems. Luckily the worst I suffered was a bit of bruising.

My stumps were still painful. I think that's pretty typical of new amputees, stumps changing sizes and going through periods where they don't fit well. You go through phases where you're going well and then you need a new fitting and that takes a month and sets you back a bit.

Thankfully Claire had managed to cancel the offer on the flat we were looking to buy before I was injured and the Army adapted accommodation for us in Hamworthy near Poole.

The next stage was to go up to Headley Court. I spent about six months there trying to learn to walk. It was new ground for everyone, not just me, because they hadn't had a surviving bilateral amputee up there before. There was a lot of going back and forth to Birmingham where my prosthetics were made and then I'd come home at the weekends. It was pretty full on.

There were people at Headley Court who had been wounded in combat but not with the same level of injury that Mick and I had. We were by far the most seriously injured guys there and we were really aware that we had a longer journey ahead.

If I was to go in there now I think my injury would be routine. Back then no one really knew what to do and what needed to be done. It was trial and error to an extent. Now there are lads in there injured a lot worse than me.

Ian Heritage: *I wasn't aware that he was the first to survive that injury in the modern conflicts. When we first went to the rehabilitation centre they said they'd never rehabilitated someone that bad and when I saw him stumble and fall I thought, 'Well, I can see why'. But they were just being honest.*

My Story: **Neil Heritage**

I was utterly determined to walk again. I had loads of physiotherapy on the muscles I needed to walk. By the time I left Headley Court I was fine going around a flat gym floor but anything more up and down was a real problem. I didn't really know what to do. I'd been told if I had better prosthetics with better components and knee joints I could improve all that.

The whole aim of being at Headley Court was to get me back to work. The Army found me a job at Blandford which I started in July 2005, so about nine months after my injury it was back to full-time work.

But I was nowhere near rehabbed. Looking back I think they pushed me out too quickly just to say I was back at work. It was done with the best intentions, but it wasn't right. The rehab goal was plain and simple: get people back to work. I think that's changed now. Now the main aim is to enable people to achieve the best functionality they can. That's an important change.

Mia was born that July. Obviously it's really hard work having a new baby and because I was on a lot of medication then a lot of things were really blurry.

Claire Heritage: *When Mia was born Neil did absolutely everything. Probably more than the average man would do for a baby. He used to wrap her in her babygrow and pick her up with his teeth, bum shuffle across the floor and carry her about places. He could pick her up so her back was in line with the floor and carry her around in her babygrow. Often he'd bring his stumps up so that she was secure and then he'd move about the floor with her all snug to his waist.*

Having Mia around was amazing, but I was finding it wasn't easy being a dad to a young child, starting back at work and learning to walk again. I didn't really know how to feel. I wanted to progress but there was no one around who could lead me or give me the benefit of their experience.

My personality changed. I definitely became more reserved. I was pretty low on confidence. I wasn't angry or aggressive, but I kept myself to myself at work and socially. I didn't go out much. We'd have friends around to our house but we wouldn't go out.

Life was difficult because the job I was doing was IT and computer systems and I didn't understand large parts of it. I felt that if I hadn't been injured people would have been kicking my arse rather than allowing me to get away with not knowing a great deal. I felt like they were finding things within my capability to do. I didn't like it particularly. I found out I had a bit of a head injury from the blast that was affecting my memory. What I was capable of doing seemed to have been massively affected. I was fine with day-to-day stuff, but anything more complicated I didn't seem to be able to get my head around in the same way that I could before. The job would have been quite comfortable for me to do before, but now I couldn't do it. It was frustrating.

I was on lots of medication for about a year and I had to go back into hospital to have another operation because I kept on getting a load of pain in my right stump. I would tell them it wasn't right and they'd X-ray it and say 'there's nothing there'. Eventually they agreed to open it up and have a look and they found a piece of shrapnel in there which was grating on the muscle and I had a blood clot. They removed those and pretty quickly the pain eased and I was able to come off all the medication. Within five or six weeks of that operation I really began to turn things around.

You don't realise how drowsy all the medication makes you until you come off it. It was as if a cloud had been lifted. I started to feel back to my old self. I'd been on 120mg of morphine twice a day, tramadol, dyclofenac, paracetamol, amotryptolyne. Four times a day I'd had to take different concoctions and it still didn't really allay the pain. Once they carried out the operation things changed almost overnight. It was another week in hospital but it was so worth it.

At work I chose to get medically discharged rather than admit I didn't know what was going on. I wanted to leave quietly, to slip out of the door. It was always made clear that when I was ready to leave I could be medically discharged. I turned up at the adjutant's door one day and said, 'I want to leave now', and that's pretty much what happened. No one tried to stop me.

Ian Heritage: *Neil needed to go to the gym most days because of the extra effort it took him to walk. He couldn't hold down a job, look after his family and keep himself fit enough to walk. That was the conundrum. Once he was back in the Army they expected a full day's work out of him. He couldn't live on camp so he had to drive home in his adapted car. He just couldn't do it all. He was pleasing no one. He wasn't managing the job properly, he wasn't getting the fitness he needed, he'd be shattered when he got home.*

It was probably three years after I got injured that I got the prosthetic limbs I'm on now, which are known as C-Legs. I got those around the time I was being medically discharged. Initially the MOD hadn't been willing to fund them but as more and more guys were coming home severely wounded from Afghanistan a decision was taken to start paying for more high-tech prosthetics. The ones I'd been on before had been incredibly difficult to walk any sort of distance on because if you made the slightest misjudgement they would fold and collapse. The C-Legs are far more adaptable. Charities like the British Limbless Ex Service Men's Association (BLESMA) and Help for Heroes were also incredibly supportive and provided around £10,000 to enable me to buy new sockets from a local company called Dorset Orthopaedics, which meant I could spend even longer on the new legs. It was a significant advance in my rehabilitation.

It took another year until I was fully confident to go anywhere. But the new legs made a huge difference. Around a year after I was discharged I started to feel happier going out into busy places with confidence that I wouldn't fall or get knocked over. It would be months between falling over rather than every half an hour.

When I was injured in November 2004 I'd just assumed that you would be looked after financially if you were injured in the line of duty.

Because I'd cancelled my personal insurance before I'd deployed that meant I lost out on nearly £500,000, but I still thought the Army would take care of me.

What really hurt was when I was still in hospital in Birmingham, a lady from one of the charities came to visit me. She told me: 'When you leave the Army you'll get a pension but apart from that, nothing.'

In February 2010 they introduced the Armed Forces Compensation Scheme to replace the War Pension system that I was on. The first line of the guide to the scheme states, 'The Armed Forces Compensation Scheme provides compensation for an injury, illness or death which is caused by service on or after 6th April, 2005.' I'd been injured in November 2004. Unfortunately it was too late for me. It was a kick in the teeth. We've tried to get the MOD to move the date back to before my and Mick's injury but they won't budge.

The new system allows for a tax-free lump sum payout of up to £570,000 depending on the severity of the injury. But, because of the timing of my injury, I wasn't eligible. Just having the lump sum would have meant I could have gone and bought a house and then had an income to live on rather than having to spend everything on the mortgage. When that happens you are completely dependent on being mentally and physically fit enough to earn an income. The new system is clearly much better because everyone is looked after depending on how badly they are injured.

It's a change for the better but it hasn't helped me. I definitely feel like I've been let down by the system. I feel it most when I'm around other guys who've been wounded after me and they are clearly a lot more comfortable and able to do a lot more than I can. That's when it hits home the hardest. Generally life is not too bad, but it would have been so much better to have been injured after April 2005. I've needed a lot of financial support from the charities.

Claire Heritage: *The compensation issue didn't help our relationship but I was also seeing changes in Neil. He became quite selfish, not in a bad way, but in an, 'I'm not going to let this defeat me' kind of way.*

It's important to remember the families have all been traumatised and been through the pain of having their loved ones hurt overseas. It would be nice if the families were more involved in the recovery process rather than the Army just whipping the men away.

We all had to adapt to a new life. I know we are not the ones who have lost our legs or arms but so much changes for us. Living with someone who has had such a big traumatic incident happen to them, you have to renew your whole way of doing everything. Shopping trips for us were no longer just me and Neil getting out of the car and we'd each take one of the kids. It became me, wheelchair, pushchair, baby, Callum, helping Neil in and out of the car. It was a whole new life for everybody.

We weren't given any opportunity to learn about that way of life. It was such a struggle. I'd been with Neil from the beginning of his injury, every agonising step of the way, but began to feel like I was being left behind. It was so hard. I understood why Neil needed to say 'yes' to everything but, while he was able to move forward with his walking, I couldn't move on from his injury. Neil had to become selfish to learn to walk again but eventually it became all-consuming for him. I still loved him as much as I'd ever loved him but we couldn't carry on the way we were. We had to split up.

CHAPTER 2:
TEAM-BUILDING

Ed and Alex were energised by the prospect of putting a team of wounded servicemen together to row the Atlantic, even though they remained unsure of the appetite within the wounded community for undertaking such a massive challenge. The initial response of just 12 applicants had not provided overwhelming evidence of support, although the calibre of those showing an interest was undoubtedly a cause for optimism. The extreme nature of the challenge – rowing almost 3,000 miles unsupported across the Atlantic – had inevitably put many off, while many potential candidates were not sufficiently rehabilitated from their injuries to even consider taking part.

There was also some uncertainty within the medical profession about the potential risks that taking recent amputees to sea for an extended period of time would pose, while there were also concerns about finding a boat suitably equipped to cater for rowers with such specific requirements.

Alex and Ed remained undeterred. Teamwork and team-building had been an important aspect of both their military careers and, after putting the infrastructure of the charity in place, they were eager to assemble their latest team.

Alex: *One of the things Tony had said to us very early on was that people can tend to get a bit rose-tinted in how they view wounded guys and how they are all heroes. Tony is very straightforward. He says, 'If the guy is a difficult character before he gets blown up, it doesn't mean he suddenly turns into a good bloke once he's injured'. Obviously you feel sorry for the fact they have had that experience but, brain injuries aside, it doesn't change who they are. Fundamentally they are the same person.*

Tony's point was that we needed to be rigorous in selecting the right people. It was harsh but important advice because we realised one of the most important aspects of putting together a crew would be finding guys who shared the same values and the same motivation as us. We needed guys who shared our vision and bought into what we were doing. If we were going to row the Atlantic together, we were going to have to get on.

It was late 2010 when Alex and Ed set the recruitment wheels in motion, six years since Neil Heritage had lost his legs in Iraq. Neil was going through a tough time in his life when he heard about the row. He was in the process of divorcing his wife Claire – largely the result of the gruellingly relentless rehabilitation process which had taken over both their lives. Since his injury, Neil had become utterly single-minded about his quest to walk again. His dedication was both inspiring and all-consuming, but it had proved too much for Claire.

'All he talks about are his legs,' she'd said when asked why they were divorcing.

TEAM-BUILDING

After taking possession of a pair of high-tech, electronically powered prosthetics known as C-Legs, the softly spoken former Royal Signaller had been given a new lease of life. His split from Claire had hurt him deeply. In many ways he still loved her, as she did him, but the extreme nature of his injuries meant he needed to be selfish if he was to have a hope of achieving the levels of mobility he believed possible.

Neil: *I'd been pretty busy doing other fitness training and had got involved with a Help for Heroes bike ride when I'd hand-cycled around the battlefields of northern France. I'd been going through a rough time at home and was in the process of breaking up with Claire. I'd spent the past few years working incredibly hard on my mobility and fitness and was starting to feel I was ready for something really big. I had a job teaching PE at a local school but was spending more and more time on my own fitness. Maybe I was trying to fill my mind by keeping busy.*

The poster at Headley Court advertising the row said, 'More than 4,000 people have climbed Everest and more than 500 people have been into space, but only 473 have rowed an ocean'. It jumped out at me for that reason, along with the charities it was supporting. People who'd helped me. I thought, 'That would be good'.

Another person who saw the poster was 26-year-old Carl Anstey, who two years previously had suffered serious injuries to his legs when an RPG launcher had misfired, killing a close friend and the young Afghan National Army soldier who'd fired the faulty piece of equipment.

In the early stages of his recovery Carl put maps up on his hospital room walls and read about great explorers like Scott and Shackleton, dreaming that one day he would once again be able to push the boundaries of human endurance after proving himself to be an exceptional young soldier prior to his injury. Carl knew he still had much to offer.

THE ROW TO RECOVERY

Carl: *I was in the coffee shop at Headley Court on a break from a rehab session. Tony Harris was sitting down big-timing it – as he does – and he said there was a row going on next year with two friends of his and asked if people wanted to get involved. There were a few guys in the room and I was pretty eager to get involved. Then I saw the posters on the wall saying 'Row2Recovery. Are you tough enough?' I applied in writing that night.*

The attraction of the adventure and journeying into the unknown was huge. I wanted to prove to myself that I could do something that extreme. I was desperate to prove that I was not just someone who'd been injured. I'd been a career soldier and experienced the highs and lows of warfare. I yearned for a new challenge.

I was absolutely adamant I wanted to do something truly amazing. The row was a massive challenge, man against nature. I wanted to do something that caught the public's imagination.

Ed called me the following week to say they were planning a meet-and-greet day at London Docklands. I couldn't wait to get involved.

Will Dixon had just started a new job at Barclay's Bank, working as part of a team helping to reintegrate wounded servicemen and women back into the civilian workplace. He'd only been injured the year before but had quickly achieved exceptionally good mobility, as many below-knee amputees do, and was already starting to think about his next challenge. Wearing a suit and tie to work, it was often impossible to know he'd been injured at all. One day a colleague who he'd been sitting alongside for several weeks asked him, 'Why are you limping today, Will? Have you hurt your leg playing football?'

'No mate, I lost it in Afghanistan last year,' he replied.

Will: *I received an email from Tony Harris, who I'd met when I was at Headley Court. I remember thinking, 'This is too good an opportunity to turn down'. It was exactly what I needed. It was suitably bonkers and just stood out as being pretty extraordinary. I agonised over my application. I was desperate to do it.*

TEAM-BUILDING

My friend, Guy Disney, was preparing for the Walking with the Wounded trek to the North Pole at the time. I was full of admiration for what those guys were doing. Guy has a very similar injury to me and had visited me in hospital soon after I'd lost my leg. Mum was there at the time. Just seeing Guy wearing a pair of trousers and walking around pretty much normally, barely being able to detect a limp, filled me with a lot of confidence and optimism for the future. It was very good for Mum as well. He was like the Blue Peter 'Here's one I made earlier' of me.

Ever since I'd been injured I'd been determined not to be defined by my injury. Here was a chance to be known as the bloke who'd rowed the Atlantic and not just the bloke who'd lost his leg.

Corporal Daniel 'Baz' Whittingham had undergone an elective amputation of his right leg just a month earlier and was still in the very early stages his recovery. Almost two years earlier he'd been blown up by a Taliban bomb, resulting in him breaking both ankles, both heels, his tibia and fibia in his left leg, shattering his pelvis and breaking his lower back.

'It was like my left side wasn't attached to my right side,' he said.

Like Tony, Baz initially attempted to keep his leg, but a series of debilitating infections saw him eventually opt for amputation. Fittingly, he underwent surgery on Remembrance Day, 2010.

Ever the joker, Baz had worn an imitation cockerel thong underneath his medical gown for the operation and painted his toenails red with an arrow drawn onto his redundant left leg which read: 'Take this one.' The last thing he'd done before slipping under the anaesthetic was tweak the cockerel's nose on his thong, shocking the surrounding surgeons with a 'cock-a-doodle-doo' sound before falling asleep with two complete legs for the very last time.

Baz subsequently had two tattoos inked onto his flesh. One, written in Roman numerals across his left arm, read 'VI I MMIX' – denoting 6th January, 2009 – the day he was blown up. The other, inked across his ribcage, read: 'The mark of a man is his ability to rise again.'

He was an in-patient at Headley Court when he heard about the row.

Baz: *I'd absolutely loved being a soldier; it felt almost primeval. You're not designed to know how to fill out your tax return but your mentality and all your instincts are designed for working in a group of blokes, together, against an aggressor whether it is a bear looking for food, hunting, building things or against somebody trying to kill you. It is how man was meant to be and you can just fall into it. Being away at war felt almost natural. Well it did to me anyway.*

Within the first month after the op I took my first steps, which was right on time, and then it was a sort of a race to see who the first person would be to get a prosthetic leg on and get walking around. There were five of us who'd been through Headley Court the first time but struggled with infections and other complications. We all came back within weeks of each other after having elective amputations, and started competing to see who could do the best. Who could walk the furthest and hop on it and that kind of thing.

I went through a stage, soon after I had my leg off, when I decided I was just going say 'yes' to everything. In one week I signed myself up for an Ironman triathlon, swimming around Jersey in a relay, rowing the Atlantic, kayaking, doing the para-canoe and I think that was it. When you pick up an injury like this you don't know what you can do so I just said 'yes' to everything. I thought, 'Might as well, it's just like being a kid again'.

With a potential crew now assembled, Ed and Alex made plans to get the Row2Recovery project into the water. The only problem was that neither of them had a great deal of rowing experience. Alex had done some river rowing at school, but they quickly realised that they needed to demonstrate credibility within the sport in order to convince potential applicants, media and sponsors that they meant business.

If they wanted to be taken seriously they needed to engage someone who really knew what they were talking about, and they were put in touch with Bobby Thatcher by Oli Jedrej – a Parachute Regiment connection of Alex's. As a World Rowing Championships silver medallist and a 1996 Atlanta Olympian, Bobby's credentials were impeccable.

Ed: *Bobby had retired from top-flight rowing and was now coaching top schoolboy crews in west London. When we spoke to him about getting involved he didn't hesitate in saying 'yes'. He had exactly the right mindset and I liked him immediately.*

Once Bobby was on board and the initial responses had been received, Alex and Ed needed to find out how serious the applicants were. They set up an acquaint and training day at the London Docklands Water Sports Centre and invited the would-be rowers to travel to London in January 2011 to begin the selection process. The start of the race was just 11 months away.

Neil duly travelled up from his home in Poole, Dorset, along with fellow bilateral amputee Ben Hilton, who'd lost both his legs in a double IED strike while on foot patrol in Afghanistan in November 2009. Carl, Will and Baz were among the less severely wounded applicants who reported for training.

Alex and Ed put the attendees up at their own flats and ensured they enjoyed a 'social' in the evening, as they were eager to see how the prospective team-mates interacted with each other.

The relatively small number of attendees did not phase Alex or Ed. After all, how many fully able-bodied people would attempt such an extraordinary undertaking? Instead, the pair were reassured by the fact that two men with such extreme injuries as Neil and Ben had shown an interest.

Alex and Ed briefed the applicants on what they could expect at sea – although in truth they knew little themselves – and outlined what they were looking for from their crew.

THE ROW TO RECOVERY

Alex: *The fact that guys like Ben and Neil were even considering it was already an amazing statement about their mental toughness and resilience. But I don't think either Ed or I actually realised their full potential.*

We were very clear with people at the start that it was not about them. We said, 'If you want to be part of this campaign we are not just testing if you are a fit bloke, we are testing if you get on, if you're prepared to do the work with the media to help support the cause, and if you're ready to be part of something bigger to help support the row'.

That's what we were going to select on. Not the fact that someone could bench press 120kg. We weren't interested in that. We needed good blokes who were prepared to do what it took to support the campaign, not just go on the adventure of a lifetime.

I remember talking very early on with Ed about what the ideal make-up of our crew would be. Neil was very subdued at that time and I wondered where the fire in his belly was. I couldn't see it at that time. I wasn't convinced he really wanted to do it. He was so understated and didn't give anything away. I wondered if he was really interested. Was he just there out of fascination? What made him tick?

Alex wasn't the only one to have doubts. Neil himself privately harboured reservations about his ability to make the team. No double amputee had ever attempted the crossing. But seeing as he'd spent the last six years of his life proving people wrong, the 30-year-old thought, 'Why not?'

Neil: *I didn't know if it was something I'd be able to achieve. I thought there would be loads of people who'd be up for it and that I'd stand a pretty slim chance of going to be honest.*

I thought there'd be a lot of people much fitter than me there and that being so badly injured would also prove a significant disadvantage. I expected the single below-knee lads would dominate it. I went along anyway and it was alright.

Thatcher set about testing the crew's basic aptitude for rowing while at the same time forensically breaking down the technique of pulling an oar through the water in order to achieve maximum power output. Each wounded veteran had specific issues relating to their own injury, with the distribution of weight and balance two of the major concerns. Carl, whose right leg was now several inches shorter than his left as a result of being blown up, wore a supportive brace but was at least able put weight through both feet. With double amputees Neil and Ben, the main issue was the lack of leg power and the angle the oars entered the water causing them to hit their stumps with each stroke. Simon Goode from British Adaptive Rowing was also on hand to talk the applicants through their options. Thatcher remained patient and thorough. The former Olympian was proud to be able to share his bank of knowledge with a group of men he admired enormously.

Will: *Bobby was a phenomenal coach, probably the best coach I have ever known. To be able to take a group of total amateurs and break down the rowing technique in an accessible way so that we just got it straightaway was brilliant.*

Getting onto the river for the first time was a fantastic feeling, but the very first time we went out there were issues with my leg. My prosthetic was really digging in to the back of my stump. I tried rowing without it on but I would get cramp and have to hold my leg up, which is unworkable. I quickly realised if I was going to do it then I would have to find a way of adapting the leg.

Ed and Alex weren't the only ones observing people's behaviour. In an early sign of his meticulous preparation and attention to detail, Carl had carried out his own due diligence on the two expedition leaders.

Carl: *Before I went up to the meet and greet I did some research on Ed and Alex. I saw the YouTube video of these two crazy guys getting into a boat and there was a great line in it that asked, 'If you'd* survived a war would you risk it all again by rowing an ocean?' I was like, 'yes'. They both seemed switched on and very organised.

I knew Will from Headley Court and knew he was a good lad who enjoyed a laugh and joke. It was the first time I'd met Neil and I thought he was a good bloke, although he was pretty quiet. I knew Baz from hospital. Everyone seemed quite switched on, which was also quite worrying because I definitely saw them as competition.

Bobby and Oli were in superb physical condition. They were in the personal training business, founded on the principle of pushing clients to their limits, and never once considered going easy on the applicants just because they were wounded. It was exactly the message Ed and Alex wanted to send out to the lads: if you're going to do this, you're going to do it on equal terms.

Ed: *Bobby didn't pull any punches at our first couple of training sessions. He absolutely beasted us. He got the lads doing sit-ups, squats and dead weight lifting. I thought it would never end. When it finally did I threw up and dry wretched for about five minutes. He didn't show any mercy on the wounded guys either. He tailored each exercise specifically for them and made sure they were put through the mill as well. By the end of the session we were all as knackered as each other. It was brilliant.*

Carl: *Bobby and Oli were machines. They ate a lot of couscous, which was weird, but their enthusiasm shone through as they were giving up their free time to help us train.*

We did a bit of rowing in the indoor water tank and sessions on the rowing machines just to get a basic understanding of technique. I'm not sure how much actually sunk in.

I desperately wanted to get on the team. It had been the best part of two years since the injury, my last surgery had worked quite well and I was finally pain-free, and I knew I was fit enough and ready to do it.

Neil also enjoyed his first taste of rowing, although problems with his seating position and the effect having no legs would have on his power output soon became apparent. While normal rowing seats are fitted on guide rails to allow the oarsman to move back and forth in order to maximise output from their legs, Neil required a fixed seat which would prevent him sliding and enable him to generate maximum power using just his arms and upper body.

Neil: *Bobby explained on that first day that rowing was about 65 per cent leg power so it was all about getting the technique right. I remember thinking, 'That's probably not great for me!' I thought that gave me a much smaller chance of being able to do it. It didn't put me off at all but clearly someone less injured would be better placed to do it.*

But I kept turning up to the sessions. It just felt good to be back around Army people. I hadn't been in that situation for a long time and I realised how much I'd missed it. Everyone was testing the water with a bit of banter. I enjoyed it.

Some of the applicants' parents, most of whom had believed their days of waving their sons off into the unknown were long gone, were beginning to get wind of the proposed expedition.

Ian Heritage: *The first time I heard about the Row2Recovery I thought Neil had no chance. I couldn't get my head around it. I thought it was bloody mad. I wondered how much more he would put me through. What brought it home was when he asked if he could put my name down as 'Next of Kin'. I thought, 'I don't need that again'. I just had to go with it. I knew from past experience not to try to talk him around.*

At the training camp, all of the injured men demonstrated that they were capable of completing intensive cardiovascular workouts which was reassuring for the fitness team. None of them asked for special treatment or moaned about what they were being asked to do. It was an important early indicator of the can-do mentality Ed and Alex were looking for.

Meeting the wounded soldiers was an eye opener for Alex on other levels too. Having been part of the infamous tour to Helmand Province by 3 PARA (The Parachute Regiment – Third Battalion) in 2006, Alex's war had also been fought before the IED threat escalated so dramatically.

Alex: *I hadn't met any guys who were anywhere near as severely wounded as our guys were. I remember us all going to Tescos after one of the training sessions and I was really hyper aware of other people's reactions around the lads.*

At the time I was like the rest of society, thinking, 'Shit, look at these guys hobbling around. Can you talk about it? Can you not talk about it?' I asked them a lot of questions because I needed to understand what was on and off limits. I asked them, 'Do you mind talking about it? What has your experience been like?'

The initial training session gave Alex and Ed the chance to size up the men who, 11 months later, they could be sharing an enclosed space with for the best part of two months. They were encouraged, if not a little daunted, by what they were taking on.

Several more training sessions were organised, including a long weekend in Dartmouth, Devon, and Alex and Ed were reassured by the fact that the rowers kept coming back, with Baz and Carl eagerly making the 10-hour round trip from Nottingham to south Devon.

Already holding down high-pressure consultancy jobs in the city, as the charity began to grow on all fronts, Alex and Ed began to feel the pressure on their personal lives. With applicants, sponsors, fundraising, media and administrative considerations, not to mention their own families, the pair found themselves locked into a seemingly endless cycle of meetings, discussions, late nights and early mornings in order to get the job done. Fortunately, both men's employers – PricewaterhouseCoopers and McKinney Rogers

— bought into the idea, and supported the two men wherever possible by granting them time off and a certain amount of leeway. But it was tough and relationships suffered.

Ed's wife Helen had found out she was pregnant in late 2010. The couple were over the moon but at the back of his mind Ed knew his nights were only going to get shorter. Both men were working round the clock, juggling their work and home lives with the increasing demands of the Row2Recovery project.

Crucially, the weekend trip to Dartmouth in March 2011 provided Ed and Alex with another chance to assess the strengths and weaknesses of each potential crew member. With the original two-man single-seat boat put up for sale, a four-man dual-seat boat had been sourced from a local boat builder. For the first time, they had a chance to test themselves at sea.

Carl: *When I first saw the boat I didn't think it was too bad. I'd slept in worse places when I was in the Army. It was a dry cabin – well, kind of dry, but it looked okay. At the time I was still pretty naive as to the routine that would be involved in order to keep clean and dry and avoid salt-water rashes.*

It was pretty brutal getting out of the harbour and onto the open seas. The sheer pounding the boat took was a real eye opener. On top of that I felt like I was taking part in this extended job interview. I was desperate to get through the selection process.

Will was also keen to impress.

Will: *It wasn't like it was a competition. We all just thought we had to be ourselves and they would pick who they wanted to take. We knew it wasn't necessarily going to be purely down to ability. There were so many factors that were out of our control like the media angle and who would be most suitable for that. I remember thinking that out of me and Baz only one of us would go because we ticked the below-knee amputee box. Baz had a really powerful story so I thought he had the edge.*

But just being part of it was exciting. It gave me a completely new lease of life. My girlfriend, Mia, commented at the time she could see I was doing something I was passionate about. I was adamant that if I didn't make the crew I would continue to help in a support role.

Ed and the fundraising team were keen to put the challenge out into the public domain as soon as possible, knowing media coverage would further legitimise the charity as well as attracting more potential sponsors.

In late May the charity secured its first significant piece of media coverage when *The Times* ran a superb three-page feature, written by respected sports journalist Patrick Kidd, which summed up the proposed crossing with the headline: 'The Atlantic Warriors Rise Again.' It was a significant step forward, as the team now had tangible evidence to demonstrate to future partners that their story was valued by the media. It also raised expectations that high-profile media coverage would be achievable.

Despite the excellent initial coverage in *The Times*, a move to have a 'hard launch' was resisted by the media and PR team. Alex and Ed clashed over the best path to take in a series of heated telephone calls and frantic meetings, once again testing the strength of their friendship. The two men were able to put aside any professional disagreements and recognise they both had the best interests of the campaign at heart.

After a protracted debate lasting several days, it was decided to hold a 'One Million Metre Row' on Horseguards Parade in June 2011 which would challenge members of the public and a host of celebrity supporters to join members of the core team in rowing on ergometers (rowing machines) for 24 hours, aiming to cover a million metres in that time.

Will took on the job of project-managing the event, an encouraging demonstration of his commitment to the cause, while plans were underway to stage a lavish black-tie fundraising departure dinner at the Royal Horticultural Halls in central London in November.

For the wounded applicants the One Million Metre Row would

also act as the last phase of the selection process, and a final call on the make-up of the crew would be made soon afterwards.

Although it failed to generate the level of media coverage that had been hoped for, despite a torrential overnight downpour the event passed off seamlessly – as Will's team's hard work paid off. Double Olympic gold medallist and former transatlantic rower James Cracknell, along with ITV newsreader Mark Austin, and England rugby players Steve Thompson and James Haskell all did their bit on the ergometers. While Alex Gregory and Pete Reed, who would go on to win gold in the coxless four's boat at the London Olympics two years later, also took time out to show their support.

Tony Harris revelled in his role as microphone compere, strutting up and down the stage rallying team members and public alike while Neil's consistent and unwavering contribution was encouraging.

Alex: *Neil's physical fitness was impressive. He was strong, aerobically fit and extraordinarily determined. He is a very quiet and unassuming guy and I had questioned early on if he had the mettle to do it. I spoke to people who knew him well such as Bryn Parry at Help for Heroes and they'd told me, 'Stick with him'. We still had an issue around how we would adapt his seat but his attitude and commitment were hugely encouraging.*

Less encouraging was the pain Baz was beginning to experience in his still maturing stump, as well as in the heel of his 'good' right leg which had also been shattered in the blast.

Ben Hilton had taken the decision to withdraw his application before the One Million Metre Row. It was a huge shame to see Ben leave but, with seven children and a planned move north of the border to Scotland, he made the entirely understandable decision to pull out. It left Baz, Carl, Neil and Will vying for two seats in the boat.

Alex: *We were aware the blokes needed to know if they were going to be part of the crew so they could make the necessary provisions regarding work, preparation and letting their families know.*

THE ROW TO RECOVERY

One of the big debates we had when we were looking at going with two guys was between Baz and Carl. I said to Ed, 'I honestly think Carl is the man because I don't know what will happen to Baz in terms of his maturity and his outlook'.

Baz is a great guy but in the early stages I don't think he really considered the reality of what it was going to take to do this. I think he was excited by the big neon lights saying 'Atlantic Rower' but I don't think he'd really thought through what it would be like. He was a bit impulsive. Carl to me was much more mature. He laughs a lot and is a bit of a joker but the reality is that he is very, very serious and focused about what he wants to do. Carl was the man for me whereas I think Baz was the man for Ed because he was such a big character.

Ed: *Once Ben pulled out we were left with four guys who were utterly committed. Alex and I began to wonder if there was a way we could take all four. We thought: 'We get on really well with all of them, they are bloody good lads.' We were meant to have got our selection down to two by this stage and were conscious we needed to let the guys know. But we couldn't choose between them so we told them that, if they were up for it, they were all in. We agreed to take all four.*

The decision to go as a six, with four wounded rowers, meant further significant and costly adaptions were required to the new boat in order to increase the number of rowing positions from two to three. Critical to this was Neil's seat, which would need to be fixed in position to the floor of the boat. With only four-and-a-half months until departure, there was still much work to be done to get it ready in time. But going as a six was a hugely important message to send and Ed and Alex enjoyed the one-on-one conversations with their soon-to-be crew-mates. The fact that Neil was more than holding his own was also significant.

Neil: *We were told we were definitely in the crew just after the One Million Metre Row. In a lot of ways it would have been good to know earlier because I think we were all a little bit half-committed until we* knew for sure we were going. The biggest drama for me was always going to be getting my seat fitted and adapted correctly. Because I have no legs I needed to be strapped in to a different seat to the other guys. We would need to consult with people at British Adaptive Rowing who were specialists in building boats for Paralympic athletes. Up to that point things like that had to go on hold. When we did get confirmation it was very much full steam ahead. I was really chuffed to be part of the team.

Carl: *I went with Ed to the Henley Regatta in July and he said to me, 'By the way mate, we're going as a six'. I felt a huge pressure lift, it was a really relaxing feeling being told I'd made it. I could stop trying to impress people and just get on with what needed doing. It was exciting.*

With the crew selected, another behind-closed-doors 24-hour simulation row was scheduled to be held in Wellington Barracks gym barely a month later when the crew would be tested on their readiness for the gruelling routine that would see them row for two hours on and two hours off in cramped, awkward conditions.

The topic of 'stump management', and how they would cope with life at sea, was high on the agenda for all the amputee rowers, but with Baz just eight months post-surgery he was the one at greatest risk of infection and other complications.

Baz: *Loads of people were telling me I was attempting too much too soon. My dad tried to talk me out of it a few times. But I was completely committed. I'd driven down from Nottingham to Dartmouth a few times and I was desperate to be part of the team. The trouble was I was getting more and more pain in my stump and suffering from ingrowing hairs which could lead to infections.*

The Wellington Barracks row was when it dawned on me I was struggling. Everything was set out in the middle of this dingy old gym to simulate life on board. I managed to do an hour with my prosthetic leg on before I started getting problems to the back of my knee. I started getting sores. I said 'I'll take my leg off' and spent the rest of the time rowing with just my arms. I just sat there staring at the back of somebody's head. It wasn't like there was anything going by, no scenery. We were in a basement gym with a little bit of light. I thought to myself, 'This is rubbish, this is horrible, I can't do it'. I just kept thinking to myself during the whole thing, 'This doesn't feel comfortable and I'm only 12 hours into it – how am I going to feel once I'm halfway across the ocean?'

Baz's difficulties weren't going unnoticed.

Alex: *We were trying to simulate the misery of life on board and provide a little window for the guys into the world they were going to enter. You think, '24 hours of rowing, two hours on and two hours off. How hard can it be?' Well it was pretty miserable.*

We had three rowing machines lined up behind each other, two gym mats at either end to replicate the cabins and we cooked, ate, slept and rowed. The only time we left that area was to go for a piss. We just did two hours on, two hours off. Neil didn't have the perfect seat, in fact he did all his training when none of the resources were there for his injury. He was rowing on seats which were slipping around and on seats that didn't really work for him. But whereas Baz really struggled, Neil never complained, he just got on with it. He never said a word. He would get off the rowing machine at 2 o'clock in the morning having done the 12-2 shift, unstrap himself, slide along the floor, get in his sleeping bag and go to sleep.

Ed: *Baz was by far the biggest medical risk. Alex and I talked about this several times and discussed what we should do. As far as we were concerned we liked him and we wanted to do everything possible to make sure he was going to be in that boat. But he was going to need more medical oversight than the other lads. He was pushing himself to the point where he was in danger of becoming a liability.*

Carl: *I drove Baz home after that weekend and he said to me on the* *way back that he was thinking of pulling out. He was having issues with his stump. He had an infection in his leg. I told him to give it a week to settle down and to have a think about things. But he had this thing about starting the row but then getting a big infection mid-Atlantic and having to withdraw on medical grounds. He didn't want to let the team down. He didn't want that weight on his shoulders. He did the right thing.*

Alex and Ed were sorry to lose Baz from the row but knew it was the right decision for him and the campaign as a whole. They had told the crew that they would not be able to take them if the row was going to have a detrimental impact on their medical condition. They consulted medical staff at Headley Court and it became increasingly clear the row had come too soon in his rehab for Baz.

So the crew was down to five, with just over three months until the start of the race and no one on official standby. However, Alex had been prudent enough when he first realised Baz was having difficulties to sound out a former recruit he had instructed six years previously at Catterick Garrison.

At 6ft tall and weighing close to 16 stone, on paper the South African-born Rory Mackenzie appeared to tick the right physical boxes to be a successful ocean rower. Not only that, the former Army medic – who had lost his right leg in an IED blast in Iraq in 2007 – was sure to be a huge asset for any crew looking to take on such an arduous challenge because of his medical expertise.

Alex: *I remembered Rory vividly from when he was recruit. Everything about him stands out. His physical size and strength makes him highly visible. He is an incredibly confident, larger-than-life character. I liked him, he's a likeable character and the corporals liked him during training. The fact that the corporals liked him was unusual because they try not to show that they like anybody.*

A lot of those South African guys have had a robust discipline in their upbringing. In South Africa a lot of these guys have come from a background where their dad would just punch them or physically lift them up by their ear. It is a highly aggressive, macho culture. It's not all good but it does mean they are superficially resilient to a lot of the physical elements of what they do. If someone shouts at them they don't whimper and wail, they say, 'Okay, I'll fix it'.

Despite the short notice, since he was injured Rory had more than demonstrated that he had the mindset required to undertake a challenge on this scale. Despite losing his leg, with help from the Battle Back initiative he'd already learned to ski and developed an appetite for adventurous training as a means of compensating for the high octane-lifestyle of soldiering. He craved the adrenaline rush.

Alex: *I warned Rory that initially he was only coming on board as a reserve. I was very straightforward with him. I said, 'We'd love you to come down to meet the guys but you have to understand it's how you get on with people as much as how well you can do the job that will decide if you make the final selection. We have got other people in the frame but if you're happy to come down as a reserve on the understanding you may not make the cut then we'd love you to'. The truth was we had no one else!*

Rory: *Alex rang up and asked if I was up for it and my immediate response was 'yes'. He told me the crew were rowing in a borrowed boat in something called the Great River Race on the Thames the following week and to get myself along. That was the first time I met the lads or saw the sort of boat we'd be rowing in. We rowed around 20 miles. I got on with all the lads straightaway.*

With the boat they'd sourced still in the workshop in Devon the crew took part in The Great River Race – a 21-mile race along the Thames from Docklands to Ham – in a borrowed boat in an effort to hone their rowing techniques further. Not having the actual boat they would be crossing in did make planning more difficult, although reassurances had been given by the boatbuilder that their adapted vessel would be ready in time. In the meantime, decisions needed to be taken as to how to fit it out.

One of the Row2Recovery media team with a background in around-the-world yacht racing, Tim Kelly, had put the charity in touch with a company called Marine Camera Solutions. It was to prove one of the most decisive moves of the campaign. Alex and Neil travelled to Brockenhurst in the New Forest, where the company was based, to learn about the equipment that would enable them to transmit live video content and high-resolution images, send and receive emails, and use a satellite phone to communicate with the outside world. But the high-tech kit did not come cheap.

Strong links had been forged by now with ITV News, who had shown an interest in covering the crossing 'depending on news value' and agreed to make a partial contribution towards the £17,000 cost of fitting the additional on-board communications equipment which would be required to truly bring the row to life for a television audience. Race sponsors Talisker also agreed to contribute to the cost, although the charity would have to carry the biggest financial burden.

Alex: *Our media team had a lot of discussion around what we could justify in terms of the cost of on-board communications – satellite phones, video cameras, computers etc. We were a charity and we didn't have the money in the bank, but we knew how important it was to get our message out there if we were going to raise the kind of sums we had been discussing. A couple of months before we left, Ed's dad, Robin, who was one of our patrons said, 'You have to do it, it's a must'.*

While Alex and Neil were in Brockenhurst, Ed and Carl travelled down to Devon to check on the progress of the six-man boat that was being adapted and kitted out for their crossing. They had been given assurances it would be ready by 17th September, but when

THE ROW TO RECOVERY

Ed arrived to inspect it, it was clear there was still much work to be done. With barely two months until they were due to leave for La Gomera in the Canary Islands, where they would begin the crossing, there was now a real concern that it might not be ready in time. But while there was little they could do to speed up the boat's delivery, there was still much that could be done in other areas of preparation.

The crew had been booked onto a Royal Yachting Association survival course in Southampton, compulsory for all the race competitors, where they would learn vital safety drills and gain qualifications in navigation and sea-survival techniques. Rory agreed to attend the five-day course even though he was still technically a reserve, and it provided some valuable time for him to bond further with the rest of the crew.

Alex: *We had an absolutely brilliant week in Southampton. It was hilarious. Will was in charge of accommodation so instead of staying in a hotel he rented us a house for the week which was perfect. Everyone had their own room except me and Ed who had to share. We spent the entire week taking the piss out of each other and taking the piss out of other people on the course.*

The first two days we had to learn to use VHF radios and appropriate procedures at sea. But if you've been in the Army the basic principles are second nature. The phonetic alphabet 'Alpha, Bravo, Charlie, Delta, Echo, Foxtrot . . . ' we could all recite in our sleep.

We had to demonstrate we knew what we were doing by sending some very simple phonetic messages. Ed and Will were partnered up and were being idiots. We were going through the process but having as much fun as possible. Ed and Will had to do this radio transmission and it went something like this: 'Hello unidentified pink French fishing vessel, this is call sign X, please identify yourself.'

Ed, being the unidentified pink fishing vessel, had named his boat 'Supercalifragilisticexpialidocious' and he had to spell it out in phonetics. 'Sierra, Uniform, Papa, Echo, Romeo, Charlie, Alpha . . .' On and on he went. I was convinced the instructor was going to tell him to shut the hell up but he just let him go on. The boys were creasing with laughter.

That week was so important from a team-bonding perspective, not just in terms of getting to know Rory but also for the rest of us to spend some quality time socialising and enjoying each other's company.

Rory fitted in straightaway. I had been really confident that he would do but there is always a doubt. My concern was that he would overwhelm people and be too big for the team. That concern never materialised.

Our aim that week was to have fun, be a team and just try to enjoy doing what we were doing. We didn't enjoy all of it. Some of the navigation stuff – the astro navigation stuff in particular – was hardcore and very difficult.

Ed and I really didn't want the guys to think we were imposing anything on them so it was very open when we discussed Rory. The guys were very comfortable with him being part of the crew.

At the end of the week we said to Rory, 'We need to have a chat about the plans so you need to go out of the room'. Everyone said, 'Let's get him on board'.

Will: *Initially I did wonder if Rory was going to be too loud because we were going to be in such a tightly confined space. It wasn't until that week's course in Southampton when we really bonded and I worked out what made him tick. Underneath the loud exterior there is a thoughtful and mature bloke.*

Rory: *There were lots of interview-type questions from Ed and Alex. I could see what they were doing, sussing me out. We had a bit of a drink-up and it was about slowly integrating and testing the waters both ways.*

It was only at the end of that week when Ed and Alex said, 'We need to talk about this. Do you want to take part?' I was like, 'Is this the actual official you're on the team bit?' They said 'yes' and I was like, 'Okay, I thought I was already in!'

THE ROW TO RECOVERY

With the crew now fully assembled, the time had come to iron out some of the individual roles within it. A number of the 17 crews who were set to assemble in less than two months to start final preparations for the race on the tiny island of La Gomera in the Canaries opted not to appoint a skipper. But the consensus among the Row2Recovery crew was that an ultimate decision-maker would be vital, especially with a crew of six. As former soldiers, it was almost built into their DNA to accept a clear chain of command.

Carl: *We sat around the table and voted on who we thought should be skipper. It was between either Alex or Ed as co-founders. We wanted someone to be calm in a situation and we felt Ed would be the calmest on board and the best person for that role. He'd had a lot of leadership experience in Afghanistan, as had Alex.*

Alex: *We had a long discussion about who should be the skipper. Ed very selflessly wanted Will to be the skipper because he represented the wounded guys. Actually I don't think there was an appetite from any of the blokes for Will to do it. They wanted me or Ed to do it. I felt like Ed was the person who wanted it the most. I would have been happy to do it but I felt Ed was the best fit.*

I thought I could perform a better role by not being skipper. I also thought that being the person with the expertise around all the media kit, which was going to be a huge job, I wanted to focus on that. Part of the mission of the campaign was to get the message out there so we needed to have focused media activity.

To raise the money we needed to ensure the crossing was successful. That was basically how we split it. Ed was responsible for making sure we made the crossing and I was responsible for making sure the message got out there. It was basically that simple.

Rory: *There was lots of talk and discussion around the captaincy but I think everybody knew it was going to be Ed. He didn't want to be in the limelight because he wanted the campaign to be all about the wounded guys. I don't know if he felt bad about it for not being* *wounded but he was quite against being skipper. But it was obvious he should be skipper and Alex second in command.*

The stuff Ed has seen and done, I don't think he can believe he wasn't wounded. But he was so good to us. An outstanding bloke.

The week also provided an opportunity to divide roles and responsibilities between each crew member. The roles were allocated as follows:

Skipper: Responsible for navigation, safety and overall decision-making (Ed)

On-board comms and media: Responsible for recording as much on-board activity and daily liaison with London-based team responsible for generating media (Alex)

Kit and equipment: Responsible for rowing-based equipment such as oars, parachute anchor, flares (Carl)

Food and stores: Responsible for food and water rations (Will)

Electrician: Responsible for all electrical equipment (Neil)

Medic: Responsible for all first aid and medical provision (Rory)

With less than five weeks to go the crew returned to London buoyed by the week they'd spent together in Southampton. But before they flew out to La Gomera, where they would spend the final two weeks readying themselves for the row, there remained a seemingly never-ending array of last-minute administrative tasks, not to mention the not insignificant matter of putting on the London dinner.

The event, for 300 guests, was held at the Lindley Hall in London. Television historian Dan Snow agreed to compere the evening free of charge, while chief England cricket selector Geoff Miller, a highly accomplished after-dinner speaker, waved his usual fee and drove down from his home in Chesterfield to talk on the night. He brought the house down.

Rugby World Cup-winning England hooker Steve Thompson, who

months earlier had spent a week at Camp Bastion along with his friend and former team-mate, Neil Back, also attended despite having being told that morning that he would never play rugby again as the result of a chronic neck condition that was causing him intolerable pain. Thompson turned up on time, was superb company throughout, and never once hinted at the personal anguish he was going through. It was a brilliant gesture.

The guests were treated to a lavish evening that saw Christie's chief auctioneer, Hugh Edmeades, help to raise more than £20,000 from the live auction alone after the charity had been able to secure an array of 'money-can't-buy' prizes including lunch at Lord's with cricket legend Richie Benaud. That prize alone went for more than £3,000.

Guests were also given a brochure which outlined the campaign and encouraged donations. The brochure also contained a 'stats pack' providing a numerical breakdown of the crossing:

FACTS AND FIGURES ABOUT THE ROW2RECOVERY CREW'S UPCOMING TRANS-ATLANTIC ROW

2.1 million – total amount of calories the crew is likely to burn

43,200 – minutes each crew member can expect to row in order to cross the Atlantic

8,000 – amount of calories each crew member will burn per day

2,560 – nautical miles from La Gomera, Tenerife, to Barbados

1,500 – freeze-packed meals

800 – sheets of toilet tissue

295 – crews have ever successfully rowed an ocean

250 – painkilling suppositories will be packed

177 – crews have set out to row an ocean but failed

120 – days it took for the slowest ever successful Atlantic crossing

50-60 – days the Row2Recovery crew is hoping to take to complete the crossing

33 – the age of the oldest crew member, Alex

26 – the age of the youngest crew member, Carl

14 – number of kilogrammes each crew member can expect to lose over the course of the row

10 – litres of water each crew member is advised to drink per day

6 – Row2Recovery crew members

4 – the number of limbs the Row2Recovery crew are missing

1 – Bottle of Talisker whisky

0 – changes of underpants

Baroness Tanni Grey-Thompson, at the time Britain's greatest-ever Paralympian and a patron of the charity, began the evening by delivering a moving speech outlining how the crew were helping to redefine public perceptions of disability. When the lights were dimmed and the crew were introduced one by one on the stage, to the soundtrack of *Fix You* by Coldplay, there was barely a dry eye in the house.

Ed: *We'd been told told time and again that charity dinners don't make money, but we had other ideas. Deborah Peters and her team had done an incredible job putting it on and we'd been able to tap into a huge network of high-flying city bigwigs with a track record of supporting wounded soldiers' charities. It was a phenomenal night.*

Alex: *The dinner proved to be a resounding success and in total, through the live and silent auctions and personal donations, we made a profit of more than £80,000 that went directly to the charity. It was humbling to know the level of support we had. In many ways that was the best night of the entire campaign. Now all we needed to do was successfully row across the Atlantic.*

My Story:
Ed Janvrin

Age: 33
Regiment: Royal Gurkha Rifles
Army career span: 2001 – 2008
Rank: Local Major
Combat experience: Two tours of Afghanistan (2005 & 2007), one tour of Iraq (2004)
Physical injury: None

I wasn't physically injured in Afghanistan, although sometimes I still wonder how, but I'd be lying if I said I've not been deeply affected by what we went through out there.

I live a pretty ordinary life now in many respects. I have an amazing wife, Helen, and a beautiful little boy, Louis. I live in Surbiton and work in the City of London. I get up most mornings before 7am, put on my suit and tie, kiss Helen goodbye and catch the commuter train into London Waterloo. I could be sitting opposite you on the train as you're reading this right now. The difference, I suppose, are the experiences I've had.

I don't think anything can really prepare you for the level of violence you encounter on an operational tour to southern Afghanistan, but by anyone's standards our 2007 Helmand tour was intense. From a fighting force of close to 150 Grenadier Guards in our company we sustained 30 serious casualties with six 'Killed in

Action' (KIA). That's 20 per cent of our troops either killed or seriously wounded.

I commanded 40 Grenadier Guards – I was on secondment from the Gurkhas – and controlled an Afghan National Army (ANA) 'Kandak', which was made up of around 370 men. We specialised in training, mentoring and leading the Afghans in one of the most dangerous and lawless places on earth. Our area of responsibility covered the town of Sangin plus all surrounding villages, including the notorious village of Jusyalay. Our job was to train the ANA up to a level to allow them to one day take over the running of the area without us.

Of the 40 British troops I was directly responsible for one, Guardsman Neil Downes, was killed and a number were wounded. None of those wounded suffered life-changing physical injuries, although a couple of them have subsequently developed quite severe Post Traumatic Stress Disorder (PTSD). The ANA boys I worked with had it even worse. Twenty-four casualties in the four to five months we were in Sangin. Twelve of those 24 casualties were killed, 12 seriously wounded.

It was the most intense period of my life. I'd been on tours of Iraq and northern Afghanistan before but they turned out to be the warm-up acts for the 2007 tour. Before that tour I thought, 'I've been in a firefight, fucking amazing'. But in fact they were nothing in comparison to what we experienced in '07.

Guardsman Neil 'Tony' Downes died under my command on 9th June, 2007. He was 19 years old and just a boy. I think about him a lot.

Our Kandak was on patrol in a very isolated location, up in Jusyalay, 2km north of Sangin District Centre. These were the badlands. I was commanding close to 400 men, some Afghan National Army and the rest Grenadier Guards. We'd just had a massive operation to clear the Taliban from the area and were helping to widen and deepen irrigation ditches to improve the water supply in the area.

My Story: **Ed Janvrin**

On this particular day we were in Jusyalay speaking to local elders when we heard a big explosion and the crackle of gunfire. A contact was going on somewhere between our position and Sangin District Centre a couple of miles away. I decided to go and investigate because it was on our way back and clearly one of our Afghan patrols had been engaged.

We were in a convoy of seven vehicles, four ANA and three British, as we travelled along a notorious supply road called Route 611. I was in the second vehicle and Guardsman Downes was in the turret of the third vehicle alongside Company Sergeant Major Scully.

The lead ANA vehicle stopped to investigate and one of their commanders, Colonel Rassoul, got out to go and speak to a group of locals who were gathered by a hut at the side of the road. I asked my driver, Corporal Cunningham, to manoeuvre around so I could speak to Colonel Rassoul and make our plan.

Guardsman Downes's vehicle moved up to take our place and suddenly, 'boom', there was a massive explosion. Then machine-gun fire and small-arms fire started raining in on our position from all around. We were in the middle of an Improvised Explosive Device initiated ambush. We were under attack from all sides. It was absolute fucking chaos.

Downes's vehicle had been blown up, and we had guys injured underneath the vehicle. A couple of the lads from my vehicle jumped out and pulled them out but as they did so all of the ammunition on Downes's vehicle started cooking off. We had grenade rounds going off everywhere.

My Company Sergeant Major, Wayne Scully – a fucking hard man – had blood coming out of his ears and he was totally ashen-faced after being blown out of the turret of his vehicle. I've got this vision of him in front of me just swaying from side to side and eventually collapsing. I got someone else to look after him.

In the meantime the ANA guys had gone straight into a fight-through. They saved our lives that day. They showed incredible bravery by going straight at the Taliban on both sides. The Taliban started retreating. My first priority was the bombed out vehicle and the casualties. I knew the ANA fight-through was being successful because I could see the Taliban withdrawing.

The driver of Downes' vehicle, Colour Sergeant Day, had managed to crawl out. He was okay but he was shouting at me, 'We're fucking missing Downes, I can't find Downes, I can't find Downes'.

The first thing I needed to do was identify where he was. It was possible he could have joined the fight-through or, much worse, that he had been taken by the Taliban.

Then I remember Colour Sergeant Day shouting, 'Downes is dead, Downes is dead'. He was by a low wall and must have seen his body. I ran over and saw this crumpled figure lying in a heap. It was Downes. He had a massive gash to his head and his helmet had been ripped clean off. His leg was missing. He was limp. I took his pulse. Nothing. I got straight back on the radio.

'Hello zero, this is alpha two zero alpha, contact, one friendly KIA, wait out'.

I remember thinking, 'Be calm when you give this, they need to know that things are under control'.

They could hear my contact report in the Brigade HQ back in Lash Kagar. It's very rare they would get so close to hearing a firefight in real time. I've subsequently spoken to a friend who was in that room that day who heard the report. He told me it was like that scene in *Platoon* when firefights are going on all around the perimeter and they're close to being over-run by Vietcong.

We sorted ourselves out on the ground and went through Downesy's kit. It was important to retrieve anything that could be meaningful to his family. Retrieving his leg was horrendous. He'd been blown a long way clear of the turret and his leg must have got caught and literally been ripped off. He'd died instantly.

I remember lighting a cigarette and sitting down after that 15-minute intense firefight had happened, making sense of it all. There was a bit of a lull and I just thought, 'Downes has just died, and there are people back home in the UK, people who love him very dearly, just going about their daily lives, oblivious to what's happened. In the next 12 hours they are going to get told the news and their lives are going to fall apart. I knew it, but they didn't know it yet'. I thought that was just tragic.

Downes was an outstanding soldier and an outstanding young man in every way. I remember seeing his CV for the first time and thinking, 'Wow', because he had 16 GCSEs. He was keen, courteous, polite and tenacious. Everything a commander could ask from a young soldier. He had a huge future in the Army and would unquestionably have gone on to achieve great things. His death was an absolute tragedy.

The inquest into Downes's death was held at Stockport Magistrate's Court in June 2008. It was horrendous. It was in a courtroom with a coroner who interviewed all the people who were involved.

Downes's family were there and it was a very hard moment. It was made a lot harder because it felt like the coroner had already assumed I was guilty of negligence. I was given a proper grilling and, inevitably, I couldn't answer every question he put to me. Could anybody? The chaos of a firefight is something only a soldier can understand. As a commander you try to make order of the chaos. That is leadership. But you can never have a complete picture of what is going on in that kind of situation. It was so difficult.

Ultimately the outcome, the cause of death, was attributed to the Taliban, but I felt my ability as a commander had been called into question. I came away from that inquest thinking, 'Fuck, I was responsible for his death'.

Thankfully Downes's family were amazing. I'd written to them previously and had gone to visit them when I got back to the UK. They were very, very good about the whole situation. It was devastating for them, as you can imagine. But they believed absolutely in the Army and were very proud of their son and rightly so.

Downesy's inquest led to me really closing things down in my mind. I just didn't want to think about it. It just made me feel like shit. For ages I was paranoid that the lads blamed me for his death. When I think rationally about decisions I took that day, I know I made the right calls. But in my heart, I was responsible and I feel terrible about it.

And while the death of Guardsman Downes was a horrendous experience that I think about all the time, in many ways I think the civilian deaths and casualties affected me even more.

Downes was a soldier. He was a good guy who was there for a purpose and his amazing family knew that and were proud of him for it. But we were soldiers, and that's the danger we face.

Seeing kids who had been mutilated by suicide bombers was fucking horrendous. That was the worst thing, having to deal with the aftermath. I remember arriving in a market square after a suicide bomber had set themself off. One of our boys was holding a dead child in his arms, bawling his eyes out. This fucking hard soldier just stood there bawling his eyes out while this child died in his arms.

I remember another occasion when a little girl, she was maybe six-years-old, brought her two-year-old brother into camp for treatment. She was pushing him in a wheelbarrow. He'd been shot through the stomach.

There is another incident that plays on my mind, which happened after we spotted an armed Taliban team crossing the river and going into a hut in an area of caves.

I called in artillery support and spoke to the Forward Air Controller (FAO) to call in air support. I was actually talking to the pilot via the FAO, describing where the enemy were. These aircraft came in and the first bomb went straight into the hut, with the second and third bombs landing in the dead ground, which was the area we couldn't see from our position, between us and the caves.

I was told that the pilot had seen Taliban in the caves in the dead ground so we were just like, 'Fuck yeah'. We'd called in fast air and destroyed that Taliban team. 'Brilliant. All go home. Fucking good day.'

The next morning we went back out to the village and the locals were in a terrible state and the elders were really angry with us. The second and third bombs had hit a group of women and children who had been sheltering in the caves.

78

My Story: **Ed Janvrin**

Who do you blame? I don't know. Was it me because I'd called in the air strike? I've been told the pilot had seen Taliban at the mouth of one of the caves, but I didn't ask them to bomb the dead ground that I couldn't see, where it turned out there were women and children sheltering. I believe 12 civilians were killed in that incident.

When I first got back from Afghanistan, and in the years that followed, I had flashbacks all the time. Afghanistan was on my mind for every second of every day. Guardsman Downes was never far from my mind. For quite a few years afterwards I was thinking about Afghanistan every moment of every day. That's eased a bit in the intervening years but it's still there. It will never go away.

I'm not alone in suffering flashbacks and having dark thoughts. Far from it. I saw a lot of bad things – a lot of us did. Why wouldn't it affect me? It's a normal human response. Sometimes I think I'm being soft but I can't deny it's there. I don't think anyone can witness those kind of things and just walk away completely unaffected.

I don't think I'm very far down the Post Traumatic Stress Disorder (PTSD) scale, but I'm on it somewhere. Don't get me wrong I'm fine. I'm functioning and I'm fine. I'm holding down a good job and making a success of my life now I'm a civilian. I don't want to overdramatise and make what I'm experiencing now sound worse than it is. I also don't want to make out that my experience has been somehow worse or tougher than anyone else's because I know that's not the case.

I also don't want to scare my family into thinking I can't cope, because I can. I am coping. But it is always there, nagging. The memories. They'll never leave me. How can you see a maimed child brought to you in a wheelbarrow and just forget about that? How can you see a 19-year-old soldier, someone you're supposed to be looking after, killed in front of you and just forget about that? The answer is you can't. Well, I can't.

When I got back from Afghanistan I think people knew I'd had a tough tour. I used to get frustrated by people not wanting to know more, not asking questions. Now I accept their ambivalence. Often, people are well intentioned. They just don't want to pry.

This is the first time I've really spoken about this other than when I went through Trauma Risk Management process in the field, which happens in the immediate aftermath of a major incident. That was a huge benefit at the time, but time passes . . .

When I'm around military people it's easier because you get the banter going. It's when I'm trying to describe something that happened on the battlefield to someone who wasn't there that I struggle. I can get emotional. I'm definitely more emotional now than I was before that tour. It's the contrast of extremes I find hard to deal with. Extreme danger to near total safety. Londoners, on the whole, don't know how lucky they have it.

There are times when I might say a bit more because the situation warrants it but even with a close friend like Alex, who has shared experiences, we rarely talk about specific incidents because there is an element of not wanting to pry. I don't want to upset Alex either. We've never asked each other directly what we went through, but we've always looked out for each other and cared for each other and asked, 'Are you alright?' 'How is that affecting you?' We have talked around it.

Alex and I are both conscious it's probably a good thing to talk about our experiences. But equally I don't think either of us are ill as such, although a couple of our close mates have been hit very hard by PTSD.

Over time I've gradually made my peace with the idea that no one will ever really understand what I experienced. How could they? I've also made peace with the decisions I made and the fact that people die in war. But I still have flashbacks, less than I used to perhaps, but they are with me.

I've had a couple of incidents recently which have unsettled me. Twice I've broken down in tears in front of colleagues, in the middle of the office, and I can't really say why. It may have been someone asking me what went on triggering an emotional response which I'm not in control of. Images flash up in front of my eyes. Usually it's that young soldier holding the dead child, crying. Sometimes it just overwhelms me.

Living and working in London now does present some challenges. There is such a contrast between the repetitive, banal nature of commuting in to work and the high-octane, adrenaline-fuelled life on tour in Afghanistan. I can get frustrated, and sometimes I wish I was back in Helmand. In the UK everything is so safe. Someone twists their ankle and it's the worst thing ever.

It's that contrast that leads to people being a bit messed up in the mind. I've got friends who are way down that PTSD scale. They have terrible recurring nightmares. I don't have that. I sleep pretty well. Some of my friends' day-to-day behaviour has been affected. They are far more reckless than they ever used to be. They ride motorbikes far too fast, relationships have broken down, they have nightmares and cold sweats. Some have turned to drink – that's when it gets more serious.

I still analyse decisions I took. Terrible things resulted from situations we were in so I look back at those situations. But I think that, given what I had at the time, I made the right decisions. If I couldn't do that I would be in a much worse state than I am. I have the invasion of my mind by these thoughts and these memories and that is annoying at times, but they get them really badly. It's troubling them very deeply.

I've got a friend who was in charge of letting the families know when there'd been a death or serious injury on a recent Gurkhas tour. What a job. He saw at first hand the devastation death and serious injury causes to families. He wouldn't just turn up and tell the next of kin and then bugger off. He'd be there every day, trying to sort things out, being there at all the hardest moments. They had something like 30 serious casualties on that tour so there were a lot of families to look after. I wouldn't be surprised if he got PTSD from that. When you're on tour you have so much to do you just crack on. You don't realise what the families back home go through.

I think my own family knew my last tour was not pleasant, but beyond that I don't think they knew much. The tour happened very early on in my relationship with Helen and I was speaking to her on the phone maybe twice a week for 10 minutes at a time, but I was trying to shield her from the whole thing. I remember firefights starting while I was on the phone and I'd be in Forward Operating Base (FOB) Robinson with mortars coming in and I just had to say, 'Sorry, gotta go' as incoming was landing. I remember having conversations when that happened, although I can't remember Helen's reaction. I don't think she realised and thought, 'Oh shit, he's in a firefight'.

Before I went to Afghanistan I watched *Saving Private Ryan.* What a great film, but I could not watch it now. No way. I would be so uncomfortable. I wouldn't even try. If it's a gangster film, I can watch that even though there's plenty of violence in it. There may be moments that I don't feel too comfortable. But a war film with uniforms and all that stuff? No.

Watching anything that is combat-related sets off these massive rushes of adrenaline and my body just reacts to it. My heart beats faster, almost to the point that I get palpitations and I start sweating profusely. All the symptoms you get from an adrenaline rush. Very restless, you just want to move.

The adjustment to civilian life has not been easy. One of the first interviews I went for after I'd left the Army in 2008 was at a trading firm in the City. I did all the interviews, the CEO was happy with me and I was on the verge of getting an offer. So they asked me to join them for a couple of drinks one evening after the traders had finished work. They were a bunch of absolute arseholes. The worst stereotypes you could imagine from the City. They were in their forties and probably millionaires from all the trading they were doing. All they were interested in was money and all they wanted to hear from me was how many people I'd killed. They were laughing about it.

I just thought, 'You are fucking idiots for asking me that question in that way'. I don't think many people would ask that question normally, but these guys didn't know me and they were asking me about it in a piss-taking way. It was so crass.

My Story: **Ed Janvrin**

I had a stand-up argument with their head trader – I can't remember his name – who had first of all asked me how many people I'd killed and then started asking me, 'How much do you want to make money?' I said, 'Money is not the primary driver in my life'. He could not understand that and just said, 'How can you look to be joining our firm if money is not the primary driver?'

I just thought, 'What the fuck?' And sure enough the next day I was told I didn't really fit the culture and they were not going to make me an offer. I was like, 'The feeling is mutual'.

I didn't want to be part of that culture. It's that world where using prostitutes is okay, cheating on your wife is okay, everything is okay as long as you are making money. That was an insight into some parts of the City I definitely didn't want to be part of. It is a sick culture.

After that I shopped around a bit. I went into PricewaterhouseCoopers as a junior graduate consultant and I found that hard, really frustrating. Every day I was like, 'Jesus Christ I really miss the responsibility'. After carrying that huge burden of responsibility in the Army, suddenly I felt completely anonymous. People were treating me like a child. People didn't get that I'm more comfortable managing more complex projects and more people than I am doing the grunt work in a business. It felt a bit like someone who had been to the South Pole being told, 'Well done, but can you work an Excel file?'

I remember that, soon after I started there, there was this big meeting and everyone was getting pretty flustered and panicking a bit about what roles they were going to play and what the outcome would be. I couldn't get interested. It didn't feel important. Just as I was about to go into the meeting I got a text message pop up on my phone.

'Yubraj Rai has been killed.'

He was one of my blokes. A young Gurkha who I knew well. I didn't say much in that meeting I don't think. All I could think about were the lads who were still out there.

I missed the passion and the sense that I was contributing. I still do in many ways.

THE ROW TO RECOVERY

In Afghanistan I remember going into firefights and it being the most exhilarating thing I had ever done. It was just amazing and I wanted more. Despite taking casualties, which was fucking shit, I don't want to say the word, but it does feel like a bit of a 'game' because you are in that normality where suddenly taking casualties becomes part of life. It's bizarre. It's an emotional rollercoaster where you have really high highs and really low lows.

I definitely thrived on that at the time. And in an odd way I think people like myself and Alex are searching for that high when we do extreme challenges like Row2Recovery. There's a restlessness that wasn't there before. We're always searching for the next thing.

When I look back at my time in the Army, it was great, but would I want to be there right now with a wife and child? Probably not. But there are definitely things I miss. That's the really odd thing about the intense experiences of somewhere like Afghanistan. Because on one hand it's fucking uncomfortable and on the other you yearn for it because life is so much more vivid in those circumstances.

As I said before, I don't think I'm very far down the PTSD line. I think what I'm experiencing is normal and I don't want to over-dramatise it. I think that's what worries me. I'm worried it gets over-dramatised in people's minds. I'm okay. I don't have stress from it, my behaviour has not changed, I'm not an alcoholic because of it, I'm not ill off the back of it. I've got a natural human reaction of not wanting to see that kind of situation again. I feel a bit odd talking about it and occasionally there will be a few tears. But I think that is pretty normal actually.

I sleep fine, I don't drink heavily and I can manage my demons. Being in a stable, loving relationship with Helen is massively important. If I wasn't, then who knows?

If I could have a confidential way of speaking to other veterans then maybe I would. But it's not an easy thing to do.

I've found a job which is finally providing me with the challenge I craved and I feel passionate again. Afghanistan will never leave me though. Once you've seen combat, and the consequences of it, you can never be the same again.

My Story: **Ed Janvrin**

POSTSCRIPT:

Letter written by Guardsman Neil Downes to his girlfriend, Jane Little, to be opened in the event of his death.

Hey beautiful, I'm sorry I had to put you through all this darling. I'm truly sorry.

Just thought I'll leave you with a last few words.

All I wanna say is how much I loved you, and cared for you. You are the apple of my eye, and I will be watching over you always.

Mary-Jane, Ian, Tom, Craig, Lee, thank you all for accepting me in to be able to care for your daughter/sister. I will not forget how nice you have been to me!

Bet now my bloody lottery numbers will come up! Ha ha.

Jane I hope you have a wonderful and fulfilling life! Get married, have children, etc!

I will love you forever and will see you again when you're old and wrinkly!

I have told my parents to leave you some money out of my insurance so have fun bbz!

Ok…gonna go now beautiful.

Love you forever.

CHAPTER 3
LA GOMERA

19th November, 2011

The Row2Recovery crew arrived in La Gomera excited and daunted in equal measure by what lay in store. The notion of 'stepping outside the gate' was one they all understood. It was the heightened state of anticipation, excitement and fear a soldier feels as he prepares to go on patrol.

This time around that choking fear had been replaced by nervous excitement but all six men felt invigorated by a renewed sense that they were once again getting ready to step into the unknown. Critically, they all felt part of a team.

After months of sometimes frantic preparations, the reality of what they were taking on began to dawn as they walked off the ferry at San Sebastian, the island's capital and main port. Every other year since British adventurer Sir Chay Blyth initiated the race in 1997 – having first completed the crossing in 1966 – San Sebastian, with its population of barely 2,000 people, has found itself besieged by rowers, families, support teams, race organisers and other hangers-on, all frantically preparing for race day.

This year there would be 16 other crews in the Talisker Whisky Atlantic Challenge race. All of them with their own reasons and motives for choosing to step into the unknown. They made for an eclectic bunch, from a six-woman crew raising money to fight people trafficking, to a pair of jovial Welsh firemen also raising money for Help for Heroes. Most were raising money for charity.

While the race organiser's PR team were selling the event as '17 crews, 17 stories', it was the Row2Recovery crew who were attracting most interest from both national and international media.

The *Sunday Telegraph*, *Sunday Mirror* and *The Times* had all run weighty pieces about the campaign before they'd even left London, while radio, television and other newspaper interviews were lined up ahead of race start day. The crew were a headline writer's dream, 'Oarsome Crew' and 'Herows of the Atlantic' being among the favourites.

There was only one problem. There was still no sign of the now long-overdue refitted boat. Despite repeated assurances from the boatbuilders in Devon, the Row2Recovery crew arrived at San Sebastian harbour to find a vacant space where the boat they'd ironically tagged 'Sea Legs' was meant to be. All the other crews were busy working on their boats ahead of departure in just 13 days time. The camaraderie was already evident, with all the crews checking out how the others had set their boats up in order to gain any advantage possible. But with no boat to work on, the Row2Recovery crew were immediately placed at a disadvantage.

Ed: *It was hugely frustrating. We'd been down to see the boat on 17th September, when it was originally meant to be finished, and been told it would be ready for our arrival in La Gomera. When we got out there* *it wasn't there. It meant we were behind the curve when it came to understanding how things like the Global Positioning System worked, how all the communications equipment worked. Neil's seat still wasn't fixed. It was frustrating. We ended up waiting three days in La Gomera with no boat to work on. It wasn't ideal.*

Despite the crew's mounting frustration at the slow delivery of the boat and the impact it was having on preparation time at sea, the unexpected delay did provide a further opportunity to reinforce the team spirit which had been so carefully nurtured by Ed and Alex over the previous months.

Ed: *We'd heard of several previous crossings, the Fogle and Cracknell one being just one example, when each of the crew members had had totally different reasons for being on board and different things they wanted to achieve. That had caused massive friction and was something we had to avoid at all costs. There's nowhere to go if you fall out with each other in the middle of an ocean.*

After the initial discussion in Southampton regarding roles and responsibilities, Ed and Alex were keen to instil a set of values – a code – for the whole crew to abide by during the crossing. The aim was to ensure any tensions or disagreements that arose would not fester and threaten morale and ultimately the crossing. Ed had set up several meetings with renowned expedition leader, Jeremy Brade, before leaving for La Gomera, and Brade's advice proved invaluable.

Ed: *As skipper I felt it was my responsibility to make sure we were all agreed on how we were going to make decisions. Jeremy was strongly in favour of a charter where everyone agrees certain principles. You almost sign up to it.*

Over the course of several coffees and several more beers sat outside a bar on the quayside overlooking the harbour, the crew established a core set of values and principles they hoped would stand them in good stead out in the middle of the Atlantic.

Here is the charter they agreed upon:

THE R2AAARGH CODE

- The team always comes first – be selfless, be honest, be supportive, be on time.
- Admin is not a place in China – clear up after yourself and others.
- Never speak ill of someone else on the crew, and come down hard on those who are.
- Enforce discipline on yourself and others – in safety, hygiene, routines.
- The skipper's decision is final.

R2R's PRIORITIES

- Safety
- Cohesion
- Campaign
- Crossing
- Race

As well as the charter itself, Ed also noted a series of important reference points which would be important to keep in mind in times of high stress or difficulty.

Log (brackets indicate proposer):
- Always tell someone if you are hurting or can't row – and all others cannot judge that individual because it was the medic/skipper's decision to stop them, not theirs. (Rory)
- Welfare of the individual is the team's problem – be honest about your situation. (Will)

- Be vigilant – you are responsible for the team and yourself. (Alex)
- Start your shift at the designated time. Always. (Neil)
- Say something positive to the person coming off shift. (Will)
- Have you done a good deed to the person who has pissed you off the most today? (Ed)
- 'Race to win' or 'Best Effort'? (Alex)
- What goes on tour stays on tour – be wary what you divulge to outsiders because you cannot control the consequences. (Will)
- Safety first, campaign second, crossing third, race last. (Ed)
- The crew's friendship when we step off Is more important than the race. (All – from crew session in Southampton)

The crew stayed in modest apartments five minutes' walk from the harbour, which in the days after their arrival very quickly developed into a bustling hub of activity with each crew tinkering, testing and preparing their boats for the arduous journey that lay ahead. The Row2Recovery crew continued to fine-tune their team rules, with Alex initiating an honesty session which saw each crew member tell the others two good points and two points they each needed to work on in order to improve their contribution.

Alex: *The charter was crucial. One of the things it stated was that no one was allowed to say anything negative about anyone else unless they were present and you were addressing the issue directly to them. It meant you couldn't close the cabin door and say, 'Ed's being a nob' to Carl or anyone else. Everything was out in the open. It was all about honesty and trust.*

As well as the charter, we did a one-on-one feedback session, which I ran. It was like speed-dating where everyone wrote something that someone was doing well and something they could improve on. We learned a lot from those sessions. No one pulled any punches.

While the crew was undoubtedly functioning well, there remained an elephant in the room: rank. The Army operates a hierarchical system based upon a rank structure of officers (traditionally drawn from more wealthy backgrounds), Non-Commissioned Officers (NCOs) and private soldiers. Officers give the orders and the NCOs and junior ranks implement them. It is an old-fashioned structure but one which has operated for centuries, as a strict chain of command is widely acknowledged as being essential to an effective, functioning fighting force. Ed, Alex and Will had all been commissioned as officers, while Neil, Carl and Rory had all served as NCOs. It was essential to avoid a 'them and us' mentality developing.

Rory: *In Southampton I'd made a gag. Alex, Ed and Will were on one side of the table and Carl, Neil and myself were on other. They were doing what officers do, letting us eat first, but they didn't even realise they were doing it. I was like, 'Soldiers first is it?! Dive in'.*

There were a few officer jokes, but Alex and Ed were quick to snub them out. That was the right move. There was no natural or unnatural segregation, it just happened.

Ed: *Rory, in a jokey way, liked to make the distinction between officers and NCOs. I don't think life's about that; I think life is about your capabilities. In the military you have to go with the hierarchy, but when you're in something as fluid as Row2Recovery or a start-up company it is all about capabilities and will to succeed. Besides, we were going to be spending the next couple of months together on board a tiny boat. We could hardly expect a salute every time we saw each other.*

Carl: *Ed made the point that we were all equal and to forget about the fact that it was three officers and three NCOs. I was quite pleasantly surprised to hear that. We were encouraged to put our opinions forward which I saw as good leadership. We couldn't get to week four of the row and suddenly have someone come out and go,*

'You're a nob, I don't like you'. With the stress and pressure we were likely to come under that would have been a disaster.

With the team dynamic working effectively, there was now only one thing missing: the boat. Finally, three days after their arrival and more than two months overdue, 'Sea Legs' was delivered to the harbour. But the relief at seeing the boat was tempered by the realisation there was still significant work that had been left unfinished. At least Neil's new seat had been installed, although it still needed testing on the water.

Alex: *Our boat arrived last and it wasn't finished. We basically had to build it on the dock and we were one of the last crews on the water. There was no point moaning or pointing fingers. How would that have helped us cross the Atlantic? The whole point of building team spirit was to help us overcome problems that arose together. So that's what we did. We cracked on. We spent 12 to 14 hours a day on the dock working on the boat. It was a massive pain but we got on with it.*

Neil: *Getting the seat right was a real drama from the word go. It was always a bit of a botched job through the training. There was never a point where we reached a satisfactory solution because the fixing for the seat kept breaking. We would screw it in all kinds of different ways but it was never really sturdy, it was always a little bit temporary.*

I had a design that I wanted. The ones I'd trialled were ones they'd used in the Paralympics with an L-shaped back support on. We all assumed the best system was to have that support for my back but I subsequently found out it is designed like that in order to provide equal competition for people who are paralysed below the waist. I realised I would get a much better stroke if I could lean back and therefore I needed one without a back. La Gomera was the first time I was able to trial the seat for real and start making little modifications.

One of my biggest worries before departure was how my back was going to hold up. I was expecting to encounter a lot of problems in that area.

THE ROW TO RECOVERY

Each crew member could expect to burn up to 8,000 calories per day, almost three times what an average person would normally burn. It would be impossible to consume that amount of calories so it was inevitable there would be significant weight loss, but with the right blend of high-energy drinks, freeze-dried meals and supplements, that loss could be kept to a minimum. It meant that getting the on-board stores and rations right was enormously important.

Will struggled to work out the best formula to pack the boat, with hundreds of freeze-dried meals, similar to the Army ration packs used on operations, hundreds of litres of energy drinks, chocolate, dried biscuits and fruit all needing a home.

Countless journeys were made to and from the local supermarkets, which struggled to cope with the demands of the last-minute buying by the 17 crews taking part in the race.

Will: *I just couldn't see how we were going to get all the food in. A week before departure we carried out a dummy run where we packed 10 per cent of the food we'd require into the boat. It was clear if we did it that way we would not get all the food in. We were told by someone who had rowed the Atlantic before that 'It will be fine' so Ed took the attitude that it would be fine. But I was getting quite stressed out.*

Alex: *Will did a great job with the food stores. Just fitting it all in to the many hatches and spaces in the cabins was a huge game of trial and error. It was quite a stressful task.*

From what I saw of other crew's rations I think we had the best mix of food out of anyone. We had hundreds of different meals, great snacks. We had variety. Will put a lot of thought into it and made it his personal responsibility to focus on the trials and development of certain products!

The men had spent several weeks leading up to the row intentionally overeating or 'carb-loading' in order to put on sufficient weight to counter the inevitable loss they would experience during the crossing. Will had embarked on the task of getting 'Atlantic-ready' with great gusto, while Neil had put on so much weight the stumps of his legs had changed shape, meaning he was struggling to fit them into his carefully tailored prosthetic sockets.

Other essential equipment such as flares, life jackets, parachute anchor, inflatable life raft and, of course, shark repellent, all had to be stowed away. Packing the shark repellent, which is a powder made up of nigrosine crystals and copper acetate which forms a dense black cloud when mixed with seawater, was another sobering moment for the crew.

'If a shark went for me he'd probably end up disappointed,' Will only half-joked. 'If he went for my leg he'd either end up with a gob full of metal or fresh air.'

Whales and blue marlin had also been known to approach ocean rowing boats on previous crossings, although to the crew's knowledge there had not been any recorded incidents of a boat actually being attacked.

But sharks and whales were low down Neil's list of worries. His biggest concern was the inevitable muscle wastage to his stumps that would occur as a result of the expected weight loss. He and Rory were both due to leave their expensive electrically-powered prosthetics behind in La Gomera, to be shipped to Barbados, meaning he would have to carry out a series of stretching and strengthening exercises while at sea. But there was nothing he could do to completely prevent the muscle wasting away, which was sure to make his life more difficult if and when the crew made it to Barbados.

Neil: *I'd put on more than a stone by eating pizzas and generally pigging out. I'd spent six or seven months trying to put on more muscle and working on my strength in order that I could get back on my legs quickly once we reached the other side. I was worried that if I lost so much weight on the row I would effectively be back to square* *one when we got to the other side and have to learn to walk all over again.*

I put myself through quite a few days of pain in La Gomera before accepting I had no choice but to start using the wheelchair again. The legs were just sort of dropping on and off because the stumps were too big to fit into the sockets. It meant they were getting pounded on the end and it was bloody agony to be honest. I wasn't sleeping much at night because the pain was pretty constant. If I'd been on holiday I would have carried on wearing the prosthetics and just gritted my teeth but I was conscious of the row and the fact I needed to rest and be in the best shape possible at the start. The best decision for the team was for me to use the wheelchair again but I hated it. I hated having photos taken of me in it. It's not what I'm about.

Neil's struggles were a stark reminder to Ed and Alex of the incredible journey he had come on just to be in a position where he could even consider undertaking such a physically challenging expedition. The way he dealt with his day-to-day problems was also incredibly humbling.

Ed: *It was a reminder that these guys had been on a journey that most people can't even comprehend and I certainly couldn't. It was a reminder that the wheelchair for Neil represented a point in his recovery which was so dark. It represented failure.*

Rory: *The locals just hadn't seen people like us before, especially not a double amputee. Neil's sockets weren't fitting but the pace we needed to get around meant we needed him to be in his chair. I know that was very tough for him. I fully understood how he felt.*

My wheelchair represents defeat to me. It annoys me when I see people in the street in a wheelchair with below-knee amputations. I just think, 'Come on lad, you don't need that'. Then again I'm in the Army and if you're going to lose a leg the best place to do it is in the British or US Army.

Despite the extra workload brought about by the delay in the boat's arrival, there was still time to enjoy a little down time, often with the other crews, in the few nightspots the tiny port had to offer.

Ed: *We were working bloody hard, although we played pretty hard as well. We went on the piss quite a bit, which was really good fun and an important part of the bonding.*

By 'going on the piss' Ed meant the crew, in traditional British Army fashion, saw it almost as their duty to be the loudest and most gregarious of any of the crews taking part in the race.

Rory: *From the second day we got out there, the workload was relentless. It was a case of take a step back, look at what we've got, and then press go and hit fast forward three times. Early starts, full, busy days. Packing, wrapping, moving, humping, dumping, painting, sanding, building, destructing. Everything. It was full on.*
We'd finish around sunset, have a shower, put on some tatty old clothes and get down to the bar and have a big night, every night. It was great because the people we were meeting, the other rowers, were all going through exactly what we were going through so we could share and compare our experiences. All of a sudden we had 20 new friends.

When the organisers put on a fancy dress themed night for all the crews six days before departure, there was only ever going to be one winner. Or three. The event was taken very seriously indeed.

Rory: *We won first, second and third prizes. I won first prize dressed as a cross-dressing sailor. I wore a little black and white pinny with an anchor on the front and a cute little bob hat, offset with a silk mini skirt and a single fishnet stocking. I must have looked quite fetching! I don't think any of the other crews had been exposed to that kind of squaddie humour and camaraderie.*

THE ROW TO RECOVERY

We were working hard and playing hard and there were some heinous hangovers. But we were always professional after a really big night and always on parade. We'd be down by the dockside, sometimes still steaming drunk, by 8.30am every morning while some of the other crews would rock up around midday. I think some of them were a bit intimidated by us but the rivalry and camaraderie was brilliant. We were all there for the same reason, no matter what shape or size: to row an ocean.

The way the different crews bonded came as a welcome surprise to the Row2Recovery boys, whose extrovert spirit and sense of fun hit exactly the right note and helped settle some anxiety in the days counting down to departure. They hit it off especially well with the Norwegian boat, 'The Sons of Norway', made up of Emil Eide Eriksen and Trond Bratland Erichsen, who Alex nicknamed 'Mega Trond', while the all-female boat, 'Row4Freedom', and the two Welsh firemen, Jamie Windsor and John Haskell, were also the subject of plenty of good-natured banter, especially the morning after a late night. Team Tom, made up of old friends Tom Fancett and Tom Sauer, also shared several beers with the Row2Recovery crew along with the Atlantic 4.

Hungover or not, Ed would always begin the day with an 8.30am briefing to ensure the crew knew what needed doing that day, and who was going to do it. With space on the boat at an absolute premium, there were only so many people who could physically be on deck working at any one time. Inevitably Carl and Neil carried the greatest burden of responsibility as they were in charge of kit and electrical equipment.

Ed: *The lads would take the piss out of me for constantly doing military-style briefings. I wanted to create some kind of structure, so we'd have meetings alongside the boat on the harbour front and the lads would be like, 'Not another fucking meeting, you have got to be kidding'. Then all the other crews would take the piss about us having meetings.*

I was definitely getting the same sort of buzz I used to get when I was in the Army. I felt like we had a high-performing team. Since Southampton, everyone had taken the time to get to know and take responsibility for their various areas and they were helping each other as well without anyone needing to step in.

People were just cracking on with what they needed to do. Everyone was taking responsibility, was motivated, aligned, got the bigger picture. Carl would be doing something on the boat and Neil would be helping him and then Neil would need help with something more technical and get Carl involved. They were just getting shit done.

I tried to create as much structure as possible because as soon as you create structure it actually creates freedom. You put the boundaries in place and then you have the freedom to do what you want within those boundaries.

I felt strongly that in the run-up to something like this you will never finish all the tasks that you set out to do. I was perfectly happy to call it a day at times and just accept you would never complete every task on the list. It's just a fact. Given that, we needed to do as much as we could but also make sure we were rested and have a bit of time to ourselves. There were little things that needed doing like loading music onto iPods and that kind of thing. I was quite happy after dinner for guys to stop working but often they would say, 'We're going back out to the boat and we're going to finish this work. Are you with us or what?'

The harder the team worked, the more obvious it became to Ed and Alex that the hunch they'd had more than 18 months before, that the wounded crew-mates could play a fully active part in the crossing, was spot on. Gradually they stopped even noticing their injuries.

Ed: *Rory, Neil and Will were moving around a lot without their prosthetics – although Will had his prosthetic on most of the time. You get massively used to it. One of the great things was that it got to a point where I wasn't treating them any differently. I was almost* *taking their injuries for granted. Sometimes I found myself thinking their differences were completely normal. Then there were times when I'd catch myself thinking, 'Bloody hell he is really injured and it is pretty inspirational what he is doing'.*

The sight of such severely injured people moving unaided around the town was also an eye-opener for the locals of La Gomera, who had not been exposed to many war-wounded before. One unsavoury incident served as a reminder that prejudice remained fairly deeply ingrained in some parts of Spanish society. As Rory, Neil and Alex were wandering back to their accommodation in the small hours after the fancy dress party, a local man made a derogatory comment to Rory about his missing leg, prompting a heated exchange.

Rory: *We were walking home, admittedly worse for wear, when this guy called me over quietly and said, 'You guys with no legs are nothing. I've been through worse, you are nothing. I've lived through more than you have.'*

I was politely aggressive towards him. I wished him 30 minutes of amputee life and promised him he would take it back. He was adamant that he wouldn't so at that point I turned my back to him, tapped Alex on the shoulder and said, 'Get him away from me before I hurt him'. He was slagging Neil off as well. Five minutes later he came up to me in tears. I have no idea what Alex said to him but within a couple of minutes the guy was utterly apologetic.

Ed: *When we were in public I did get reminded of our crew's injuries. In Spain, to see a double amputee on their prosthetics is very unusual. Quite a lot of people would stop and stare. That was a bit of a reminder.*

But it made me feel proud to be associated with such a good bunch and proud for them. They have picked themselves back up and stepped back into the breach. Not quite the same breach, but a breach nevertheless.

LA GOMERA

Alex spent much of his time away from the rest of the crew, in near constant liaison with the support team in London in an effort to ensure the £17,000 worth of communications equipment, which had been fitted on board and would prove vital to the crew's aim of sharing their message through the media, was functioning properly.

Carl and Neil worked tirelessly to ensure brackets were fitted, holes plugged, hatches water-tight, safety equipment stowed, the water desalinator installed and countless other jobs which should have been sorted before they arrived in La Gomera were taken care of.

Carl: *Most of the other crews were out on the water testing their boats for the whole of the second week, making sure everything was spot-on. That was the whole point of going out there two weeks early. We were still stuck alongside the dock, working on getting the boat ship-shape. It annoyed me. I wanted to have three or four days to chill out before we left but that never happened. It was a botched job.*

With just four days to go before departure the boat was finally ready to be trialled at sea, giving the crew the long overdue chance to test some of their new kit, including Neil's seat, on the water. In an early sign of what lay ahead, things didn't go to plan.

Alex: *On our first night-time row a whole load of stuff broke, Including Neil's seat. We had to come up with a solution. We were talking about having it mounted on a special seat which went onto the rollers, but it was too high and didn't really work. The ultimate decision we went with was to bolt it straight onto the decking. That worked well. He had a seat belt across his stumps to keep him strapped in.*

While a solution finally appeared in sight for Neil's seat, substantial alterations still needed to be made to the stanchions and brackets that would fix the seat to the floor of the boat. Two days before departure, Will managed to source a new bracket which he was in the process of adjusting on the harbour wall when he knocked it over the side and into the murky water.

Will: *I was certain it was a goner. It was so deep there that I couldn't see any way of retrieving it. It was a heavy metal bracket and it sunk to the bottom very quickly.*

It was at that point that the crew were to realise, if they hadn't already, that Rory's addition had brought a sheer physical presence that would prove invaluable.

Rory: *Will had taken about a day to blag that bracket. We were at panic stations because Neil's chair was still not completely right. Two guys who worked at the dock had put together this fancy, custom-made bracket after Will bribed them with beers to make it. It was a Eureka moment. The chair worked. Almost literally in that same moment this bracket just went 'plop' into the water and we all gasped and watched it sink.*

It had to be recovered. I'd been in the water before and knew the depth of it so I got hold of a diving mask, duct-taped a torch to my hand so I didn't lose that too, and took a massive gulp of air and dived in. It was deep, maybe 15 metres, but I didn't come up until I had it. It was very, very murky under there but the bracket glinted in the light almost as soon as I hit the water so I could see it.

When I was at Headley Court I used the swimming pool at least once a week as part of my rehabilitation because it's weightless and friction-free. I was a very confident swimmer by the time I got to La Gomera.

Rory re-emerged, plonked the bracket on the quayside, and hauled himself onto the metal walkway that ran alongside the harbour, to the disbelief of the small group of onlookers who had gathered upon noticing the commotion.

Rory had, in Neil's words, the 'easy' job of overseeing the

on-board medical supplies. But with three amputee rowers in Neil, Rory and Will, another severely wounded in Carl, and two novice rowers in Alex and Ed, the Row2Recovery crew were going to be exposed to more medical risks than any of the other crews.

Back in the UK, Baz was struggling. Just as he'd been due to fly out to join the crew in La Gomera to wave them on their way, he'd been struck down with yet another severe infection of his stump. It was painful, angry and inflamed, and needed yet more treatment with strong antibiotics and painkillers. It completely vindicated his decision to withdraw from the race.

Alex: *The word all the wounded guys come to fear and a word I only really came to understand by getting involved in the campaign is 'infection'. When most people say 'infection' it means they've got a cold or a cut or whatever it may be. When an amputee says 'infection' they mean, 'I am at serious risk of losing another part of my body'. Getting a bad infection at sea could be seriously problematic.*

Rory: *Infections were obviously a worry. An infected stump in the middle of the Atlantic would be far from ideal, but we had strong antibiotics and a really good medical kit to deal with that eventuality.*

My biggest medical concern before we left was somebody sustaining a serious head injury at sea. Being tossed around, smashing their head, there would be very little we could do about it.

I knew we were going to get salt sores on our backsides and other places and there was nothing we could do about them other than try to maintain a disciplined cleaning and washing routine. We had the right kit to do that, which was fresh water and baby wipes. That was just something we were going to have to endure.

As departure day drew closer it became increasingly apparent that the Row2Recovery crew were making quite an impact at home and abroad. As media interest rose, money started pouring in via the charity's website at a rate of almost £1,000 per day. It was hugely gratifying for the crew to know the attention surrounding them was also helping to drive the fundraising part of their mission.

ITV flew reporter Geraint Vincent and cameraman Jim Healey out to cover the departure.

'Last week Libya, this week La Gomera!' the affable Vincent quipped upon his arrival. His own life was dominated by near endless travel to far-flung, often dangerous places, and the crew admired his sense of adventure and optimistic outlook. Vincent was also able to take a joke at his own expense, which went down well, and he quickly gained the crew's trust.

Newspapers were also showing an increased interest and a double-page feature in the *London Evening Standard* as well as a piece in the respected Spanish paper *Marca* – in which the crew's endeavours were compared to those of Christopher Columbus – demonstrated the boys were starting to achieve global recognition. The *Sydney Morning Herald* also carried an article about the crew.

But more important in the short-term were the last-minute adjustments needed on the boat, catching up on some sleep and welcoming anxious friends and families who had begun to assemble in the days before departure. The crew were aware of the need to be sensitive to their families concerns.

Jilly Dixon: *My big concern was that Will was putting himself in danger again. The last time I'd said goodbye to him things hadn't really gone that well. There was so much that could go wrong this time too. I really thought we'd left all that behind as a family and I was quite cross for a time. I thought he was being quite selfish because he'd put us through so much and I didn't think he needed to do that.*

Will: *When I told Mum I was going to do the row I don't think she was overly taken by the idea. In fact I think she burst into tears. I don't blame her. She was always supportive and accepted it was something I wanted to do, but I'm sure she'd rather I hadn't. She knew my mind*

*was made up. I hated seeing Mum upset, but this was something I
needed to do. In her heart she knew that.*

Despite the reservations several parents and partners held about
the expedition, they were all keen to support wherever possible,
fetching bottles of water, running errands, collecting prosthetics
and washing clothes. They even set up an impromptu sewing club
on the harbourside, quickly dubbed 'Sew2Recovery', with Ed's mum
Isabelle and dad Robin, Will's mum Jilly and girlfriend Mia, among
those who spent countless hours sewing sheepskin linings onto
foam pads to act as bespoke seat covers that would go some way
to protecting their loved one's backsides.

With less than 48 hours to go before the start, the crew began to
focus on what lay ahead. Apart from head injuries and Infections,
the biggest safety concern was capsizing. All the crews were under
strict instructions to keep the cabin hatches closed whenever
possible as the air-tight cabins, combined with 200 litres of ballast
water stored in each boat's hull, would act as a self-righting
mechanism in the event of a capsize. The most likely cause of a
capsize would be a freak wave, which they could do little about, or
poor steering which would leave the vessel beam on (side-on) to a
wave and prone to taking its maximum force. Each crew member
would be tethered to the boat at all times while on deck, with a
clip they could release in emergencies.

The crews would also be crossing some of the busiest shipping
lanes in the world, and the threat of being sunk by a passing liner
or cargo vessel was very real. All the boats in the race had to be
fitted with specialist 'Sea Me' active radar devices which artificially
magnified their size on other vessels' radars and acted as vital
safety devices if they came too close to an ocean liner steaming
across the ocean. Without them, there was every chance they
would be missed by busy commercial liners not used to such tiny
vessels in the middle of the ocean.

Ed had also been monitoring the weather closely for several

days. December is traditionally the best month to start the row because the hurricane season has usually ended and the trade winds and currents are flowing from a north-easterly direction, providing valuable propulsion as the crews travel east to west across the Atlantic. This year was no different, although after consulting a local weather expert Ed noted some packed isobars – a sure sign of storms – on the satellite heading in the direction of La Gomera.

To make matters worse there were also reports that the El Hierro volcano, located approximately 60 miles to the south-west of La Gomera was erupting, causing sulphuric gas to rise menacingly to the surface of the sea from deep underwater and potentially posing a threat to small vessels. The crews were given strict instructions to navigate well south of the threat.

The race organisers would provide a safety yacht, 'Aurora', to stay around the fleet, which would inevitably spread out over many miles from a very early stage, and provide assistance wherever possible. But as disqualification from the race would result if assistance was taken, a call would only be put out as a last resort. Aurora would stay in radio contact with all the boats, and would prioritise the support they provided depending on the immediacy of the danger crews may or may not be in.

Alex: *I think we were all pretty confident. For our crew it was exciting rather than intimidating. We'd all been in situations where we'd stepped into the unknown before. We'd done it loads of times. It sounds a bit glib to say it but at least no one was going to try to kill us. That was an upside already.*

It gave us a massive psychological boost. Other crews didn't necessarily feel the same but we got a lot of confidence by drawing on our previous experiences. There was also a perspective thing.

The night before the scheduled departure the race sponsor, Talisker Whisky, laid on a leaving party for the crews and their families to enjoy some quality time together. In keeping with their stay in La Gomera, the Row2Recovery crew didn't hold back, continuing a tradition Neil had begun months before by singing 'Happy Birthday' to Carl every single day. A message was passed to the Spanish band entertaining the crowd and within seconds the red-faced former sniper was hauled up on stage, handed a pair of maracas and forced to grin through gritted teeth as he was serenaded by the band and his fellow competitors.

Carl: *Hilarious. The birthday gag came about on a Help for Heroes surfing trip me and Neil had been on to America a year earlier. In restaurants, bars, clubs, everywhere, I would get free shots. One day I was given a big birthday cake with 'To Carl' written on it. We were surfing one day and I had a birthday in the water. That soon got picked up in La Gomera. I hated it. Despised It. I think that's why it carried on as long as it did. Neil's a bastard. He told the guys what had happened in America at the departure dinner. He told Alex, who told one of the organisers, and he told the band. They got me up playing the maracas. Neil was crying with laughter.*

But despite the fun and games, there was also a tangible sense of trepidation among all those present as they readied themselves for one of the biggest tests of their lives.

Will: *There were definite comparisons to getting ready to go on an operational tour. That feeling of the unknown as you step out of the gates. There were a whole variety of unknowns which you've trained for but you don't know when they're going to hit or what form they're going to take.*
I remember the night before we were due to leave I slept very badly, which is strange for me. I was very nervous in the morning when we got up, really nervous. The evening before I went around to the flat Mum and my sister Catherine were staying in and I just could not do any small talk with them whatsoever. In some ways I was more apprehensive than when I went to Afghanistan because I felt more outside my comfort zone doing this. There was also a strong sense of

guilt that I was putting my loved ones through this all over again. Not so much my girlfriend, Mia, who was awesome, although I'm sure she was very worried while we were away.

Rory: *In some ways this was even harder than going on an operational tour. At least then I'd trained properly and, to an extent, knew what to expect when I went to Iraq. I'd come late to this and hadn't done all the training the other guys had. Damn right I was nervous.*

Ed's wife, Helen, had come out to visit with the couple's six-month-old baby, Louis, along with her own parents and Ed's mum and dad.

Ed: *It was brilliant having them all there. They were so supportive. Poor little Louis was totally out of his comfort zone. It was hot and he was in a completely new environment.*

Because of my experiences in the Army I've got quite good at approaching what is on the surface a major undertaking but just going, 'It's not a big deal, I can sleep'. Some people can't sleep the night before something big. I was fine apart from Louis's crying, but it wasn't as if I was up all night worrying.

My mind was really focused on getting the crew ready, getting everything ready. For right or wrong I took the responsibility as skipper seriously and I think I probably had more of an eye on the risks than the other guys. The 'what ifs?' I was playing out permutations in my head all the time. 'What if this happens? What if that happens?' Always contingency planning. It probably meant I wasn't great company.

There had been rumours flying around at the Talisker party the night before the official start day that a big storm was sweeping up from the south-west and threatening to delay the race. It was the same storm Ed had seen on the satellite. The race organisers were forced to postpone the start by 24 hours. While it was frustrating, with the Row2Recovery crew still working on their boat the prospect of a late start was actually quite welcome.

Will: *I got down to the harbour at around 7am and the first person I saw was one of the race organisers. The wind had been really heavy that night and he let it slip that we wouldn't be going out that day. He was going to call a meeting and asked me not to tell anyone. Of course I went and told the crew straightaway, and everyone else I saw actually. I was gutted because I knew it involved going through that waiting again.*

For some reason I slept much better the next night and I was much more composed when we actually came to the start so maybe it was for the best. We were more ready because if we'd left that morning we would have had even more work to do on the boat because we were still working on it until midday. It was just fiddly stuff like last-minute packing and working on some of the fittings, but it had to be done.

When it came to saying goodbye to our families it was pretty emotional. I held it together but it was touch and go. Seeing Mum cry was difficult. Mia pretty much held it together, until I left anyway. There was a real relief about finally getting going. I wasn't upset about leaving my loved ones behind, but I was upset about them being upset. It brought home what we'd all been through collectively over the past couple of years. It had such close parallels to me leaving for Afghanistan. The whole goodbye, going into the dangerous unknown. That definitely wasn't lost on me. I was very excited about what was coming up but also very aware of what I was putting my loved ones through.

The physical act of saying goodbye was incredibly tough but once we were on board and pulling the oars it was game time.

Carl: *There were a lot of pats on the back and good luck messages between the crews. One crew also put a dead fish in another one's boat and the Welsh crew of firemen drew a penis onto the Atlantic 4's rudder.*

I didn't have any family out in La Gomera because I wanted to be able to focus on the row itself. In the end that was a good decision because of the amount of work that was required.

THE ROW TO RECOVERY

Neil: *Even up until a couple of days before it seemed such a long way away that we were actually going to be rowing. To actually be there doing it, it did feel like a day that was never going to come. People said getting to the start line was going to be the hardest bit and that was partly true. It was definitely in my mind that no one had ever done it with my injury before. Not that many people had done it full stop! But it was a big motivator knowing that I was pushing the boundaries.*

I think I was a little bit nervous, a bit excited. It was nice to be in the race. If we'd done it on our own it would have been even tougher. All of the crews had become quite good friends by this time. We'd been together for a couple of weeks by then. I've spoken to a few of the other crews subsequently and a few of them said they were terrified on the way out to the start line. I don't think I was ever scared particularly. But having said that I'm not sure I was looking forward to it. I just wanted to get on with it.

My Story:
Will Dixon

Age: 28
Regiment: The Rifles (Third Battalion)
Army career span: 2008–2012
Rank: Lieutenant
Combat experience: Afghanistan (2009)
Injury: Below knee amputation of the left leg

Suddenly there was an almighty explosion and the wind was knocked right out of me. Our armoured vehicle had been hit by an IED. It hadn't been penetrated but it was lifted up into the air and then there was a massive crash as it came back down again onto the front tyres. There was a smell of cordite and my ears were ringing.

I looked to my left where my driver, Rifleman Middleton, was sitting and asked him if he was okay. His glasses were hanging half way down his face like something out of a *Carry On* film. He was fine.

I looked in the back to find out if anyone was injured. 'Yep, we're okay boss. No injuries.'

Then, I heard myself say, 'Right, I'm not okay. My leg's fucked'.

Very quickly the pain started to hit me, maybe three or four seconds after the explosion. Everything slowed down and my body was sending me messages I'd never received before. I was trying to make sense of them. I couldn't really feel anything below my knee other than this intense throbbing pain in my right heel.

111

THE ROW TO RECOVERY

The pain increased rapidly and soon I was in agony. I knew it was a fairly serious injury. I'd never experienced pain like it. I'd fractured my cheekbone playing rugby and dislocated my shoulder but this was something else entirely.

I had a quick look down and what I saw didn't make sense to me. My boot was still on but my foot wasn't where I thought it was and everything just looked wrong. The impact had driven my heel into the floor of the vehicle and shattered both my heels. I had a severe compound fracture of my leg and my foot was smashed to pieces. I didn't look down again. I guess that was the last time I saw my foot. I knew my leg was a goner.

There was blood, not masses, but it was pooling in my boot. They injected me with my own morphine in the top of my leg. It wasn't enough.

One of the first things that entered my head was, 'This is the end of my tour'. I remember being really pissed off about that.

The boys carried out the treatment on the spot and I got pulled into a medic's vehicle. The medic was called Gabby and she was phenomenal. All the lads were around me telling me I was going to be alright. They were superb.

People were being quite firm with me saying, 'We're all okay, get yourself sorted'. I trusted everyone around me. I knew they were good guys who would make the right calls. I was also in a stupid amount of pain so I wouldn't have been any good even if I'd wanted to be. I remember at one point saying, 'I'm going to have to just scream here'. So on a few occasions I just lay there going 'Aarrggghhh!' at the top of my voice.

I never thought I was going to die, I just wanted the pain to stop. It was probably about half an hour before the chopper arrived. It seemed like ages. I was put on a stretcher and carried to it. The next day they cleared that area – because it had been dusk when it happened and all this was happening in darkness – and found a load of pressure plate IEDs right along the route they'd taken me out on.

The chopper journey took a while but the American crew were

awesome. They were cracking loads of jokes, going, 'Man, when you get back you're going to get so much pussy'.

We landed and I was put in an ambulance. As I was being taken out of the ambulance they knocked my leg on the side of the door and I went absolutely apeshit. My last memory before I was knocked out is of me ranting and screaming at these people who'd knocked my leg.

My next recollection is of being woken up by the doctor saying, 'You're in Bastion hospital and I'm afraid we've had to amputate your leg'.

'Don't worry,' I replied. 'I knew that was going to happen, thank you very much'.

I remember being very polite to everyone and feeling really grateful to have this level of care.

One of the first things I asked when I regained consciousness was, 'Do my mum and dad know?' I insisted on telling them myself so they wheeled my bed over to a phone and I phoned them. I was so nervous. I didn't give myself too much time to think. The phone rang about three times and Mum picked up. My heart was thumping. I knew what I was about to tell them was going to change their lives. I wanted to get to the point without being brutal, but again I didn't want to let them know something was wrong too early and then drag it out.

Jilly Dixon: *I was neurotic about missing a phone call when he was in Afghanistan. Everywhere I went I would put the phone through to my mobile so I was always contactable. Sod's law, once Will rang and I missed the call but he left a message. But in fact it was fabulous because I could replay the message over and over again just to hear his voice.*

Mum answered and initially she was just really happy to hear from me. We hadn't spoken for a while and I'm sure she'd been waiting for me to call.

She said, 'Will, how are you?' I said, 'Not too bad, although I've picked up a bit of an injury'. She said, 'Oh dear', but the way I'd said it she must have thought it was nothing too serious.

I said, 'I've fractured my right heel and I've also had my left leg amputated below the knee'.

I could hear her voice trembling and followed up with, 'Mum, I'm okay, I'm going to be home soon'. Dad took over the phone and said, 'Will, I've got your mum, we're fine, get yourself home. Is there anything we can do?'

Jilly Dixon: *My overriding feeling was, 'Thank God he's alive'. I knew his brain wasn't affected and he promised me he had no other injuries. None of his major organs were damaged.*

It was terrible, it was such a shock and I had to make him repeat it a few times before I handed the phone on to Rob. We were just numb. I was physically sick. I couldn't cry. I was just physically very ill after we put the phone down.

I told Mum and Dad I'd be home in 24 hours and that I was absolutely fine and there was nothing else wrong. I just wanted to allay as many of their worries as possible. I knew I was causing them anguish and I felt so guilty about that.

It took a while before I actually got to see the damage after the operation because my leg was very heavily bandaged up. I had this big bulbous stump and I could still very much feel my foot even though it wasn't there. I was also still in a lot of pain. I was on a lot of drugs but I was very, very positive. People would come to see me and I'd have this beaming smile on.

I was a below knee amputee. One of the lucky ones. I had friends who'd suffered the same injury and I knew that, while my rugby playing days were over, I would be able to live an active life in the future. Having that knee joint intact was absolutely crucial to my future.

In Bastion Hospital alone there were guys who were far worse off than I was. While I'd been out on that Quick Reaction Force (QRF), on the day I was injured, a suicide bomber had struck and killed two guys from the Recce Platoon. I knew them, they were in the same company.

There was a guy on the ward from 4 Rifles who'd been shot through the neck and shoulder. He was able to talk, but he was in a lot of pain. I remember saying, 'Shit are you going to be alright?' and he came back with, 'You're the one with the missing leg, mate'. I was like, 'Fair play'.

My biggest worry was for my blokes. I felt very disconnected from them. I'd gone from spending every waking minute with them and knowing exactly what was going on and then suddenly they were there without me.

I was flown home and spent a couple of weeks in Selly Oak where I was given a further reminder of how lucky I'd been. There were some bad double amputees, young lads with horrific injuries and guys with complex infections because they'd been blown up and all the dirt and river water had got into their wounds and caused severe complications.

Rob Dixon (Will's dad): *There were some terrible sights in there. Awful. The people on either side of him had no legs at all. One lad was missing his testicles. It was terrible.*

I went home after a few weeks in Selly Oak and started doing my dressings at home. Seeing my stump for the first time out of its dressing was quite tough. It's not the most attractive thing, let's be honest. I'm not squeamish or especially vain but it's not my best feature. Poor old Mum had to come and do a lot of the dressing changes and stuff. I let her look after me because she wanted to and she was incredible in so many ways.

I felt like a child again. I had to crap into a commode and Mum would have to take it out and deal with it. I wasn't mobile. It had to be done.

Mum was very straightforward and no nonsense about it and would say to me, 'I know you're a grown man, but I'm going to have to deal with your poos. It's not going to be much fun for you and it's not going to be much fun for me but let's just get on with it'. That was it.

We both just accepted it because if I'd let it play on my mind I probably would have found it difficult. I had just lost my leg and I knew Mum didn't resent doing it and I would rather have been at home than in a hospital.

Jilly Dixon: *It was very frightening. I was quite nervous. I had no medical training whatsoever and until this happened I'd always been quite squeamish. His wound was not a pretty sight. It was a peculiar blast injury so there were all sorts of folds and flaps of skin which we had to clean regularly, each day before dressing it. Will was brilliant. He knew much more than I did. He had a huge cocktail of tablets that he needed to take at different times throughout the day and night. He had to inject himself in the stomach every day.*

I was terrified of infections so I was manically cleaning everything in sight and changing his sheets twice a day. We had decided to get a downstairs bathroom fitted out for him with a wet room to shower in but it wasn't ready so I had to bring him bowls of water so he could wash himself. There was a commode which I had to empty for him. It didn't worry me at all but for a young man of 25 that is not what you want your mother doing. I know it sounds silly, but I was just so grateful I was able to do something for him. It was all I could do.

He didn't really have any low points. I was actually quite concerned about that because I thought he must have them. The only point I saw him break down was when he heard that one of the battalion sergeants had been killed. He went into his room and howled.

I had the occasional low moment but, on the whole, every day since I was injured has been a good one. I'm alive and I have another crack. I'm not trying to play the martyr but it's plainly obvious that it could have been so much worse. I feel a responsibility to those who weren't as fortunate to live every day of the rest of my life to the full.

My Story: **Will Dixon**

In my battle group we had over 30 killed, including attachments from the bomb disposal teams and some of the mentors who were attached. The battle group was around 800. We had over 100 battlefield injuries. There's a fairly wide scope of what that can involve but it means that at some point they would have been evacuated back to Bastion, even if they subsequently returned to the front line. About one in eight could expect to be killed or fairly seriously wounded. That's pretty sobering.

Afghanistan and Iraq were both kicking off and in the news constantly while I was at university. I was always reading about guys on operational tours, guys my age, and I was impatient to get on with something serious in my life.

I remember saying to people at the time, 'We're sending our young soldiers out there, I would be much happier if I was leading them'. It wasn't arrogance, I was just confident I would make a good commander. I believed I could flourish in the Army.

Dad had been the commanding officer of The Gloucester Regiment. I was very proud of him. There was never any pressure from him for me to go into the Army, but I'd grown up in that environment and felt comfortable in it. I'm very similar to Dad I think. The reasons he'd joined were the same reasons I joined. The sense of adventure, a desire to lead and a real sense of service. I'm a patriot, but it means different things to different people. I feel strongly about this country. It drives a lot of what I see and what I do. It's about being a positive citizen and giving more than you take.

All the staff at Sandhurst had been through Iraq and Afghanistan so we were instructed by some very experienced colour sergeants and platoon commanders who'd seen war up close. They were bringing their knowledge back from the battlefield and it was up to us to absorb the lessons they'd learned.

We heard the casualty numbers that were coming back and I remember thinking, 'That could be me soon'. But it was what we wanted. We lapped up the stories and were eager to hear about every tiny detail of what we could expect to encounter. As soon as someone came back from a tour you'd always want to quiz them and find out more. It was exciting.

After Sandhurst, I joined 3 Rifles and found out pretty much straightaway that we would be deploying to Afghanistan within about a year. I was happy about that. In some ways I'd have liked to have gone sooner.

By the summer of 2009 Sangin had developed a reputation as the hot spot within Helmand Province. It was where the majority of the casualties were being taken. This was where we were going. We took it as a credit to our battalion that we were being sent to the toughest place. We thought we were the best and that was why we were being sent there.

My parents came up to Edinburgh, where I was based, the weekend before we left and we went out for a meal. When I'd told them I was deploying to Sangin they'd started following it really closely on the news. They were seeing a lot of soldiers getting killed or injured and I'd tried to allay their fears. I felt selfish for putting Mum through it. Essentially you're pursuing a job you love even though you're causing your family a degree of concern and worry. It wasn't easy at all.

Jilly Dixon: *We were very conscious of what was going on in Afghanistan. The reason Will hadn't told us he was deploying sooner was because a friends of ours' son had been killed in Iraq. I knew what he was getting into. We were acutely aware of the dangers he faced.*

It was incredibly difficult saying goodbye to Mum. She never made me feel guilty, but you can tell someone you're going to be alright as many times as you like but you can't promise someone you're going to be alright. The 2 Rifles guys had been on tour before us and had taken a shitload of casualties, the most casualties of any British battalion that had deployed up to that point. We were going into the same area as those guys.

Dad was strong, but he was going through it as well. Seeing Mum worried always has an effect on me. I was pretty emotional but you want to stay strong because you want to appear confident. But you also have to acknowledge their concerns and reassure them you're not taking the risks lightly. It's a difficult balance. We had a very long hug, I remember Mum giving me a big squeeze and I just tried to draw as much out of that moment as possible. At the back of Mum's mind I knew she was thinking, 'I hope to God I get to see him again'. I was thinking exactly the same about her and Dad.

Jilly Dixon: *I'd read a brilliant but unsettling piece by Anthony Loyd in The Times. He was out there with 2 Rifles at a particularly bad time. His sign-off to the piece was something to the effect of, 'I wouldn't want a son of mine being a soldier in Sangin.' I just thought, 'Oh my God'.*

Saying goodbye was ghastly. It was so tough. We were stood just outside the officer's mess and I remember looking really, really deeply into Will's eyes and just clinging on to that. I can still see that look in his eyes now. He knew exactly what we were feeling.

My parents were an amazing source of strength. I could not have done it without them but at the same time I didn't want to put them through it. It's so much harder for the families because all they can really do is sit back, read the headlines and worry. I was so aware of that.

Soldiers are required to write a letter to their loved ones so if they do get killed they have something to remember them by. It was the hardest thing I've ever written. It wasn't long, probably about two sides of A5. I'm not a great writer.

The thrust of what I was trying to say was that I'd been killed doing what I enjoyed and I was incredibly lucky to have had them as my family. It was along the lines of, 'I don't want you to be bitter, I need you to move on'. I knew Mum would really struggle and would need someone to blame, but I wanted them to know that everything would have been done to help me and that they should go on and live their lives. I think I also apologised for not being able to leave them any money!

THE ROW TO RECOVERY

I started and stopped that letter so many times. It's very difficult to get into the right state of mind to write something like that. It's incredibly emotional. I was in pieces for parts of it. I'd stop and have to walk away.

We spent the night before deploying in a hotel near RAF Brize Norton. The rooms were pretty basic with single, uncomfortable beds with a sheet and woollen blankets. I lay awake wondering who had slept there before.

I'd lost a good friend, Mark Evison, who I'd been through Sandhurst with, a few weeks before. He'd been shot while on patrol and died of his wounds. Mark was very much in my thoughts that night. His death had troubled me. It struck me that if someone as good as Mark could be killed then anybody could. It was arbitrary. I'd always thought of Mark as being invincible. I wondered if he'd slept in the same room that I was in before he'd deployed.

Jilly Dixon: *As a mother you just want to protect your young, whether you are a human being, a lion or a dog. It is instinctive. This felt as if it was going against nature seeing your son going off to a war which the majority of people in this country didn't support. I knew there were a lot of very nasty people who would be trying to kill him.*

I spoke to my platoon a couple of times before and after we'd deployed. I thought it was my job to at least say why we were there. I gave them the party line.

I remember at the time being pretty sure of why we were there and what we were doing. It was about the security of this country and the security of the region. Afghanistan is a very strategically positioned country because it borders Iran, Pakistan and Tajikistan, which also borders Russia, and it touches China as well. If it's allowed to go lawless then we'll see what we saw before 9/11 which was al-Qaeda being harboured by the Taliban. I told my platoon that was the reason we needed to provide a stable region so terrorism was unable to thrive there. That may have been the textbook line but I genuinely believed it.

My Story: **Will Dixon**

I said to the lads, 'There will be times on this tour when the shit hits the fan, people will get hurt and maybe killed, and people will question what the fuck we are doing here'. It was important to set out the reasons we were there because that wouldn't change no matter what happened on the tour.

I've had more time to think about it since and I kind of go around in circles. You want to think we made a positive difference and that we were there for the right reasons. I know our battalion conducted itself admirably. New schools were built, healthcare centres as well. History will judge us I suppose.

The heat in Afghanistan hits you straightaway when you get out of the plane. The first impression on arrival at Camp Bastion was that it was fairly comfortable. There were lots of bottles of water around. It was a huge, dusty place. The Americans were there as well on a separate part of the base and we realised just how vast the support operation was for the guys going to the front line. We had a tour of the hospital which was important. The facilities were amazing. It was reassuring for the blokes to see that.

We spent about 10 days at Bastion acclimatising and getting ready to deploy to the battlefield. While we were there I bumped into a really good friend of mine from Sandhurst, Will Hignett, who ended up being awarded a Military Cross off the back of his tour. He'd had a very tough tour and was in absolutely no danger of sugar-coating it for me. He just said, 'It's fucking brutal'. He was coming up to his six months, pretty much done. He told me the entire place was like a low-density minefield. It was good to see him but, if we needed it, it was another stark reality-check. He was quite solemn. He was still cracking jokes but you could tell he'd had a tough tour. He'd lost weight and was clearly exhausted. I remember speaking to the other platoon commanders, Danny and Tom, and going, 'Fuck me, that doesn't sound much fun'.

You never know what you're going to be like in your first contact. You think about how you'll react under fire, how you'll react when you need to pull the trigger. You just want to respond well. You question it. Will I just shit my pants? I hadn't heard of anyone who'd choked in that situation but clearly some people would react better than others.

Along with the other platoon commanders I deployed before the rest of the lads to shadow the battalion we'd be taking over from and get an understanding of the land and the threat we would face. We had a big contact on one of the very first patrols I went on. We went into an area they hadn't really been into that much up to that point on their tour, right up into the badlands.

We deployed at night so that when daylight came we'd be in position and it was about a three-mile walk out from our base. The idea was to get up close to the enemy before they knew we were there. We didn't have one specific target, but we wanted to show a presence in the area. We got into position and occupied a few compounds and did a few searches and at one point we went up this very high tower. It had great arcs of fire – clear visuals – around the whole area but obviously, being a tower, it stuck out quite a bit. Before long we were attracting a fair bit of attention and before I knew it I was in my first contact.

It was mainly one way, with a Taliban sniper taking a series of potshots at us. We fired some rounds back because we could see his position from where the smoke came up from his rifle and where the dust kicked up from the rifle's recoil. But we were basically being reactive. The bullets were very close. There was a real fizz when they went past. It was strange. That was the first time I'd heard that sound. They were hitting the wall behind us. There was a big radar dish on this building that must have been there from a long time before. I remember ducking back down the next time the rounds came in and I was standing behind the radar dish. I came back up and looked behind at the dish and the rounds had peppered it precisely where I'd been standing. That was quite exciting. I managed to put a few rounds back down into his area which was good.

I didn't freeze, which was the main thing. It probably helped that I was surrounded by experienced guys. I was very glad I had experienced my first contact before my soldiers got out there. The fact I'd had a contact and had reacted effectively would have reassured them I'm sure.

The image of the radar stuck in my mind. It was bloody exciting and actually quite fun but I remember sitting back afterwards and thinking, 'That was bloody close'. Danny, one of the other platoon commanders, also came into contact on the patrol he was on and he had a ricochet that cut his nose and his lip. The bullet had gone that close to him.

Then, later on that same day, from that tower we saw a British armoured vehicle get hit by an IED. We had a full-on view of it. There was a huge explosion, a huge dust cloud. We were quite far away on a high point from about 500 metres. The bang was unbelievable. I physically jumped in the air when it happened. It was a hell of a shock.

We heard pretty much straightaway over the radio network that there were casualties. It was such a big explosion I remember thinking there was no way anyone could have survived it. Amazingly, they all did. One of the crew was a guy called Ed Addington, a Rifles officer who has since become a good friend after we met at Headley Court. He was the most badly injured out of all of them. He had two very badly fractured legs and broke both heels. Thankfully he didn't need amputations.

That was about five days into my tour.

The sound of the IEDs going off was one you came to dread. You'd hear them all the time and every time you heard it you would just pray no one was hurt. Then you'd wait for the dreaded 'man down' on the radio. That would be frequent.

Leaving camp to go on patrol was probably the hardest part. It was wearing. The IED threat was constantly on your mind and the chances of getting into a contact of some description were high. It took its toll, psychologically, on some guys, no doubt.

We'd had a big IED clearance operation one day. It was a company operation and Staff Sergeant Olaf Schmid was attached to my platoon. Staff Schmid had been one of the characters on the camp for a while. He was an Ammunition Technical Officer with 11 Explosive Ordnance Disposal (EOD). He was a phenomenal guy, very, very bright and lively. Brave and articulate.

We knew the area was basically a no-go because it was so heavily seeded with IEDs. It had a reputation which had been passed on from the Battle Group before us. We confirmed 14 devices in just a few hours of patrolling. It was a seriously busy day, really tense with devices everywhere. My job was to provide the security for Staff Schmid and his team to deal with the devices. He was attached to one of my sections while I was positioned nearby.

Normally an EOD team would blow up the device remotely rather than waste time diffusing it. We were told over the net Staff Schmid had found a device and was going to deal with it there and then. They'd found themselves in a pretty difficult situation, surrounded by command wire IEDs. He went to deal with that device because the other lads were in danger, pretty much holed in by these command wire IEDs.

I could hear him over the net saying, 'Yep, I'm now going up to it, I'm going to test it'. When he went to blow it, it didn't blow the first time. He had to reapproach the device and it was then that we heard the explosion. Normally before you detonate a device you give a warning that gets sent down the radio net so that everyone knows a device is about to be blown. We hadn't got that warning. My initial thought was, 'Fuck, I didn't hear the warning for that, he must have set it off early' and I immediately got on the radio and it came over 'man down'.

My section commander, Corporal Rowe, was with him at the time. We said 'ZAP number?' which is normally the first two letters of the individual's surname and then the last four numbers of your army number. Corporal Rowe came on and said, 'Boss it's Staff Schmid, I don't know his ZAP but I've just seen his body fly up in the air, he's a goner'. Corporal Rowe had to deal with the situation on the ground and I had to get to them as quickly as possible.

We had to recover Staff Schmid's body in a very difficult and dangerous environment. We thought the device had potentially been detonated by the enemy and we could see other command wires around the place so it was hugely difficult. Corporal Rowe handled the situation amazingly. The soldiers underneath him were incredible. They were tasked with getting Staff Schmid into a body bag and we had to organise the evacuation from there. It was a fucking nasty job. Young riflemen. It was a very tense time, a dangerous time, with a lot of emotions. Staff Schmid's team had just seen somebody they loved blown up in front of them and were clearly upset.

My job was to control the situation. My platoon sergeant was in another area with a different section. I didn't want to bring too many people into the area where Staff Schmid and the rest of the lads were because it was too dangerous. I left my section outside and approached with just one man with me through a cleared route. It was a very high stress time that, waiting to get him out of there. It was brutal. But the guys didn't waver, they knew what they had to do. They just said, 'It's alright boss, we'll fucking crack on with this'. Young privates speaking to Staff Schmid's team, who were all pretty shocked, taking control and telling them what they needed to do in a very firm but sympathetic way. I could not fault the leadership they showed on the ground there. That whole section did incredibly well that day. I was very, very proud of them.

There were two lads, in their very early twenties, who were tasked with the job of collecting him up and that will probably stay with them for the rest of their lives. Staff Schmid's death had a huge impact on the battalion. He'd been due to go home the next day.

Jilly Dixon: *The knock on the door is what you dread. A few weeks before Will was injured there had been a very bad day in Afghanistan. It was late on a Sunday evening and, living where we do, deep in the countryside, you don't often get people dropping by. Certainly not when it's dark on a Sunday evening in the middle of winter. But there was a knock on the door and both Rob and I stopped stone still. We just stopped breathing.*

It was Mr and Mrs Perkins, an elderly couple from next door. It was most unusual for them to do that.

THE ROW TO RECOVERY

Rob Dixon: *Mr Perkins had brought a couple of pheasants around.*

The day I got injured we were involved in a company-level operation to clear a main road of devices. My platoon's job was as a mobile QRF tasked with responding to any incidents in Mastif Armoured Vehicles. It turned into a very busy day.

We were basically trying to restrict the Taliban's movements by putting in patrol bases along their key supply routes. There were a lot of firefights going along the main road we were clearing and there were a lot of contacts. We had RPGs whizzing above our heads because the Taliban knew what we were up to and were trying to stop it. They were defending those areas pretty vigorously. We were taking a lot of casualties.

One of my platoon's Mastif's had been hit in the middle of the day by an IED strike. It happened right in front of me. We rushed out and went over to it and managed to get the doors open. Everyone inside was okay, badly shaken up but basically okay.

Not long after that our vehicle was hit.

By 2009 the medical chain for dealing with casualties was very well practised. I knew that after Selly Oak I would go home for a bit and then I'd go to Headley Court. I knew from friends who'd suffered the same injury that I'd be up and walking about sooner rather than later, and that's what happened.

I got measured up for my leg after a few days at Headley Court and within a few more I'd been given my first prosthetic and I was up and walking on it, albeit a bit at a time. But I could put it on and walk backwards and forwards across the room. It was amazing.

I remember the first time I got up and walking I made a video of myself and sent it home to the family because I wanted to show them as quickly as possible that I was up and mobile. It's why they call a below knee amputation a 'scratch' at Headley Court because you do get up and about very quickly.

I got to know a lot of the other guys going through their recovery. The banter is pretty merciless. You weigh up your injuries and there were constant arguments between different people over who was most severely wounded. Stealing people's wheelchairs, stealing people's legs, winding up blind people. I never felt I could because I wasn't wounded enough to do it but the guys were always playing pranks on people.

We got taught different tricks you could do with your stump. One of my favourites was the Loch Ness Monster impression where I'd stick my stump up out of the water in the pool and move its head around.

To start with I thought a lot about getting back out to the front line. I think a lot of guys think like that. But over time those thoughts diminished. I realised I would never again command an infantry platoon and that was all I'd ever really wanted to do. It was time to move on with my life.

CHAPTER 4
ROUTINE

Day 1: 5th December, 2011

The emotion was palpable at San Sebastian harbour as the crews awaited their turn to be called to the start line. Nerves, excitement and just the hint of fear proved a heady concoction for the Row2Recovery crew as their departure time drew near. The tears had been shed, the hugs exchanged. After months of planning, training, searching and fixing, it was time to get down to business. Sixteen of the 17 crews had made their way to the start line, when the call came.

'Row2Recovery,' the tannoy announcer bellowed.

Rory handed his prosthetic leg to Steve from the support team as Carl held out his arm to help his friend aboard. Neil strapped himself into his now fully modified seat as Will took a deep breath and tried to enjoy the moment. His heart was pounding, his palms were sweaty, but he loved it. He felt alive. Alex and Ed exchanged a knowing look before Ed settled into the central of the three rowing positions. This was the moment the two men had dreamed of ever since that cycle ride in the Surrey hills.

'Good luck lads,' Ed called and patted each man on the back. 'Oh, and happy birthday Carl.'

Will looked across to his mum, Jilly, who was standing on the harbour wall waving frantically, her dark glasses barely hiding the tears trickling down her flushed cheeks. His girlfriend, Mia, put her arm around her as the rest of the Dixons waved and cheered. Will was racked with guilt for leaving them again. But he had to do this, they all knew that.

Rory's best friend, Dorothy, smiled as she considered how far her old pal had already come on his remarkable journey, and how far he still had to go. Back home in Spain, Rory's girlfriend, Lara, stared blankly at her phone. She was not looking forward to the next few months.

Ed's parents, Robin and Isabelle, stood arm in arm, full of admiration for what their son had already achieved and full of worry for what lay in store. Helen cradled Louis, who'd be without his dad for Christmas, but any sense of sorrow was overshadowed by an overwhelming sense of pride.

'You'll be so proud of your dad,' she whispered, managing to hold back the tears as the red-haired toddler grinned back at her.

The crew received an enormous ovation from the large crowd gathered to witness this bizarre spectacle. Many of the locals had seen it all before. But no one could fail to be humbled by the determination and adventurous spirit of the rag-tag collection of rowers currently bobbing away 200 metres from the harbour wall waiting for the signal to begin the adventure of a lifetime.

The Row2Recovery boat pulled out of the harbour entrance on its way to the start line and was immediately dwarfed by the passenger ferry docked alongside.

'They look so tiny and vulnerable,' Jilly Dixon thought to herself as she wiped away another tear.

ROUTINE

Ever the showman, Rory turned to face the large crowd gathered on the harbour wall and flexed his huge biceps. 'Row2Recovery,' he screamed, and again the crowd cheered.

'Nob,' said Will.

Sam from the support team had commandeered a motor boat for Geraint and the ITV crew and they came alongside to ask the crew a few questions as they waited nervously on the start line.

'How tough do you think this will be?' the reporter shouted.

'Easy,' came the unanimous response, grins spread wide across their faces. It was not the answer Vincent was looking for, but he chuckled to himself regardless. In the few days he'd spent with this hardy band of former soldiers he'd grown close to them. In truth, he was nervous too.

Suddenly there was a piercing din as the klaxon sounded for the race to begin. At 12 o'clock precisely the crowd cheered again as the first strokes were pulled in the 2011/12 Talisker Whisky Atlantic Challenge.

Will: *When the starting horn went we were straight into our stroke with Ed, me and Neil taking first shift. I made sure I splashed Geraint as we pulled away.*

In those first adrenaline-fuelled hours of rowing we could see the other boats and were checking them out. We thought we would be quite near the front but there were quite a few crews in front of us which surprised us. In the bigger scheme of things it was completely irrelevant but from an ego point of view we wanted to look good while the other crews could see us.

The legacy of the storm that had delayed the start were huge waves and strong tail winds gusting at more than 40 knots per hour. They were perfect conditions for an experienced crew to achieve maximum speed, but for Row2Recovery's novices it was a baptism of fire. Almost as soon as they were past the headland of cliffs protecting the harbour they were confronted with some thunderous waves. Within a few hours they were alone with the elements as the tiny volcanic island of La Gomera gradually began to disappear from view and the flotilla of boats that had waved them off reluctantly returned to port.

With the El Hierro volcano 60 miles to their south-east they also had to consider the small matter of an underwater eruption. It all added up to a fraught start for all the crews.

Carl: *Pretty much as soon as we got going, we were into it. No messing around. I'd only been on the oars a couple of hours when I turned to Alex and said, 'This is fucking brutal'.*

With so little time spent at sea prior to departure, the crew needed to learn fast how to surf down the front of the waves and manoeuvre into position to ensure they didn't get beam side on to the next one, leaving them vulnerable to capsizing. The boat's auto helm – an automatic steering mechanism which could be set to a specific navigational bearing – was switched on to ensure their course was corrected if they found themselves going beam on to the waves.

The crew had been kitted out by sailing and yachting clothes manufacturer Gill, while Oakley had graciously donated six pairs of custom-made sunglasses. The kit was superb, but such was the intensity of the swell, it proved impossible to stay dry.

The plan was to row non-stop across the ocean, apart from a brief stop on Christmas Day, breaking only to swap between each three-man shift every two hours during the day and every four hours at night. While three of the team were rowing, the other three would sleep in the two small cabins.

Shift A: Will (stern – stroke), Ed (middle – main steering), Neil (bow)
Shift B: Carl (stern – stroke), Alex (middle – main steering), Rory (bow)

Alex and Carl would sleep in the stern (rear) cabin when not on shift, as would Ed and Will, while Neil and Rory would take turns in the single bow (forward) cabin at the front of the boat which the crew had dubbed the 'Barbados Suite'.

ROUTINE

Carl was the first to be struck down by seasickness. He was lying on his side in the stern cabin after his first rowing shift when a wave of nausea hit him. The crew had been taking anti-nausea pills for several days before departure, but it didn't make it any more bearable. All the crew were struggling within hours of the start. Alex lay in the cabin with Carl, fighting against the growing desire to vomit, but Carl gave in straightaway. Desperate to get the inevitable over and done with, he flipped open the cabin hatch, stuck his head out and vomited what was left of his morning's breakfast over the side. Sympathy wasn't exactly forthcoming.

'Must have been all that birthday cake you ate mate,' Will quipped.

'Fuck off,' Carl replied, wiping the remaining sick from his chin.

Within six hours of the start, the technical problems started. On his first shift, Neil noticed his seat was lifting up as he pulled back on his stroke, causing the handles of his oars to repeatedly pound into the tops of his stumps. Red wields quickly began to form as the bruising emerged. He gritted his teeth and kept rowing.

Neil: *It was impossible to stay dry and as a result the sores started emerging pretty quickly. Because of the position of my seat it meant my oars were entering the water at a steeper angle than the other guys. It meant my stumps took a real pummelling. Things were really uncomfortable. We were constantly soaked to the skin and I thought to myself, 'What the hell have I done here?'*

Then one of the stanchions fixing Neil's seat in position snapped, leaving just three holding it in place. Neil took the opportunity to saw down the remaining three stanchions and lower the seat into position. It meant he was able to take a clean stroke without bashing his sensitive stumps.

Neil: *When things needed fixing in the cabins the seasickness really kicked in. The anti-vomiting tablets stopped me being physically sick*

133

but I still felt rotten the whole time. I spat some stuff up a few times but was never actually sick. I managed to fix the seat that night but it was a constant worry.

Ed: *I kept catching my knees with my oars which was really annoying for me but for Neil the oars were smashing across the end of his stumps, the most sensitive part, and all I'd hear was a dull groan. When I was hitting my knee I was screaming out and Will also threw his teddies out a few times. Neil never threw his teddies.*

On the first night Will's footplate also broke as his prosthetic leg pushed up against it. Like Neil, he spent several hours unscrewing and then re-positioning the metal plate before he could start rowing again.

There were also small leaks in the front hatches which needed plugging, while the bilge pump needed to pump water out of the foot wells seemed faulty and, most worryingly, the auto helm kept flicking on and off causing the boat to list alarmingly.

Carl: *Trying to fix anything in that cabin was so hard. It was so hot and stuffy and such a confined space. I tried to fix a circuit board which had about 12 screws on it and just felt awful. Even the smallest tasks were difficult. We were using small spanners and torchlight rolling around on top of some pretty big waves in the dark. My head was pounding and it was impossible to hold down any food.*

One of the hatches that we'd been working on in La Gomera hadn't been sealed properly and was filling with water. It was coming through two holes into the cabin where all the wiring was connected to the desalinator and the communications kit. We were in danger of losing power on the very first night.

As the realisation dawned that despite all the hours they'd spent working on the boat on the harbourside there were still significant problems, Carl could barely contain his frustration.

ROUTINE

'This is unbelievable,' he said to Alex as the hatch continued to leak, threatening the electrical cables in the foot-wells and seeping into the auto helm's housing mechanism.

'What have we done to deserve this?'

Between them they managed to stem the leak and bilge out the excess water but the boat's auto helm continued to cause concern. The display panel was flickering on and off while the mechanism was making an unusual whirring noise. They carried on rowing but within minutes it had failed completely. One of the lines from the rudder to the steering plate snapped, causing the boat to spin around and position them beam side on to the huge waves. It was precisely where they did not want to be.

'Fucking hell,' Carl shouted nervously. They'd barely been rowing for 15 hours and already they were in trouble.

Carl: *That's when it hit home that we were in the middle of the ocean in this tiny boat. I couldn't believe how vulnerable I felt out there.*

'Shall we not capsize just yet?' Carl snapped at Alex, not at all happy. It was two o'clock in the morning, pitch black and both men were already exhausted.

'Let's change it over, we've got a spare one,' Alex shouted back, struggling to make himself heard over the din of huge waves crashing over the boat. Behind him, Rory pulled hard on the oars, secretly wondering why on earth he'd said 'yes' to this ridiculous idea.

They set about changing the auto helm over, cursing their bad luck. Within a few hours the back-up auto helm had failed as well.

CAPTAIN'S LOG

Auto helm broken, stroke footplate broken, Neil's seat broken.
Position: The El Hiero way point (27°12'N 17°40'W) bearing 260 degrees
Distance covered: 40 miles from start point, 16 hours rowed
To Barbados: *2,510 nautical miles*

Day 2: 6th December

As if the technical problems were not enough to worry about, the sheer size of the waves also took everybody by surprise. Before they'd left, the crew had heard drunken tales from previous transatlantic rowers of 30 to 40-foot-high monster waves flipping boats over with terrifying ease but they'd taken them with a hefty pinch of sea salt. The common consensus among the Row2Recovery crew was that a lot of ocean-rowing stories were exaggerated. They soon realised they should have taken the warnings about the size of the waves a little more seriously.

Neil: *We would go up onto the crest of a wave and be able to see everything around before sliding down the face into a trough where you could barely see the skyline.*

In some ways the actual rowing was the easy part. It was the day-to-day routine the crew found most gruelling, with normally simple tasks such as cleaning teeth and keeping bodies clean made almost impossible by the cramped conditions, salty air and constant battering from the waves. Holding down food was also difficult as nausea continued to plague the crew.

Alex: *We struggled to eat enough in the first few days because we just felt like shit all the time. We were spending two to four hours every day fixing stuff. Everything was so uncomfortable.*

The fact that the crew would be rowing naked for much of the time had fixated the media before departure but was barely given a moment's thought by the men themselves. Managing the inevitable chafing and friction sores on their skin, made worse by the moist salty air, was one of their number-one priorities. Rowing naked wouldn't stop the sores, but it would help reduce them.

ROUTINE

Alex: *You were hot, you stank and you had a naked bloke sitting right next to you the entire time. It was basically everything you don't want in life.*

The failure of both auto helms meant Alex and Ed in the middle seats would – if they were to complete the crossing – have to steer the remaining 2,500 nautical miles with their feet, instead of relying on technology. There were pedals either side of the middle rowing position connected to the rudder. Previously the auto helm had been programmed to alter course automatically. Now the middle rower was required to press down with either foot in order to steer the boat. Alex and Ed came to depend on the information passed back by the rower sat in front – Will or Carl – who could see the compass and Global Positioning System inside the rear cabin. All in all, it meant far more energy would be used up steering the boat and plotting a course, inevitably making the crew less efficient. It also meant even greater responsibility for Ed and Alex.

Alex: *If you go from auto helm steering to foot-steering and you're tired and rowing at night that is a lot to think about. For the first couple of nights after the auto helm broke I didn't row at all. All I did was steer because I was absolutely knackered. I didn't feel like I could row safely if I was trying to steer as well. The guys all said they'd rather we just focused on steering.*

Ed: *The next question was whether the foot-steering mechanism was strong enough to take us the whole way. We were foot-steering from two days in and my calf muscles were agony. There is quite a lot of resistance and it is not a natural movement, certainly not having to put all your strength against it. I was getting searing pain in my right leg from doing that.*

Alex and Ed were forced to add an extra stretching regime of their own to mitigate against the effects of the added pressure on their calves, but the foot-steering only added to their discomfort.

Supporters were able to monitor the crew's progress and race position on a map on the sponsor's website, and it was evident that the Row2Recovery's route had gone from being gun-barrel straight in the very early stages to noticeably more meandering.

Ed: *You can't help but steer a slightly less efficient route if you are doing it manually from a compass. If someone's concentrating on that it's inevitably going to detract from their rowing. It was a serious blow so early on.*

CAPTAIN'S LOG

Third position behind Corinthians and Box Number Eight. Spare auto helm fails.
Position: (26°51'N 18°01'W)
Distance covered: 51nm in past 24 hours
To Barbados: *2,459nm*

Day 3: 7th December

While the campaign had always been about far more than where they finished in the race, the crew's competitive juices had not been diluted by the inconvenience of losing a leg or two – quite the opposite in fact. Ed and Alex had banked on this, and while completing the crossing would always take precedence, both men had been keen to include 'race to win' in the team's charter.

Ed: *Almost as soon as we'd got out to La Gomera and started mixing with the other crews we got caught up in the race element. Seventeen crews set out as part of the race and I didn't see any reason why we couldn't beat them all. We knew it was a marathon and not a sprint and we knew we had so much to learn and so many things could go wrong. But, in those early days, we were racing to win.*

ROUTINE

As the crew settled into a rhythm on the oars it soon became evident that sleeping was not going to be straightforward. The constant buffeting of the waves and the stifling conditions inside the noisy cabins would take some getting used to. The crew also took time to adjust to the two hours on, two hours off, shift routine. Everyone came to dread the '15-minute warning' wake-up call.

Alex: *On operations, the tempo is so high that when you're told you've got two hours to move you are so shattered you can normally just click your fingers and you'll be out like a light. In Afghanistan we would sleep in 50-degree heat. It's tough but you get used to it.*

But the boat was without doubt the worst environment I've ever slept in. It was like going to the gym, doing a two-hour session and then being told you could go to sleep in the sauna. 'And by the way you need to be cleaned up and ready to go again in the gym in two hours'. It was totally relentless. I'd be rowing and thinking, 'I'm quite tired now, I could do with a lie down'. But once you were inside the cabin it was was unbelievably hot yet you had to keep the door and hatches shut in case the boat capsized. You'd end up rolling around, sweating and struggling to sleep thinking, 'I wish I was back on deck'.

We slept on what was effectively a bit of gym matting which only had a certain amount of life in it. Pretty soon it completely compressed and was like lying on a concrete floor. When I woke up I'd always have a dead arm or dead shoulder or dead leg. If we'd capsized and someone had pins and needles, they'd have potentially been in serious trouble.

Carl: *We all felt tired and pretty grumpy. Conversations were kept brief between the two shifts. It would just be a grunt or 'Alright, how are you doing?' You'd do your row, get off your shift, talcum powder your feet, wet wipe around your groin area, backside and armpits. Sleep-wise it was quite hard but you did get accustomed to it. The first quarter of an hour after a shift was spent cleaning yourself in the cabin. I'd get about an hour and a half of sleep and then I'd hear Will shout '15 minutes', then '10' then 'five'.*

THE ROW TO RECOVERY

Sometimes I'd wake up thinking I was on shift and I'd get changed and go out fully clothed on deck and be told, 'You've still got an hour to go'. Other times I'd dream I was rowing while I was asleep. I'd wake up thinking I'd been rowing all that time only to realise I was about to start a shift. That was soul-destroying.

While the Barbados Suite had its advantages, the downside was that waves would smash over the bow of the boat, making it considerably more turbulent than the rear cabin.

Rory: *I literally hit the roof of the cabin several times. I'd be fast asleep and wake up as my head slammed into the roof. Outside I'd hear, 'Whhooooaaahhh, that was a big one!' I'd manage to get back to sleep, but straightaway I'd hear that knock with Neil saying '15 minutes' and I'd think, 'Bullshit, I have just gone to sleep'. I'd close my eyes again and instantly it would be 'Five minutes'. At that point I had to start getting ready because Neil would be waiting to come into the cabin. It wasn't fair to keep your buddy waiting.*

The forward seating position Neil and Rory occupied when they were rowing was also vulnerable to the breaking waves and soon earned the tag 'The Kill Zone' due to the constant risk of being soaked.

Rory: *It was gruelling, horrible. It was rough. First of all the sleep deprivation kicked in and the relentless monotony of going into the wet cabin where I couldn't relax or completely unwind.*
Gradually I realised that the best time to switch off was when I was rowing. I'd listen to an audio book of Sherlock Holmes or Shackleton's adventures and be so enthralled that everything else would just be happening around me. I'd get into a rhythm and zone out completely. Then Carl or Alex would say, 'Give Neil the 15-minute shout' and I wouldn't believe it had been two hours on the oars.

CAPTAIN'S LOG

Water-maker fails but is reset, leaks found in aft cabin repaired using bolts (poorly fitted bilge pump).

Position: No entry in captain's log
Distance covered: 54nm in past 24 hours
To Barbados: *2,405nm*

Day 4: 8th December

Physically squeezing into the cabins in the early days proved difficult because of the sheer amount of food and equipment tightly packed in to last the crossing. The more they ate, the more space they gained. The boat sat low in the water as a result of the weight of the uneaten food, which was helpful when trying to ride out the big waves but also made Alex and Ed's job of foot-steering even tougher.

Moving freely around on deck was also hazardous, especially for Neil. As a double amputee he was used to hauling himself around on his hands at home and had assumed it would be a simple enough task to do so on board.

Neil: *I'd thought that because I can get around pretty easily on my bum everywhere else I'd be able to do the same on the boat. But the amount of sharp, pointy bits on board made it horrendous. I soon ended up with wounds all over my backside. I got injured all the time. I realised that unless I needed to go to the rear cabin to fix something or use the satellite phone then I should stay around the seat by the door of my cabin. There were only a handful of occasions when I wasn't in that space of the boat.*

We came up with little games to counter the monotony of rowing, counting how long we'd been going, how far there was to go, times, distances, that kind of thing. I started ticking over sums and equations in my head, working out estimated times of arrival in Barbados.

CAPTAIN'S LOG

[No entry]

Position: No entry in captain's log
Distance covered: 63nm in past 24 hours
To Barbados: *2,342nm*

Day 5: 9th December

Will and Carl's rear rowing position enabled them to see inside the aft cabin when on shift and keep an eye on the GPS and compass providing the bearing required to take full advantage of the prevailing winds and currents. Without an auto helm, the information was also essential in avoiding another incident like the first night when they'd found themselves in serious danger of capsizing.

Will: *Carl was very strict on what angle the boat was on and officious whenever it was getting beam on. He was quite concerned about capsizing and often during shift changeovers the boat would spin around because we'd be concentrating on changing over rather than keeping on our course.*

With no en-suite bathroom on board, the crew also needed to accustom themselves to answering the call of nature 'al fresco'.

Alex: *Ed was the first one to go for a shit. It was always going to be the sort of unpleasant thing he'd take pride in. We found a way to get quite comfortable, quite quickly. There were two primary positions. One, if you went towards the bow behind where Rory and Neil sat, you could squeeze your body between the base of the boat and the rail so you were wedged in, hold onto the handle, and go over the side. I used to deliberately try to go there. Firstly because it felt the most stable and secondly because I could speak to Rory while I was going. I'd deliberately look at him and put him off his rowing.*

ROUTINE

The other position, which Carl insisted on using, was near the stern on the right-hand side. It meant the wind was behind so every time Carl went to the loo not only could I see him doing it, but when the wind was blowing straight in my face the smell would hit immediately. Carl seemed to choose the most inopportune times to go. Ideally you'd go when someone else wanted to so you would have two people leaning out on opposite sides to balance the boat.

Carl: *We worked out you could use the waves as a bidet. You could poke your arse over the side and let the waves wash over. One time I was doing that when a massive wave smashed into me and I was completely soaked. That went down well with the others.*

With the toilet routine mastered, the crew were also beginning to notice the effects of the salt water combining with the constant friction caused as their backsides rubbed against the seats. The sheepskin seat covers lovingly sewn by their families before departure helped, but were never going to alleviate the problem altogether.

Carl: *We all developed little dots on our arses from an early stage. That was the start of the deterioration as the salt and the rubbing took its toll. Very soon we all had very sore backsides.*

The only way we could have avoided any problems was if we'd worn clean underpants for every shift. With the lack of launderettes in the middle of the Atlantic that was impossible.

A sore backside wasn't the worst thing for me though. My balls started stinging like mad. I was in agony. It was genuinely the worst pain I'd ever had in my life, even worse than when I was injured. At first I thought it was thrush or some kind of fungal infection but it wasn't. I was on strong painkillers like tramadol to try to alleviate the pain. I was also on antihistamines and anti-fungal tablets but they did nothing. The only cure for it was fresh water and the camomile lotion Alex's sister had given him.

CAPTAIN'S LOG

Up to second position behind Box Number Eight. 3 hours spent trying to fix auto helms but no luck. 4-hour shifts at night are too destructive. Will try 3-hour shifts.

Position: 26°18'N 20°46'W

Distance covered: 56nm in past 24 hours

To Barbados: *2,286nm*

Day 6: 10th December

The initial plan had been to row for two hours on and two hours off during the day, with four-hour rowing shifts in the cooler night-time conditions to allow an extended period of sleep when off shift. But as the crew struggled to get used to the gruelling routine, Ed realised the four-hour night shifts were taking their toll. A decision was taken to reduce each night shift by an hour.

Alex: *There were quite a few times I noticed Carl's head go down while we were rowing. He was in the stroke position, setting the pace, so I'd have to stay in time, but I'd see his head drop and then his arms would go to different heights and he wouldn't even be squaring the blades in the water, they'd just be slapping on the water. He was sleep-rowing. I'd shout 'Carl' and he'd jump back into action.*

CAPTAIN'S LOG

Winds have turned to north-east so still running with weather but making better ground south. Attempt to repair auto helm failed. 3-hour shift pattern at night better.

Position: 25°40'N 21°32'W

Distance covered: 56nm in past 24 hours

To Barbados: *2,230nm*

Day 7: 11th December

Will, as the only amputee on board using a prosthetic, struggled with his balance in the early stages of the crossing. He was able to impart some power through his left leg when rowing but inevitably most of the pressure went through his stronger right leg meaning his weight was always slightly off kilter. It made him considerably more vulnerable to being knocked off his seat, normally much to the amusement of the others. But one week into the crossing another huge wave caught him off guard and served as a reminder to everyone about the hazards they faced.

Will: *When a big wave hit more often than not I would get knocked off my seat, much to Ed and Neil's amusement. It was actually quite frustrating and occasionally quite painful as I got whacked on the head a few times.*

This particular time we got hit by a wave, I was knocked off my seat and involuntarily let go of the right oar. It flew out of its bracket and the rope that was holding it on, which was only really a small piece of string, snapped. Before we knew it, it had been washed away. Alex, Carl and Rory were off shift and were woken up by me shouting 'Nooooo!!' at the top of my voice. They thought something really serious had happened.

I wanted to turn the boat around to go and get it but against the current and the waves there was never any chance of that and the oar was soon out of sight. It was the moment we realised that if we did lose a man overboard it would have been him that would have to get back to the boat rather than vice-versa. It brought home how dangerous our predicament potentially was.

Neil: *Will shouted, 'Let's turn the boat around,' and I thought, 'We've got no hope of getting that'. We spent five or 10 minutes trying to get the oar back but it wasn't going to happen. The currents were so strong it was scary. It absolutely flew away from us. There was no way any of us would have been able to swim that fast, injured or otherwise.*

Will was pretty upset but we still had three spare oars so in my mind we were alright. It was the first time I'd seen Will down because he is such an upbeat bloke normally. I think he felt a bit guilty and that he'd let the lads down. It was just one of those things. We gave him grief immediately of course.

Will: *I did feel like I'd let the guys down. They were pretty merciless in dishing out the abuse. Carl stuck the camera in my face straight afterwards and Alex sent the footage back to the support team in London. I was over it within a few hours but it did affect me. I should have made sure it was tied on better. There's a doubt in my mind as to whether the gate holding it in place was closed tightly enough. I hadn't checked it was screwed tight. It was a lesson for all of us because I know I wasn't the only one who hadn't checked the gate every day.*

Alex was sleeping in the cabin at the time but was woken by Will's shouts.

Alex: *Will was quite dramatic. He screamed, 'Nooooo', and I thought we had a man overboard. It panicked me so much, but he'd actually just lost an oar. I said, 'It's not that bad mate, get over it!' From then on, every so often you'd just hear 'Nooooo' from down in the cabin or up on deck. Will took it in his stride. He just copped the abuse in the knowledge it would inevitably move on to someone else.*

That refusal to take anything too seriously was really important to team morale. It's a part of Army culture and stops an individual thinking they're bigger than the team. So when Will's oar went over we just laughed about it.

CAPTAIN'S LOG

NE winds force 4-7. Punchy when at 7. Difficult night last night. Cabin getting uncomfortable. But spirits v high. Lost an oar today.
Position: 24°52'N 22°31'W
Distance covered: 56 nm in past 24 hours
To Barbados: *2,174nm*

Day 8: 12th December

While the high seas and strong winds made for hazardous rowing conditions they also meant that if they were harnessed correctly they would increase the boat's speed and help cover valuable mileage in the early stages.

The crew kept in constant contact with their support team in London. They were encouraged to hear that they were maintaining a high level of media interest courtesy of the footage Alex was sending back, which was immediately posted on the charity's website and Facebook page. And ITV News continued to dedicate a series of 'And finally' sections on their 6.30pm and 10pm news bulletins, with Will's lost oar receiving plenty of coverage.

The channel became so convinced of the value of the crew's story it insisted that none of the footage be shared with other channels as they had contributed to the cost of the communication equipment. It was a frustrating development, but one the support team grudgingly accepted, making the judgement that the ITV coverage was in itself generating a fantastic buzz around the campaign and driving a lot of the other coverage.

Back on board, another huge wave almost saw Ed lose an oar, although this time the extra attention paid to the gate holding it in place following Will's mishap 24 hours earlier ensured the skipper could maintain his grip before it slipped away.

Encouragingly, the crew were holding their race position in third place, just ahead of the Atlantic 4.

Will: *We came to the top of a wave and spotted the Atlantic 4 barely 100 metres away from us. It was surreal to see them so close, having been completely alone for more than a week.*

We shouted across to them, 'There's some terrible weather coming, you need to put yourself on to your para anchor for safety'. I'm not sure they'd have believed us even if they had heard us but it was fun trying to wind them up. We got on the radio and started sending unhelpful messages like, 'Pirates spotted, proceed with caution'. They were great lads, but all's fair in love and ocean rowing!

'Worse things have happened at sea' was one of our favourite phrases.

CAPTAIN'S LOG

Nearly lost second oar and spare cooker to a wave today. We installed electric bilge pump and cleared hatch of water. That was very good for morale. 2 hours of work.

Position: 24°15'N 22°22'W

Distance covered: 56nm in past 24 hours

To Barbados: *2,118nm*

Day 9: 13th December

The early-morning shift from 6am to 8am was one of the most enjoyable for the crew as the sun rose to provide more than enough light to navigate but not so much heat as to make rowing seriously uncomfortable. On day nine the Shift B team of Alex, Carl and Rory emerged from their cabins bleary-eyed and sleepy but ready to get on the oars again. Alex and Carl grunted at Ed and Will as they shuffled past them, ready to get their heads down for some well-earned rest.

Carl immediately noticed a large sea bird hovering around 10 metres off the port side of the boat.

Carl: *I remember looking at it and wondering what it was up to. Perhaps it thought we would toss it some food. I don't know. It was a big old creature though. I think it was a cormorant.*

Carl thought no more about it and instead began his customary routine and started rowing. Soon, with his iPod plugged in, he was leading Alex and Rory in a steady rhythm from the stern position.

1. Alex in an armoured Snatch Land Rover in Afghanistan

2. Neil before his injury, next to some of his bomb disposal equipment in Iraq

3. Ed with an Afghan National Army counterpart

4. Carl training with his sniper rifle

5. Will holds a 'shura' with Afghan National Army counterparts

6. Rory by a Warrior Armoured Vehicle, similar to the one in which he was blown up in Iraq

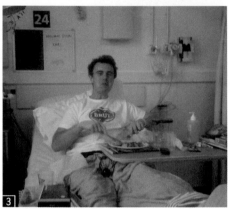

1. The remnants of the suicide bomber's vehicle that wounded Neil in Iraq in 2004

2. Will's Mastif vehicle after it was blown up by an IED

3. Will sits up in Selly Oak Hospital, already looking on the bright side

4. Will's amputated left leg just days post op

5. Will sees his family's beloved Labrador for the first time since his injury

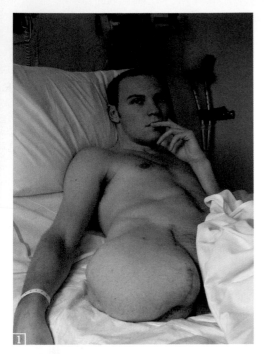

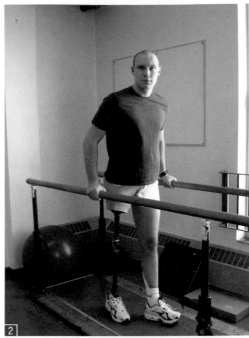

1. Rory at Selly Oak Hospital
2. Rory begins his long rehabilitation process
3. James Cracknell and Mark Austin join Baz and Will for a promotional shot
4. Neil rows through the night at the Million Metre Row
5. The crew look mean and moody for a *London Evening Standard* photo shoot

1. The crew finally get a chance to test the boat in La Gomera Harbour

2. The pre-race fancy dress competition was taken very seriously indeed

3. Carl and Ed share 'a moment'

1. Ed's family form the core of the 'Sew2Recovery' team

2. Rory emerges triumphantly from the deep with the bracket for Neil's seat

3. Will and Neil consider how best to pack the boat three days before departure

4. Another meeting! Ed, Neil and Alex discuss the weather conditions with a local expert inside a cabin

5. Carl is serenaded at the departure dinner – it's his birthday yet again!

1. Ed and his son, Louis, on departure day

2. Will gives mum, Jilly, a hug before departure as Ed and his family say goodbye

3. The first strokes are pulled just minutes after the start

1. Will and Neil get into their rythmn

2. The stores are packed high in the stern cabin, making conditions extremely cramped

3. Neil inspects the damaged auto helm

1. & 2. A couple of staged festive shots were well received by the media

3. Carl inspects the broken water purifier in the stern cabin

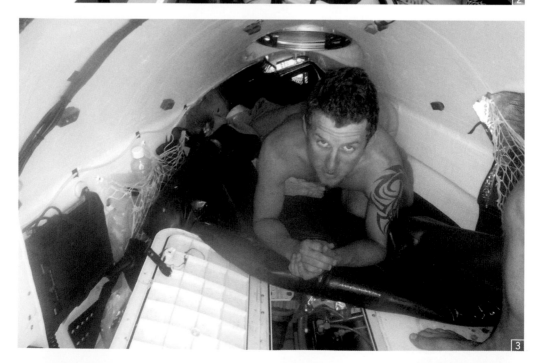

1. Rory and Ed salute the tall ship Tenacious

2. Carl has a go at deep sea diving

3. The thirsty crew try to shield themselves from the sun as they wait for emergency water supplies

1. The Aurora arrives and Graham begins the re-supply

2. The view from the Aurora, showing the rough sea at the time of the re-supply

3. The broken rudder

4. The first attempt at re-fitting the rudder, with Carl in the water

1. Homeward bound. Moments after crossing the official finish line

2. One of the Atlantic Four lights a flare to welcome the boys home

3. Fellow rowers salute the crew on their way into Port St Charles Marina

1. Sir Cliff Richard pops the champagne cork as the celebrations begin

2. Moments before touching dry land for the first time in more than 51 days

3. Carl treats the supporters to a champagne shower

1. Ed lets out a primeval scream as his dream of rowing the Atlantic is realised

2. Rory and his girlfriend Lara, embrace

3. Carl high-fives Sam from the support team as his dad and Geraint from ITV look on

4. Will hugs his tearful girlfriend, Mia

5. Neil promises his daughter, Mia, he won't do it again as his son, Callum, looks on

1. The first supper! Burgers and beers on dry land!
2. Sir Cliff congratulates Rory, while Alex's mum Ginnie looks on
3. Ed hugs Helen and reacquaints himself with Louis
4. Carl's dad, Chris, hugs his son next to proud girlfriend Tori

1. Families re-united. A happier ending than the last time they'd said 'goodbye'

2. Beyond injury, achieving the extraordinary

ROUTINE

Alex: *I looked up and out of the corner my eye I could see this bird flying pretty low in our general direction. It never crossed my mind that it would do anything other than fly past us or over us.*

Before anyone could react the cormorant had flown straight into the side of Carl's head, knocking the startled rower off his seat before flailing stunned in the foot well. Carl jumped back.

'What the fuck was that?' he said, spinning around in Alex's direction assuming he'd had a prank played on him.

'It's a suicide bird, mate!' Alex responded. Trying to stop himself from laughing out loud. Rory had less success, howling with laughter at his friend's misfortune.

Carl: *I couldn't believe my bloody eyes. This huge bird was flapping around in the foot well, squawking and flapping about. There were feathers everywhere. I don't know who was more petrified, me or that bloody bird!*

The three men considered bringing an oar down on top of their unwanted assailant's head. After all, it would have made a tasty meal, but they took pity on the unfortunate creature and Carl managed to lean down and flip the still confused bird over the gunnels at the side of the boat. Momentarily it looked as if the impact with Carl's head was going to prove terminal, but before long the bird had gathered itself and, after a couple of exploratory flaps, hauled itself off the water and back up into the air where it belonged.

But that was not to be the end of Carl's woes. As he settled back down to begin rowing again he again leapt off his seat as a searing pain ran through his hands.

'Arrgghhh,' he yelled. 'I've been electrocuted!'

'Don't be silly mate,' Rory replied, still barely able to contain himself at the memory of Carl's head-on collision with the bird.

'No, I'm serious,' Carl replied. But before he knew it he had lurched back again as a pain jolted through his body after he'd put his foot down on the wet foot well beneath his rowing position.

The pattern continued for the next 20 minutes.

Alex: *The highlight of the trip for most people was when Carl got electrocuted and attacked by a bird. It wasn't just the fact he got electrocuted that was funny but it was his reaction to it. It made him so angry. You could see it happening. 'Oh he's been electrocuted, it's going to happen again in a minute'. Sure enough. Zzzzz. He'd scream. It was just entertaining.*

With zero sympathy forthcoming from his fellow rowers, an increasingly exasperated Carl decided to wake the sleeping Neil and ask his advice. Neil wasn't best pleased at being woken up but raised a smile when he saw Carl's state of distress.

'What's up mate? You look like you've seen a ghost!' he asked.

Carl explained he had been electrocuted repeatedly, choosing to leave the bird attack story for another time, and Neil listened solemnly. While he was instinctively amused by the situation, he was also conscious of the fact that, with overall responsibility for on-board electrics, he needed to get to the bottom of it.

Within minutes, he had the answer. Some of the wires in the stern cabin had been fed through underneath the cabin door and were touching the floor of the damp foot well where Carl was sitting. One of the cables had not been safely tied off, leaving live wires open to the elements. Sheepishly, Neil produced a roll of electrical tape from inside his cabin before safely sealing the end.

'There you go mate,' he said, before disappearing back inside his cabin as an incredulous Carl shook his head and frowned before slowly beginning to row again.

When the shift finally came to an end, Will, Ed and Neil emerged to start one of their own. Within minutes they had their own wildlife encounter as an 18-foot long basking shark slid underneath the boat. All of the men knew they were harmless, but it was a breathtaking moment nonetheless.

CAPTAIN'S LOG

Carl attacked by a bird, Will and I spot a shark, electric bilge pump already showing worrying signs of slowing down. Have decided as a crew to eke out more efficiency. Tweaking shift patterns, better rules about maximising rowing time etc.

Position: 23°33'N 24°28'W

Distance covered: 63nm in past 24 hours

To Barbados: *2,055nm*

Day 10: 14th December

With Carl's day of pain still fresh in their minds the crew settled back into a steady pace on the oars. But it didn't take long for another hammer blow to strike. A radio message from the race organisers confirmed that Team Tom had capsized and its crew had needed rescuing after spending several hours drifting on a life raft.

The Guardian **newspaper, 14th December:** *Two transatlantic rowers were plucked from the sea in a dramatic rescue early on Wednesday after spending the night in a life raft they were forced to scramble into when their eight-metre boat was struck by a giant wave and capsized.*

Tom Fancett, 23, from London and his Dutch friend Tom Sauer, also 23 and a student at St Andrews University, were picked up by a cruise ship nearly 500 miles south-west of the Canary Islands, eight days after departing for Barbados in the 2011 Atlantic Challenge race.

In a message to race organisers Sauer told how the pair, who made up Team Tom, were changing places in the boat when disaster struck on Tuesday evening.

'The ocean was quite calm. We were in great spirits after the first eight days in the race. Suddenly our boat was rocked by an enormous wave, the size of which we've never seen before. Our boat was thrown over and capsized. The cabin flooded.

'We desperately tried to turn the boat back up again but to no

avail. In fact it started to sink. We managed to get the life raft and life jackets out during some very nervous and difficult moments. We entered the life raft and saw our dream literally sink in the ocean.

'We floated for about 10 hours in the night on the life raft until we were rescued by the Crystal Cruise ocean liner. We are obviously very disappointed but mainly we are just very happy to be alive and very grateful to our rescuers.'

Neil: *Hearing about the two Toms really brought home to us how vulnerable we were. It also reinforced the lesson that we had to keep our hatches closed at all times. That was the mistake they'd made. They'd been hit by a massive wave with a hatch open while they were changing shifts which meant the cabin filled with water and the boat was unable to right itself. Up to that point we'd been a bit lax about that because it was so hot you just craved air in the cabin. That had to stop.*

Will: *We were gutted for Team Tom. We knew how much the race had meant to them. We'd met them down in Devon before we'd left and we had a lot of time for them. They did get picked up by a cruise liner and taken to St Maarten in the Caribbean so it wasn't all bad for them, but it was a massive wake-up call for us.*

CAPTAIN'S LOG

Hard night again. Shifts at night are brutal. But spirits good. Nearly ¼ of the way there! Don't think we broke anything in the last 24 hours – that's a first.
Position: 23°00'N 25°40'W
Distance covered: 66nm in past 24 hours
To Barbados: *1,989nm*

Day 11: 15th December

As the crew gradually grew accustomed to the routine, they found they were averaging close to 60 miles a day, meaning they would complete the crossing in around 45 days if they maintained that rate and they were holding their race position towards the head of the fleet.

Neil: *After a couple of days I'd looked at the radar and seen that we were still right next to La Gomera. We'd made millimetres of progress. It was a massive morale boost to see us starting to eat into the miles.*

CAPTAIN'S LOG

Today is Will's 'rebirth' day – 2 years since he lost his leg. We celebrated with a Mars bar. Wind still v strong. Force 5-7 generally, which is pushing us along v nicely but makes for quite frightening nights esp before the moon comes out. Some of these waves could easily capsize us. Slowly getting used to the routine of cooking, sleeping and rowing. Conditions are Spartan as there is no room on deck.

Position: 22°34'N 26°51'W
Distance covered: 61nm in past 24 hours
To Barbados: *1,928nm*

Day 12: 16th December

Will: *In the lead up to Christmas we got ourselves into a really good rhythm. We were gunning it. We had great conditions with the wind behind us and we started to enjoy ourselves. We'd acclimatised to the heat, the seasickness, the salty skin and started to really get into it. We were really competitive and enjoying racing.*

I felt safer in the daytime but I preferred rowing at night because it was so much cooler and you could get into the longer shift. I had some really good music. Stuff like Chase & Status, the Arctic Monkeys, Bob Dylan, a lot of Jay-Z, lots of hip hop. I played up to the idea I was listening to rubbish all trip. Whenever anyone asked me what I was listening to I would say, 'Steps', or, 'Lee from Steps' new album'. I think the guys genuinely did believe that was what I was listening to. On the longer shifts I would try not to listen to music for the first hour or so. We would either talk or just have some quiet time to ourselves without music. Then I found when I put the music on it would give me a bit of a boost.

I found sleeping reasonably straightforward, but because it was such an unusual environment and sleep was so snatched it did cause some amusing moments. Ed woke up once shouting, 'Further down, further down' from the cabin. He'd been dreaming that he was steering the boat. He confused everybody on deck by shouting, 'Guys, hard down on the left, hard down on the left'. The rowers didn't know what the hell he was on about.

CAPTAIN'S LOG

At 0630am we reached the ¼ way point. Celebrated with chocolate and more rowing. Trying to clean stuff now. T-shirts, towels, bodies.

Position: *22°12'N 27°57'W*
Distance covered: *59nm in past 24 hrs*
To Barbados: *1,869nm*

Day 13: 17th December

The salt sores on the crew's backsides were proving extremely uncomfortable, but not intolerable. Regular washing with clean water, generated from sea water by the all-important desalinator unit in the rear cabin, provided temporary respite from the soreness and irritation. However, Rory had begun to experience severe discomfort in his right buttock, which he initially put down to the amount of muscle and tissue he'd lost when his leg was traumatically amputated.

The back pain Neil feared most had not materialised as the decision to opt for a 'backless' seat paid off – he was able to rock back and forth with the oars, generating more power and imparting less pressure on his spine. But there was little he could do about the muscle wastage he was beginning to notice on his stumps other than try to maintain the exercise regime he'd been prescribed

ROUTINE

before departure. In the tight, awkward conditions on board that proved far easier said than done.

Mercifully, his troublesome seat was holding firm, while all the food and supplies they had consumed had left the boat sitting higher in the water and stopped his oars entering at an awkward angle that would leave his stumps at risk of being battered.

The crew remained disciplined with their personal hygiene routines, knowing only too well from their time in the Army that if they let that slip, their physical condition could go downhill extremely quickly in such a harsh environment. White spirit proved a highly effective means of sterilising stumps and preventing infection. It was applied liberally at the end of each shift.

Will: *Initially I was really worried about the rubbing at the back of my stump but I realised that by folding the rubber socket back at the top of the prosthetic it provided a nice cushiony bit and stopped the rubbing. It meant the stump would slip out quite a bit because inside would get very sweaty, but it worked. I could put weight through it. My right knee got quite swollen at times because I was definitely putting more weight through that side.*

The main thing I wanted to avoid was any kind of infection so I was pretty fastidious about putting surgical spirit on my stump every time we stopped. I'd come off shift and go straight into the cabin, put a towel out and lie down on it and take my prosthetic leg off. That was always the first thing I'd take off. If I had any clothes on I'd take them off, take my shoes off. Then I would get the wet wipes out, put a bit of water on the wet wipe and then my priority was my arse. I'd wet-wipe my arse and also often surgical spirit it, which we discovered worked quite well. Any cuts I might have I'd put surgical spirit on.

Neil: *There was a bit of movement behind the back of my stumps and that was where all the worst of the salt sores were. Cleaning them with surgical spirit dried them out pretty well. It was horrendous having to put surgical spirit directly onto open sores but it did the job and staved off infection.*

Keeping clothing dry was almost impossible, especially as any suggestion that they were trying to gain any advantage by using T-shirts as makeshift sails would have been met with instant disqualification from the race. But despite the sores, the wet clothes, the discomfort and the heat, the crew retained their sense of humour wherever possible.

Alex: *I'd been to the toilet over the side, wiped and thrown the paper into the sea. We had some alcohol gel for disinfectant and Rory said I should put it on my arse because it would help clean it. He kindly offered to do it for me. He sprayed this gel on and it was like pouring acid directly onto it. Rory seemed to find that amusing.*

CAPTAIN'S LOG

Good admin done today: towels, T-shirts and bodies washed. Still trying to eke out efficiencies. Our daytime routine on the oars still takes distractions such as bilge pumping, water re-supplies etc which mean we only have 3 rowers rowing 50% of the time. At night this goes up to 90% I'd say. No space on deck = uncomfortable.

Position: 21°49'N 29°07'W
Distance covered: 61nm in past 24 hours
To Barbados: *1,808nm*

Day 14: 18th December

Alex and Ed were both concerned that Rory's condition wasn't improving. The intense pain in his backside was getting worse and it was increasingly clear that this could become a serious problem. He was loading himself up on painkilling drugs just to get through each hour of the day. As team medic, Rory was the one responsible for making the ultimate call if someone should stop rowing. He'd never considered that it might be him.

Rory: *The pain was excruciating. Initially I thought it was being caused by the bone being so close to the surface of the stump causing it to bruise badly. I was using a whole load of foam pads which I would lay out meticulously on my seat before sitting down for a shift. But I was struggling to get any respite from the pain.*

CAPTAIN'S LOG

Rory suffering with his stump but the others are good – we're on top of our niggles. Days are getting warmer and the cabins are starting to get unbearable (yet this is just a taster!).

We're changing time zones today – so fitting in an extra hour of rowing to move the clocks back on our shift timings. Key media week approaching Christmas.

Position: 21°32'N 30°15'W

Distance covered: 60nm in past 24 hours

To Barbados: *1,748nm*

Day 15: 19th December

CAPTAIN'S LOG

Over 1/3 of the way now. 1,700nm to go, 870nm done. More chocolate. Wind and sea state has dropped to about 3-4 – calmest it's been so far so very pleased with mileage achieved. We're daring to hope for a quick crossing – sub 45 days?! It's in the hands of the weather Gods.

Position: 21°15'N 31°25'W

Distance covered: 65nm in past 24 hours

To Barbados: *1,683nm*

Day 16: 20th December

Despite all the technical failings on the boat, the communications equipment continued to function efficiently. And on the morning of Day 16 the crew were given a telephone number by their London support team which they were told they must ring from the satellite phone at precisely 2pm for an 'important ITV interview'. No more details were forthcoming.

Will: *Sam from our support team was being a bit secretive. He kept saying, 'Guys this is a really important interview, make sure you don't miss it' and we were thinking, 'We're not going anywhere else, son!'*

I was told to make sure I was being filmed when I made the call. When I heard Geraint's voice on the other end I wasn't too surprised. He explained he was at Clarence House and I just assumed he was covering another story and fitting this conversation with us in around another job.

Geraint said: 'I'm sitting here with someone who wants to speak to you, it's Prince Harry'.

We'd been briefed that it would be a big interview with Geraint and ITV newsreader Mark Austin so when I spoke to Harry I thought we were just chatting before the actual interview started. I was really relaxed and just chatted away as if he was another soldier, which he is. Harry said how proud everyone was of us and joked: 'Make sure you win, otherwise don't bother coming back.'

We really appreciated him taking time out to speak to us, although I felt bad because Neil never ended up speaking to him. As usual I hogged the call by just gobbing off. There just never really seemed to be an opportunity to pass the phone over.

Neil: *I was actually chuffed that Will spoke to him. I watched him on the phone and he was so relaxed, much better than I would have been. It was a good thing he hogged it, definitely. He's good at that sort of thing.*

Will, in fact, was so relaxed that when the footage was received back in London, it became evident that some of it was unusable due to a severe 'itching' problem.

Will: *It was the first time I'd worn pants for about two weeks and they* *just felt so clingy and uncomfortable. After the interview I said to Ed, 'I'm pretty sure I was scratching my balls for that entire conversation'. As it turned out, I was.*

Rory and Carl had been in the water cleaning the boat when I'd made the call so they had no idea what had been was going on. Rory climbed back on board and asked, 'What's been happening?'

I replied, 'Nothing much. Oh the third in line to throne called to say hello . . . '.

The crew had initially been cautious of speaking to the media. The Army mentality of 'team first – individual second' does not sit comfortably with the idea of self-promotion. But Alex and Ed both knew that in order for the campaign to achieve its maximum impact, all the crew members would need to be comfortable in the limelight.

Will: *It was made clear from an early stage that if we wanted to get involved we would have to embrace the media because it was our most potent means of getting the campaign message out. I totally got that and was very aware I needed to be available for it. I started out quite reticent because I was conscious of how other soldiers would perceive us. You can often come across as a bit of a tool by talking up your injury. I was always aware that there were people more severely injured than me and I didn't want to be seen to be milking what had happened to me by doing those interviews.*

By the time of the crossing I'd learnt to relax and enjoy them. Some of them were actually quite fun. It helped when one of the interviewers called me 'Brave Will Dixon'. The lads picked up on that and from that point on I was always referred to as 'Brave Will Dixon'. I was delighted that tag stuck!

CAPTAIN'S LOG

Media + admin day today – had a recorded call with Prince Harry, taken by Will, to be shown on ITN News at Ten tonight. Also a call with BFBS [British Forces Broadcasting Service]. This meant we stopped rowing for three hours and took advantage of the pause to do some essential admin. Clean the hull, make sense of our cabins, redistribute weight. Wind has dropped right down and shifted to south-easterly. At best we'll only be doing 50 miles per day with this weather. Hot.

Position: 21°01'N 31°12'W

Distance covered: 46nm in past 24 hours

To Barbados: *1,637nm*

Day 17: 21st December

As the weather conditions calmed, progress slowed. The wind eased and the seas flattened. It made for less bumpy rowing but slowed the boat's speed and, with little breeze, conditions on deck and inside the cabins became stiflingly hot.

Matters were not helped by Rory's continuing difficulties on the oars. The runners under Will's seat were also causing him issues when rowing, and while the constant refrain of 'Morale is high' was maintained, frustration built as the pace slackened.

CAPTAIN'S LOG

Will's seat has played up with the ball bearings needing changing. This has meant repairs on the go again – not operating where we could be at the moment. V disappointed in distance covered – we average 2.7kn where all three are rowing but the daily average is 2.0kn which means we are spending at least 12-15 mins per hour not rowing.

Position: 20°48'N 33°00'W

Distance covered: 46nm in past 24 hours

To Barbados: *1,591nm*

Day 18: 22nd December

Inevitably there were occasions when the crew's spirit and togetherness was tested.

ROUTINE

Carl: *As we were changing over shift, Ed clearly told me that the bearing on the compass needed to be 80 degrees west. We needed to steer that course. If we went below a certain degree we were guaranteed to go beam on to the sea and get hit by the waves. They'd dropped off in the last 24 hours but there was still the occasional one more than capable of capsizing us. If we went at 80 degrees we had the wind and waves at the optimum angle and would stay as safe and dry as possible. I said to Alex a couple of times, 'We're dropping off the wrong bearing, we're going to get wet in a minute'. He just ignored me.*

I kept telling him the correct bearing and that we were off but he insisted it should be 60 degrees.

Ed and Will were down below giggling like a couple of schoolkids, obviously enjoying the brewing argument. That was also bloody annoying!

Alex dug his heels in. 'Carl, for fuck's sake, I've been steering for three weeks, I know what I'm doing,' he said.

'Alex, I am telling you we are on the wrong course here,' Carl retorted.

'No we're fucking not.'

'Yes we fucking are you dickhead,' Carl snapped back.

Carl: *The next day I asked Ed in front of Alex what our bearing should have been.*

'80 degrees,' he said.

'Oh was it?' said Alex, and shrugged his shoulders before looking at me.

Alex: *I said, 'Carl, I've been steering for three weeks, I'm pretty sure I know what I'm doing'. I can't remember what he said back. I don't remember who was right or wrong but I didn't like being treated like an infant.*

Afterwards it was quiet for about half an hour and I realised I was going to have to make the first move and said, 'Sorry mate'. 'No problems, I was being a wanker,' he replied. That was it, we moved on.

The brief spat was soon forgotten, but it was a reminder that despite the meticulous attention to detail the crew had put in to ensure team unity, flare-ups could still happen in an instant. The incident was never referred to again.

CAPTAIN'S LOG

Preparing for xmas – had to take xmas shots for media yesterday, and been figuring out what we will do on the day. Still looking for efficiency gains – ditched some more weight (eg gas) and looking to maximise time on the oars. Carl saw a pod of dolphins.

Position: 20°27'N 33°50'W

Distance covered: 51nm in past 24 hours

To Barbados: *1,540nm*

Day 19: 23rd December

Rory's discomfort was showing no sign of relenting and, despite valiantly continuing to row whenever possible, the likelihood of him becoming a passenger was growing with every passing shift.

Rory: *The pain was getting progressively worse. I tried everything to get comfortable but nothing worked. Every time I sat down it felt like someone was sticking a dozen needles in my backside. These angry red sores had formed on my arse but they definitely weren't normal salt sores. My routine just to sit down would take five minutes.*

Sometimes I'd be close to tears while I was rowing. But everyone had their headphones on so no one else knew. I didn't want to be baggage, sat there cooking everyone's meals and not rowing. A mid-Atlantic housekeeper for a bunch of naked soldiers. Imagine that. No thank you.

It was really, really painful. It was very difficult for me to say, 'I can't row' because the two guys in front of me, Alex and Carl, were also having a shit time. But eventually the pain got so bad I couldn't row and I had to tell Alex.

He said, 'If you need to rest then rest' and I sat there feeling like shit. I couldn't go into the cabin because Neil was in there, so I had to just sit out on deck. It was hugely demoralising sitting there getting pummelled by waves and soaked through in The Kill Zone.

After the second shift I skipped I realised I had to do something so I started having a really good feel around my backside. The wounds were dry, and when I started to pinch the actual sores I could feel something below the surface.

Suddenly it dawned on me. The pain was being caused by shrapnel left over from the blast. I'd been diving in Egypt the week before we left for La Gomera and the pressure from being 30 metres underwater, followed by the dive to retrieve the bracket in the harbour, must have forced it all to the surface. Charities actually take injured servicemen scuba diving with the express purpose of drawing out shrapnel, a consequence of the pressure you experience when going so deep underwater. So that was the answer, but the question was, how the hell was I going to get it out?

CAPTAIN'S LOG

Frustrating day trying to push south with a S Easterly wind – beam sea all day, v uncomfortable. Rory's condition remains a concern.

Position: 20°01'N 34°30'W
Distance covered: 43nm in past 24 hours
To Barbados: *1,497nm*

Day 20: 24th December

With Christmas approaching, thoughts turned to home.

Neil: *We could phone home on the satellite phone but the line was quite distorted. The kids could barely understand a word I said. As it* *got towards Christmas it got pretty hard being away from them. I felt really guilty, I felt like I should have been at home. It was not like I was still in the Army and didn't have a choice.*

Ed's thoughts were also with his young son, Louis, and wife, Helen, but he never once doubted he was doing the right thing.

Ed: *To someone who has lived a cotton-wool existence it would probably be shocking that I chose to go away for two months so soon after the birth of my son. But to someone who has just come out of the Army after doing six-month operational tours every 18 months it is no big deal at all. In my mind, we were doing it for a much bigger cause so the sacrifice of not being around for two months was justifiable. Secondly there's an element to being a good dad where first of all you need to be present but second of all you need to be a good role model. For me, doing something like Row2Recovery was part of that.*

CAPTAIN'S LOG

Another long frustrating night. Had a downpour for best part of 3 hours which would beat a jungle downpour hands down. Soaked to the bone. Now heading due W and making preparations for tomorrow.
Position: 19°50'N 34°30'S
Distance covered: 51nm in past 24 hours
To Barbados: *1,446nm*

Day 21: 25th December

By Christmas Day, Rory was near his wits' end. The shrapnel under his skin was causing the open sores to bleed. He'd tried applying Vaseline to smooth the lumps, cleansed with water and taken an array of painkillers, trying to stay as *compos mentis* as possible while not telling the rest of the crew. High as a kite on the drugs but still in excruciating pain, decisive action was required to prevent him becoming a full-time passenger. By running his hand over the surface of the inflamed skin he estimated there were four or five peppercorn sized pieces of shrapnel trapped under the surface. With the help of some arterial forceps and a small mirror, he set about removing the offending items as the rest of the crew downed oars and tucked into a novel Christmas lunch of pork scratchings, foie gras, chocolate and a drop of the sponsor's whisky.

Rory: *I took out two strong painkilling pills but the slow-release gel had dissolved in the wet which meant the painkiller entered my bloodstream pretty much immediately. Almost as soon as I took them I was in la-la land. I popped my head out of the cabin door, the sun was on my face. I hadn't eaten anything and I was drugged up to the eyeballs. Ed was very concerned. Alex was going to the toilet right over where my head was and said, 'Mate, you are really fucked'.*

Ed came over for a serious talk. He wanted to know what the hell was going on. I told him I had shrapnel coming out of my arse and I'd taken all these painkillers. I had to justify myself to him, which was totally fair enough. He was skipper and he was concerned.

I was so spaced out I just said, 'This isn't happening, it needs to come out'. So while the rest of the guys were eating their weird Christmas lunch concoction. I took two more 100mg tablets of dyclofenac and within 40 minutes I was like Pete Doherty, flat on my face and wired to the moon.

I picked up this little plastic round mirror, flipped over onto my back and lifted my stump towards my belly button, as high as I could get it, and tried to have a look at what sort of state these shrapnel wounds had left my backside in.

I had an exfoliating glove that you buy in Boots to exfoliate your skin and I started scrubbing. The wounds were about the size of my little finger and each piece of shrapnel inside was about the size of a small grain of rice.

I scrubbed and scrubbed with the glove and then got the arterial forceps, sterilized the tips and shoved them into the wounds. Closing them and pulling. In surgery you clench and close them to lock off an artery so it doesn't piss blood. I was using them to try to get hold of the shrapnel and pull it out. I dug frantically, scrubbed hard, washed the blood, no holding back. It was incredibly sore, despite the painkillers, but after a few hours it had done the trick. In all I took five pieces out. The release was instant and immense.

While Rory was below deck, the rest of the crew tried to make the best of their situation by donning party hats and eating the rations they'd set aside especially for the day. The support team had arranged for them to receive a phone call from Ben Fogle, who knew all about the misery of spending Christmas Day in the middle of the ocean.

Will: *I didn't really enjoy Christmas Day. We stopped rowing and it all felt a bit forced. I don't think we felt like we had anything to celebrate and it all felt pretty hollow. The deck wasn't big enough for everyone to feel comfortable and I just wanted to get going again.*

Neil: *We did the hats and all the rest of it, but it all felt like just another day on a boat. It didn't feel like Christmas at all. That was one of the worst days of missing the kids. I thought back to recent Christmases when the kids would be running around and coming in to wake us up early. It was difficult.*

Carl: *We talked about family and friends and what we'd usually be doing on Christmas Day. I didn't miss it to be honest. I wanted to enjoy the experience as much as I could. Ed and Neil missed their kids but we were okay. I'd got used to being away at Christmas when I was in Afghanistan.*

The highlight for me was the phone call from Ben Fogle. He told us that Christmas Day was the worst day of the crossing for him and I knew how he felt. He also told me there was no better feeling than that first step onto dry land. That still seemed a very long way off though.

After taking a two-hour break from rowing the crew were eager to get going again before nightfall. Carl and Alex went down into the rear cabin with the intention of grabbing some rest before their shift began.

Carl: *Straightaway I noticed the water desalinator was making a strange noise. It had been problematic on day one, but since then it had been relatively problem-free. Just as I was about to ask Alex what he thought was wrong with it I just heard 'zzzzeeeeuupp'. It didn't sound good.*

The water desalinator, crucial for making their drinking water from seawater, had stopped working. If the crew couldn't get it working again they would be faced with the grim prospect of having to hand-pump water through it for the rest of the crossing. Carl and Neil immediately set to work fixing it in the confines of the rear cabin, stripping it down and putting it back together. They replaced the fuse and several valves along with other working parts and were delighted when the troublesome machine eventually coughed and spluttered its way back to life four hours later.

They had fixed it, for the time being at least, but the unreliability of one of the most important pieces of kit on board was a worrying development.

CAPTAIN'S LOG

Christmas Day – what a rollercoaster 48hrs.

We took 3 hours to celebrate xmas and have a large meal together – was great to have everyone on deck and chomp through foie gras, xmas cake, chocolate and our favourite dehydrated ration – cottage pie!

Then the water-maker failed. Cue despondency. Got it up and running again thank God . . . This whole boat is being held together with string and gaffer tape!

Position: 18°43'N 39°23'W

Distance covered: 41.5nm in past 24 hours

To Barbados: *1,405nm*

My Story:
Rory Mackenzie

Age: 30
Regiment: Army Medical Corps
Army career span: 2004 – 2012
Rank: Corporal, Combat Medic Class 1
Combat experience: Iraq (2007)
Injury: Above knee (high) single leg amputee

Back in 2007 I was a company medic attached to the Staffordshire Regiment in Iraq. One night we were on patrol, sitting in the back of our hot and dusty Warrior armoured vehicle, exhausted and all dropping off. We were like nodding donkeys. Then suddenly 'boom', this almighty explosion with dust everywhere.

We waited for the inevitable impact but nothing happened. The angle of trajectory must have been just too low so it missed, just.

I texted my brother, Stewart, as soon as I got back to base to let him know I'd just been in an IED attack but was okay. I got another couple of hours sleep and then went back out again on another patrol.

It was about 3am by now, and when I climbed into the back of the Warrior I saw this lad, 18-year-old Michael Tench, fast asleep where I usually sat. I always liked to sit behind the gunner because I could look at his screen and see what was happening outside. As the medic I could reasonably have said to Michael, 'That's my spot mate, move' and he would have moved. But he was fast asleep and

THE ROW TO RECOVERY

I just thought, 'Fuck it, I'll let him sleep'. So I sat down opposite him and off we went as normal. It wasn't long before I drifted off myself.

Suddenly there was an immense explosion. It set car alarms off in Zubayr which was almost 10 miles away and lifted our vehicle up what felt like sideways and plonked it back down. I was knocked unconscious by the power of the blast.

I came to and discovered what was left of Michael was on top of me. I remember just being able to pick him up so easily. I realised he was dead and that something very bad had happened.

I sat up. It was dusty and smoky and I couldn't see. My ears were screaming and there was a stench of burning flesh. I grabbed my thigh, it was burning like hell. I still had my upper thigh. I grabbed it and gurgled, 'My leg, my leg'. My commander was stood right in front of me and I grabbed his ankle and just shouted, 'Casualty, casualty'.

The smell was intense. Cordite, blood, burning flesh. I was bleeding out and I knew it. By now I was in the fourth stage of shock when you can't see, can't speak, can't move. It's the stage before death. It normally takes around two minutes to die from an arterial bleed and they told me later I was out for 10 minutes just pumping blood.

Guys were screaming 'Medic!', but I was the medic and I was the 'man down'. My mate David 'Shove' Lovell, the section medic, jumped into the compartment.

One of the guys who had been sitting next to Michael had got a shard of my shin in his face which had gone through his nose and lodged just beneath his brain. He's blind in one eye now. The guy on the other side of him was completely covered in copper pellets. The guy sitting next to me was absolutely fine apart from some superficial burns to his legs.

I was drifting in and out of consciousness but could hear everything going on around me. In my head I was very conscious and very alert. I kept repeating to myself, 'This is serious, stay awake, stay alive, this is serious, stay awake, stay alive'.

I could feel Shove lifting my hand and feeling for a pulse, I could hear him say, 'No pulse'. I could feel him moving my neck and pressing his fingers to feel for a pulse. I heard him say, 'No pulse' again. I heard him radio in – 'Two dead' – and then carry on treating the other guys. I started to panic. But because we were mates Shove came back one last time and started checking again for a pulse. Still nothing. It took everything in me just to exhale some air. 'Urrrggh'.

'Fuck, he's alive,' I heard.

Shove jumped out of the mortar hatch and picked me up by my body armour with his huge hands. As he picked me up my head slumped forward and my arms were hanging down and I no longer felt part of myself. Now I was standing outside the Warrior watching Shove pull my body out. I knew it was me because I could see my surgical scissors and glow sticks hanging out of my pockets. It was the weirdest thing. I watched him pull me out of the mortar hatch and as soon as my knees were through I went back into my body and could feel myself being moved around again.

Shove pulled me across to the roof of another Warrior and jumped behind the turret holding me down. He rolled me over and had a good look and saw how much of my leg was missing. He put a tourniquet on me but accidentally put my cock and balls in, tying it right up and tightening it. I jarred awake again and groaned. He realised what he'd done, loosened the tourniquet, removed my tackle and tied the tourniquet back on.

We had air support from two Merlin helicopters and Shove called one of them in to land but they refused. They said they'd only land at the Shatt-al-Arab Hotel where we were based. They put down a load of smoke to provide cover for us to extract on the ground and I was rushed straight into the hotel where one of the Merlins had landed.

I remember there was an idiot of a medic who was too scared to take me down off the top of the Warrior. I was lying sideways across it. He shouted, 'Get him down' and grabbed me by my fucking stump. I just went, 'Arrggghhh'.

Screaming, I was put on to a stretcher. Straight away the doctor, Pete Starkey, put two lines in. As soon as those lines went in I could feel life coming back into me. I could feel vision starting to come back. They were hard-lining saline solution into me and I could literally feel my life coming back.

During the medical handover from Pete to the Merlin medical team I heard them say, 'One dead, one casualty – traumatic amputation'. It was only then I realised I'd lost my leg because the whole way racing back to base Shove was constantly holding my head down as I was groaning, 'My leg, my leg', and trying to sit up to have a look.

Shove just said, 'It's okay mate, it's fine, don't worry'. I knew it was fucking hurting but I didn't know what was going on. When I heard 'traumatic amputation' I just thought 'fuck'.

As the fluids kicked in I began to get some vision back. I was carried on to the back of this Merlin and I remember this gorgeous blonde nurse, she was like an angel, reaching out. I took her hand and just didn't let go. She chatted to me for the whole flight. I actually ended up awarding my campaign medal to her. Hazel Smart was her name.

I was flown to Basra hospital. I was aware of where I was because I'd taken casualties to the hospital plenty of times. I got taken into the trauma bay and I remember a female Naval doctor who said, 'You're doing incredibly well, you're being so brave'. From the point of detonation to the point I was on that surgeon's table was 17 minutes. This was the difference between life and certain death.

During that time I'd lost virtually all my blood. The medical term is 'exsanguination'. It's the most common cause of death on the battlefield. I needed a series of massive blood transfusions. So I had £750,000 worth of blood products pumped into me and later had blood platelets flown up from Qatar just for me. A total of 37 units of blood were put into me. The body only holds seven units. They gave me a trial blood product called Factor VI which coagulates your entire system. It kept me alive.

As I lay on the trolley the doctor said, 'I just want to have a look behind you', so she rolled me over and the last words I heard before I woke up in Selly Oak were, 'Oh, fuck'.

I grew up in South Africa, in a town called Krugersdorp on the outskirts of Johannesburg, and I was infatuated by the military from a very young age.

My first job had been in a gun shop – Military Equipment Stores – selling weapons, hunting rifles, side arms, you name it. I was only 15 years old but the managers would head out for a lunchtime drink, hand me a 9mm pistol and I'd stuff it down the back of my trousers and I was in charge of the shop. At 15 years old for goodness sake! They'd leave me for the afternoon.

We'd go to firing ranges and use the weapons so they knew I was competent with them. We had a 12-gauge pump-action shot gun out the back so if it really got ugly I'd have that. I used to clean the guns, everything.

My inspiration for joining the Army was my manager at the shop, Bruce, who had been in the South African Defence Force and fought in the South African border wars in the 1980s. They were really bad wars and Bruce saw some terrible things. He had very severe PTSD.

I couldn't understand how you could be so mentally destabilised after all those years.

After that I had a string of unfulfilling jobs and then in March 2004, aged 22, I just thought, 'Fuck it, I'll go to England and join the Army'. I packed a bag and left without organising anywhere to stay. I landed in London, looked on a tube map and saw Covent Garden so I headed there because I thought there would be gardens where I could sleep. I ended up walking around all night.

The next day I walked into Holborn Army Careers Office. A staff sergeant asked me what I wanted to do and I said, 'I want to kill people and jump out of planes', and he said, 'Paras for you'. I didn't know anything about the Parachute Regiment, the ethos of it or the history or the training.

I passed the initial interview and they told me to pack my bags and head up to Catterick Garrison in North Yorkshire to begin my Parachute Regiment training. I'd had a long-standing problem with my leg – a stress fracture I'd picked up road-running – and after 10 weeks I couldn't hide it any more. I spent five months in rehab before getting put in a new platoon with Captain Alex Mackenzie as my platoon commander. I went through the training and got to about week 12 when my leg had just had it. I was on five or six strong painkillers a day plus painkilling gels but I couldn't hide it any more.

The doctor told me I had to leave the Army but I refused to accept that. I'd got the bug for it. My personality had changed. I loved it. I loved the military life. I'd had a lot more aggression instilled in me and my confidence had picked up.

I basically refused to accept a medical discharge so I persevered and was told I could join one of the service corps. My dad had been a doctor in the Royal Army Medical Corps so I decided to give it a go.

I trained as a class 2 Combat Medic and was posted to Preston for about a year before my Sergeant Major came up to me and said, 'The Staffordshire Regiment are on the lookout for company medics and they want guys with some infantry knowledge. Would you like to go on a tour with them?'. I said 'yes' straightaway.

I went down to Tidworth in Wiltshire and trained with the Staffords before deploying to Iraq as the company medic for C Company in October 2006.

I was going to Basra in southern Iraq and was warned it was going to be a beefy old tour.

My first experience of dealing with casualties in Iraq was tough. Two Royal Marine boats had been contacted by an IED packed full of ball bearings while patrolling under a bridge along the Shatt-al-Arab waterway. I was standing on the pontoon and these two boats crawled up to us in a terrible state. I stood looking at the oil and diesel and blood which was shin deep. There was a body floating face down, and a couple more who'd completely bled out into the boat. I remember thinking, 'They look like training dummies'.

One lad was holding a guy slumped behind the steering wheel and talking to him. I went up to him and felt for his pulse and was like, 'No mate, I'm sorry, he's dead'.

The ones who were severely wounded were dead but the only

other wounded guy had a ball bearing go through his jaw which was basically being held on by a piece of skin. We put a collar on to hold his jaw on and gave him a surgical airway which I assisted our doc, Kat Lane, with. You have to make a surgical incision in the throat to clear the airway. It was horrific. The Padre was reading the last rites as we were doing it.

I started humping the dead bodies up to a tent we'd erected to put them in, taking the tags off and giving them to the Regimental Sergeant Major. The infantry guys I was attached to saw me doing this and straightaway they were like, 'Cool, we've got a good medic because he's not shy to get stuck in'.

I suppose that incident was the equivalent of a rifleman's first firefight. You're not sure how you're going to react in those circumstances. I hadn't flapped, I'd done my job. In a way it was a relief to get it over with.

The whole camp went into shock as a result of that incident. Three Royal Marines and 34-year-old Staff Sergeant Sharron Elliott had died. Staff Elliott was the first female British soldier to be killed in combat in Iraq. It hit everyone hard.

That was only a couple of weeks after we'd arrived and from that point on the intensity ramped up massively. Our base got hit by mortars pretty much every day. On average we'd get around 16 a day and on one day we had 28 mortars hit the base. They were incredibly accurate. It got so bad that all of the soldiers in the tented accommodation were moved into a hotel and slept in the corridors like rats. They were hardcore living conditions.

I was terrified of those mortars and rockets. I had a huge big window with this beautiful view of Basra and I just thought, 'Fuck this, if I can see them then they can see me'. So I moved into the toilet, lifted it out and plunged it full of newspaper and plastic and had this sweet little room. I lived in that toilet.

I got very used to the casualties but I could never get used to the mortars and rockets. When we went on patrol we would run from the hotel past the accommodation to where the vehicles were and the insurgents would mortar as we ran. You would end up running for your life, jumping into the back of a Warrior, closing the hatch and sitting there while mortars flew in all around.

Eight days after our Warrior was hit, I woke up in Selly Oak hospital with the nurses sucking fluid out my lungs as they pushed me forward and hit me on the back saying, 'Cough, cough, cough'. I coughed up some rubbish. It was all very hazy.

My mother and brother were by my bedside and my mother was holding my hand. I remember looking down and seeing this crisply made bed with my solitary leg wrapped in it. I just looked at that vacant space next to it and said, 'Ma, do you know I lost my leg'.

'Yes, my son,' she replied, 'but thank you so much for living'.

It was nearly six months since I'd last seen them. A few days before someone from the British consulate had knocked on their door in South Africa to tell them I'd been involved in an IED incident and had lost my leg. My brother had said, 'No, he's not, he's fine' and showed him the text message I'd sent him saying: 'just been in an IED strike but don't worry I'm ok'.

They said 'no, he's been involved in another one and he's lost his leg, through-knee. Here are your plane tickets.'

They didn't expect me to live. No one expected me to survive. My mother and brother were both in shock.

It turned out that while I'd been transported back to the Shaat Hotel on the roof of the Warrior exhaust fumes had got into the wound as well as all the crap from the dust and soil. Infection set in.

In fact I had three different infections tracking their way up the bone marrow of my femur. The only way to get the infection out was to cut my thigh bone shorter and shorter. They scrubbed it, they did everything they could. They did it seven times in two weeks. They'd open the stump, scrub it, cut it, test it – positive. Open it, scrub it, cut it, test it – positive. At last, as they were looking into options involving removing part of my hip, the test returned negative.

When I came around from the last bout of surgery my stump was in agony. The pain was unbelievable. It felt like it was burning, on fire.

I was given 10 milligrams of morphine but it did nothing, so I had another 10mg. In fact I had the entire allocation of morphine you can take before you overdose and it had absolutely no effect.

There was nothing anyone could do to alleviate my pain so they closed the door and left me to it. I was writhing around the bed. It was hardcore pain. Eventually the morphine knocked me out again but the pain never really eased. To this day I'm not totally pain-free.

When I was put into the recovery ward I was wheeled in and the three guys opposite were patients I had dealt with in Basra a couple of weeks before. They said, 'What are you doing here?'

One day a Special Investigations Branch investigator came onto the ward and demanded a DNA sample. I was like, 'Why?' and he said, 'We think we've found your foot in a boot in the back of a Warrior and we need to identify it'. I was like, 'Cool, can I have it?' He said, 'No it's in Iraq and it's going to be incinerated'. But it was my foot and I wanted to keep it. Also, those were my favourite boots.

My mother and my girlfriend at the time, Storm, went on a recce of Headley Court and Storm took loads of photos, came back to Selly Oak and told me how good it was and about the pub around the corner where all the guys go.

I was really excited and keen to get there because I knew this would be the next phase of my recovery – getting out of hospital and trying to get some part of my life back, even if I was nowhere near being able to accept what had happened to me.

I had a lot of pent-up aggression, frustration and anger. When I was discharged from hospital it became even more apparent. I would snap. Those snaps would be horrendous, really aggressive. I never became physical but I used a lot of verbal nastiness directed at my mother and Storm. For months I struggled to contain my rages. It was the early onset of PTSD.

I'd gone from being at the peak of physical fitness to learning how to walk again. It was as if I'd regressed to being a baby again. It fucked me up big time. I had always been physically active and strong. I was into rock climbing, mountain biking, always down by the beach and jumping off rocks. I knew I was lucky to be alive but I kept thinking that my life was over. It was like being a child again. I even started making a list of things I'd never be able to do again. That was not helpful.

I was so skinny and weak. My brother would make me juices of pure broccoli to try to build my energy. They tasted horrific but they worked.

The first time I went out in public was to the Bullring shopping centre in Birmingham. I've never been out in a wheelchair since. It's a symbol of defeat to me. I don't need to be in a wheelchair.

I felt humiliated. People were looking at me. You don't often see a young man missing a leg in a shopping centre. Anyone who stopped would get the story. I had a T-shirt made saying, 'I survived a roadside bomb'. There was a massive need for me to be accepted and for people to understand.

I remember stopping at a service station on the way to Headley Court and getting on the crutches I had. I had this massive wound across the stump that needed a lot of care and attention at that stage. As I got out of the car and moved towards the forecourt I slipped and landed straight on my stump. Day one out of hospital and I'd opened it up again.

Getting to Headley Court was a great feeling but it was only the start of my recovery. The shortness of my stump posed a lot of challenges for the prosthetists because I had less muscle and sinew with which to move what was left of my leg. Having a couple of inches of extra stump would have made a huge difference.

Around that time, physically and emotionally I was very weak and I was angry, although I didn't understand the anger. The impact of my anger was felt by those around me. My mother borrowed a car from some friends and drove me around. Pray God she didn't turn left when she was meant to turn right because if she did she would just get it. I would unleash all my wrath.

One time my mother drove too close to the side of another car and it took the mirror off the side of ours. I lost it. 'I fucking told you to move over'. I never saw my mother cry in front of me, but I have no doubt she cried on her own as a direct result of my behaviour.

There were a fair few moments at Headley Court when I would get so frustrated with the prosthetic leg I would just take it off and fling it across the rehab room. I was a difficult patient, especially when it came to my family. I had real problems accepting what had happened to me.

Back then not that many Commonwealth soldiers had been injured and in a way I was forging a pathway for them and their families. The Army had flown my mother and brother over and when Mum got here she said, 'I'm not leaving until I see him walking again'.

It was really hard for my family. They got moved around and were eventually put up in one of the service quarters at the back of Headley Court. I spent eight months there and Mum eventually went into depression because of my rages. She would fear me. I'd put on this nice, big brave strong face to the therapists, nurses and the prosthetist, but then I'd go to the house to visit my family and just vent my anger pretty much from the moment I went through the door.

I was an arsehole. I was just angry and feeling sorry for myself. I was a horrible, nasty person. The painkillers didn't help my state of mind either. I was just unhappy. Pissed off. I didn't realise this at the time but my mother went home because she became scared of me. My poor mother.

Things were not going well inside my head and prosthetically things were going horrendously. I had such a high and complicated stump. The leg needed to be really, really light and it was so frustrating. The stump constantly changing shape didn't help with the fitting either. I had built up my strength again and but was struggling with the prosthetic limb. I knew what it was like to use it but I had to use two crutches which defeated the whole object.

The first time I went out drinking after I was wounded was a bad night. I met two of my ex-Para mates from basic training. I got the train up to Waterloo from Leatherhead with Storm for some do and then met these guys afterwards. I was wearing shorts – always shorts in those days – and I met these guys and they said, 'Let's go to Acton Town' to a place called the Redback. So we got a taxi there from the Waterloo. I'd had a few beers.

I was on crutches and very self-conscious. I got out of the taxi and bumped this guy with my shoulder and straightaway said, 'Sorry mate'. He looked down at my missing leg and said, 'I'll make you sorry you fucking cripple'. Boom. Big mistake. I just saw red. I threw down my crutches and I smacked him really hard in the face. He was sparked out. I'd done martial arts for many years as a teen so I could throw a punch. I connected beautifully. Then the police came. We told them the story and they said, 'Okay, you guys need to go. We know about him, he's a troublemaker around here, you need to go somewhere else'.

I am careful when I drink now because I can be too sure of myself. Psychologically I know worse shit has happened to me. I've survived an IED so who can touch me? It's arrogant and something I'm working on. I don't like who I am when I get like that.

Gradually I started to get some clarity about the future and told the doctors and nurses at Headley Court that I needed Cognitive Behavioural Therapy (CBT). I didn't want PTSD to affect future relationships or my future children's lives because I understood it could happen 10 years afterwards if you didn't deal with it there and then. It can come back to haunt you.

They sent me to see a psychiatrist but he wasn't going to give me CBT, he just gave me more drugs. He gave me anti-depressants, anti-anxiety pills. He would sit down and look at me going, 'Hmmm, right, hmmm'.

I said to him: 'Sir if you hmm and ahh me one more time I am going to get up and walk out', or wheel out.

His hmming and ahhing wasn't helping me and I told him so. I needed him to ask how I was and not, 'How are the pills?' I told him, 'I don't give a shit about the pills. They are doing what they do. How am I? That is what you should be asking.'

The next time I went to see him he asked me if I had heard of The

My Story: **Rory Mackenzie**

Priory. I said I hadn't. He said, 'It's a psychiatric hospital where they normally send pop stars with drug habits, but they also cater for Post Traumatic Stress Disorder'. So I said, 'You think I've got PTSD?' and he said, 'No, I don't think that but we'll be able to eliminate it and it's more of a therapy-based programme'.

There were all sorts of bizarre sessions there like movement classes and word therapy, all sorts of weird shit. But there was also a lot of one-to-one therapy. Those were the sessions I benefited from.

I weaned myself off a lot of the pills. I had been taking some horrendous medication which was originally developed as an anti-depressant but they realised it also had some painkilling qualities. I was taking it for the pain but it was making me very groggy in the mornings and I was finding it impossible to get up. It was probably a combination of depression and the medication that made me really lethargic. By weaning myself off the drugs I immediately started feeling better within myself.

I knew about PTSD but the psychological adjustment to losing a leg was all new to me. The occupational therapist explained that the root of everything was that I wanted to be understood, accepted.

There were times when I wouldn't leave the house on my own for long periods of time, purely down to self-consciousness. I was embarrassed about the way I looked. I'd have kids come up to me and look under the trouser leg and laugh. 'What happened to his leg?' Outwardly I was laughing but inside I was massively self-conscious.

Even to this day I don't mind shopping on my own, but I'm more self-conscious than when I have someone to distract me. I know that on a good day I can walk as if nothing is wrong. I have a stick so it's obvious something's going on.

It's part of me and I've accepted it. But it took me three years after being wounded to get to that point.

I decided to stay in the Army, partly because I thought it would help me get the prosthetics I needed which are incredibly expensive. So I went back to work at the Keogh Barracks Medical Centre, just for two hours a day for the first three months.

Around that time I received an invitation via Help for Heroes to go adaptive skiing in Bavaria, Germany, under a new military programme called Battle Back. I didn't waste a second and jumped at the opportunity. I had no idea what to expect or what I was actually getting myself into. As a South African you don't put skiing at the top of your 'to do' list, so I was apprehensive about the whole thing. Within five minutes of the initial brief I was at ease, I knew this was going to be a healing experience.

Learning to ski and coming off all that medication were really the turning points for me. I began to gain far more confidence when I was outside on my own. I'd had loads of problems with my stump fluctuating in size and shape in the early days but as the years passed and the stump settled that also made life so much easier.

It was the start of me being able to get on with my life. I began to realise my journey still had a full course to run.

CHAPTER 5
DARK DAYS

Day 22: 26th December

Rory's relief at being able to row pain-free was tempered by the issues with the all-important water-maker. With each man needing to consume between eight and 10 litres of fresh water per day to adequately replace the fluids they were losing while rowing in the searing heat, it was a critical piece of equipment. Without it, they would be forced to use a hand pump to manually produce drinking water, but that was a laborious process that would have a negative impact on both boat speed and crew morale.

Then, to add to their woes, after darkness fell on Boxing Day they were hit by a huge tropical storm.

Ed: *There was thunder, lightning, and rain like the worst jungle storm*

I'd ever seen. The waves were really picking up and you could barely see the person in front of you because the rain was so thick. The wind turned us 180 degrees and started pushing us back in the wrong direction. It was full on.

After the relatively benign conditions of the previous few days, the crew suddenly found themselves in the teeth of a storm. Powerful head winds made it almost impossible to make progress in the right direction, meaning the para anchor was urgently required just to prevent the boat going backwards. The para anchor, attached to the boat by two guide lines, was dropped into the water where it fanned out and swung the nose of the boat around to hold it in position against the currents.

For more than two hours 'A Shift' – made up of Ed, Will and Neil – sat and suffered as golf-ball-sized rain drops pummelled them on deck. After what seemed like hours the storm relented slightly and they were able to retrieve the anchor. But, just as the line was being hauled in, it snagged underneath the boat, requiring Ed to get into the water and feel his way under the hull of the boat to release it. He was in the water for several minutes, being battered by the rough seas and rain. If the parachute itself had wrapped around the rudder or parts of the steering mechanism the boat would have been left floundering, leaving it vulnerable to capsize. Ed's decisive action averted disaster but it also left the skipper cold and shivering in the cabin.

Ed: *I had my shoes on and a safety harness which clipped me to the boat. I put a torch in my mouth and jumped in backwards, keeping both hands on the boat. I flipped my feet up against the side to stop myself getting knocked out as the boat smashed up and down on the waves and worked my way along the side to get to the front. I was able to untangle the lines before shimmying back to the middle of the boat.*

I had to be pulled back on board and helped to dry off because I was so cold. The guys were very good – they got me into the cabin to dry off, get dressed, warm up and try to get some sleep. Then they got the para anchor back in and got rowing again straightaway.

CAPTAIN'S LOG

Boxing Day yesterday was rounded off with two seats needing repairs (ball bearings on wheels) and an almighty storm. The wind turned 180 degrees, against us, and picked up to 20-30kn, while the rain was so heavy you could hardly see the other end of the boat. The weather calmed down but the rain has stayed with us. Everything is wet but spirits remain high: the kit might fail but we won't.

Position: 19°35'N 36°44'W

Distance covered: 37nm in past 24 hours

To Barbados: *1,368nm*

Day 23: 27th December

The storm passed and the winds reverted to their previous north-easterly status (tail winds), so the crew were quickly able to get rowing again. By now Rory no longer required any painkillers and his all-round contribution on the oars improved considerably as a result. It meant Alex and Carl's 'B Shift' was once again operating at maximum capacity. Which was less than could be said for the desalinator – despite the work Carl and Neil had carried out on Christmas Day it was continuing to play up. Normally it would produce up to 50 litres of water per day but its output was becoming more and more sporadic and unpredictable. It was an increasing concern for the ever-vigilant skipper.

Ed: *We had this saying on on board, 'The equipment may fail, but we won't'. I had 100 per cent confidence in the crew and their ability to complete the crossing, but the persistent technical failures left me considerably less confident in the kit.*

As if to confirm Ed's fears, just before sundown the bilge pump – essential for pumping out rain or seawater from the waves that broke on the boat and which had been problematic from day one – failed. It meant the crew now had to bail out the gallons of water which flooded the foot-wells of the boat every day by hand. They began to wonder if they were jinxed.

At least now the sun had come out and the sea had calmed enough to enable the crew to hang some of their clothes out to dry on deck for the first time all crossing.

CAPTAIN'S LOG

Electric bilge pump failed. Attempts to revive it have not worked although we are still trying. Water-maker is still being difficult although as long as we are getting water that is all that matters.

Position: 19°24'N 37°40'W

Distance covered: 54nm in past 24 hours

To Barbados: *1,314nm*

Day 24: 28th December

After three days of increasingly temperamental output from the desalinator, it again failed to start when Carl turned it on before his morning shift. The crew finally had to accept that they had a serious problem.

Ed: *Normally the water-maker ran for around two hours during the day, every day, to produce the 50 litres or so that we needed. It was a critical piece of equipment. When it failed we all thought, 'Oh shit'.*

Once again Carl and Neil were tasked with trying to fix the infernal machine. They decided to contact Jim McDonald, widely recognised as a 'desalinator guru', who had told the crew they could call him 'any time' while at sea. They'd taken him up on his offer on Christmas Day, when they'd phoned him as he was about to tuck into his turkey lunch. After apparently solving the problem, he was disappointed to hear from them again so soon afterwards.

Carl explained to Jim that once again the motor that ran the pump had stopped functioning. They could still produce water by working the machine with its emergency hand pump but it would take five hours of tedious manual work every day just to produce the amount of water they needed to survive.

Carl: *Neil and I tried everything we could think of. We called Jim and spent hours going through our options. We were in the cabin trying to fix it for about four hours. They were horrible conditions to work in. Hot, disgusting, hairs everywhere. Wet wipes that hadn't been thrown out. It was really uncomfortable lying on those hot, sticky, mats. It was so hot in that cabin and we were both sweating heavily which made the salt sores worse and worse. My balls were stinging, my arse was hurting, my hands were hurting. The other guys could see us labouring away and every so often we'd just go, 'Sorry guys it's not working'.*

We had a checklist of everything that could possibly go wrong. We worked our way through it methodically. We thought the unit itself was broken, but then we thought it couldn't be the unit itself because it was brand new. So then we thought it must be the motor or the pump. Jim didn't seem to think the pump was the problem. Eventually we worked out that the motor was reconditioned. We'd been given a second-hand motor. It was kit failure again.

Neil: *Salt had got into the pump and done some damage. If we could have properly washed it through we may have stood a chance of rescuing it. We oiled it, but just couldn't get it going. It got to the point we had to say 'enough is enough'.*

After several hours of hot, unpleasant work, the pair accepted defeat and the crew reluctantly resigned themselves to hand-pumping for the rest of the trip.

The situation left Neil bitterly frustrated.

Neil: *To spend so long working on it and come out without a result was intensely frustrating. It was a low point. I wasn't getting any grief at all from the other lads, which was definitely a bad sign.*

CAPTAIN'S LOG

We reached the ½ way point today. Hooray. And our water-maker finally gave up. Boo. Now hand-pumping our water. It will not break us.

Position: 19°05'N 38°37'W
Distance covered: 54nm in past 24 hours
To Barbados: *1,314nm*

Day 25: 29th December

The prospect of hand-pumping the water was another serious blow. The crew knew that the all-female 'Row for Freedom' crew's desalinator had also failed, forcing them to hand-pump for the majority of their crossing. For the Row2Recovery crew it would mean that in order to maintain their boat speed, someone would have to man the pump for five hours a day while off shift. Sleep would inevitably be reduced.

Ed: *All the way across we'd tried to stay in the mindset of, 'Everything's breaking, but we will make it. We'll find a way.' We weren't letting ourselves get down but when the water-maker packed up it was a massive blow. The thought of hand-pumping all the way to Barbados just didn't bear thinking about. But that was what we faced so we had no choice but to think, 'We're in it so let's get on with it'.*

As it turned out, they only had to use the hand pump for a single day. Almost unbelievably, it lasted less than five hours before snapping in Ed's hands.

Neil: *It just fell to pieces in Ed's hands. It must have been faulty. People have asked us since what we were doing with it, but we were* *just using it normally. It just seemed to be one thing after another. It was a pretty bad few days.*

With no means of producing drinking water, the crew were forced to break into the ballast water, 200 litres of which was held in bottles under the deck in case of emergency. Under the rules of the race, for every litre of water they drank, a substantial time penalty would be added to their overall race time. The crew immediately implemented a strict water rationing regime and considered their options. Because so many of their day-to-day meals needed hydrating with hot water, they also faced a dramatic reduction in their overall calorie intake until a solution could be found. All of them had already lost more than 10kg since the start.

After protracted discussions with the race organisers by satellite phone, a plan was hatched to fly a new desalinator unit out to the Cape Verde Islands. This would then be collected by the race support vessel Aurora and transported to the Row2Recovery boat, currently positioned almost 1,000 miles west of the tiny African islands.

CAPTAIN'S LOG

Hand-held water-maker failed and broke at midday today. Gutted. Making plans for a support yacht to get us some spares. Will survive on our 200 litres ballast till then. Rationing to 3 litres per person per day, so 11 days to get us spares. Food is limited to snack packs only, which is all fresh, so about 2000 calories a day. No dehydrated meals.

During daylight hours activity is reduced to minimum to avoid sweating. At night we will row at slow pace. Weather has picked up with ENE winds. Force 4-5 pushing us at 1.7kn without us rowing

Support yacht is in Cape Verde and plan is to fly spares out to meet it. Doubtful this can be done and yacht cover 1000 miles in time . . .

Position: 18°43'N 39°23'W
Distance covered: 48nm in past 24 hours
To Barbados: *1,211nm*

Day 26: 30th December

With parts proving hard to come by and flights sporadic, the initial plan to fly a new desalinator out was quickly shelved in favour of the Aurora resupplying the crew with bottled water, with the crew surviving on the strictly rationed ballast water while they waited for the support yacht to arrive.

The idea of resupplying from a passing commercial vessel was ruled out because of the risks involved in a rowing boat drawing alongside an ocean liner in potentially difficult seas.

Neil: *There was no panic. We had a bit of a brainstorming session with everyone throwing their ideas in. We established that we had 200 litres of water in the ballast and a bit more left over that we'd already made. We were told it would take around eight days for the Aurora to get to us so we factored in an extra couple of days and cracked on with rationing. Will and Ed did a superb job of planning our water rationing and adding in contingencies.*

Instead of a race, the crew now found themselves in a survival situation.

CAPTAIN'S LOG

Another solution shaping up. The support ship Aurora resupplies us with ballast water. We'll have to survive for 8-10 days on 3L each only and minimal rations until she gets to us. She'll then replace our 200L (which will mostly be gone) and add another 150L to that. This may be enough to get us to Barbados if we can maintain 50nm per day.

We've managed to eke out rainwater and remaining water today so won't break into ballast until tomorrow first thing. This

*has given us another day's grace . . . The 50nm covered today
was purely from the force 5/6 winds – we are not rowing to
save water. Tonight we start rowing at night only.*
Position: 18°22'N 40°10'W
Distance covered: 50nm in past 24 hours
To Barbados: *1,163nm*

Day 27: 31st December

With uncertainty surrounding the timing of their resupply, Ed took
the decision to reduce each crew member's water entitlement from
the initial ration of three litres per day down to just two. Unable
to wash the salt off their already sore bodies, and unable to
rehydrate their dried food, it didn't take long for even more rashes
to appear and the weight to start dropping off even faster. As they
moved progressively further south to take advantage of the trade
winds, the air temperature also continued to rise, making life on
board extremely arduous.

In fourth place at this stage, any hope of winning the race also
disappeared as the crew significantly reduced their rowing output
in an effort to preserve energy and water ahead of the resupply.
With the race designated as 'unsupported', they would technically
be disqualified anyway the moment they accepted help from
Aurora.

Carl: *It became a case of, 'Forget the race, let's make sure we get
across'. First or last, the campaign would be a success If we completed
the crossing.*

The further south the crew got the more they began to notice
the presence of flying fish, which would often thud into the side of
the boat or even somtimes leap from the water onto the deck.
When this happened, if they went unnoticed there were some
unwanted consequences.

Carl: *The flying fish were good fun to start with but they became a bit of a pain. Sometimes you'd be rowing along and one would whack you square in the head. They were especially annoying at night when they'd land on the deck and flip around manically. If you didn't spot them and they died they could end up in the footwells where they'd rot and cause a horrendous smell. That was pretty disgusting.*

Just as spending Christmas Day in the middle of the ocean had proved somewhat surreal, the idea of celebrating New Year's Eve at sea did not hold a great deal of appeal. The crew did take some time out to see in the New Year in with some unlikely snacks, but all they served to achieve was to make everyone even thirstier.

CAPTAIN'S LOG

We have taken our clocks back an hour. We celebrated New Year's Eve with pork scratchings, beef jerky and strong banter. And some whisky.

We've started on our ballast, rationing ourselves to 2L per man per day until we better understand when we will get resupplied. As we can't have dehydrated meals, our calorific intake per day has more than halved. Good progress today thanks mostly to Force 5 and 6 winds. Morale high – crew is v resistant.

Position: 18°04'N 41°16'W
Distance covered: 66nm in past 24 hours
To Barbados: *1,097nm*

Day 28: 1st January

Down to two litres of water per person per day, the crew were consuming around eight litres below the amount they had been recommended to drink. Rory and Will were constantly thirsty, while the others found the hunger harder to deal with. With the air temperature exceeding 40 degrees centigrade, the crew began monitoring each other for signs of dehydration such as headaches, lethargy and significantly darkened urine. They tried to stay out of the sun and wind wherever possible in an effort to limit sweat loss. Remarkably Neil, the most severely injured of the wounded men, was the one least affected by the lack of water, often having some left over at the end of his shift which he would donate to a communal water container.

Ed: *Throughout the spell on water rationing Neil proved to be a machine. He never complained, not even a sideways glance. If something needed fixing he was always, 'I'm in there, no problem'. Not only did he use less water than anybody else, but he was the one who wanted to row the most during that period. It was hard to stop him.*

Will: *Salt was building up everywhere and it was incredibly difficult to get rid of it. You could jump in the sea for a dip but it only temporarily eased the discomfort because there would still be a layer of salt on you. Rashes built up. It was a very sore period of time. We had lots of wet wipes but they were nowhere near as effective when they didn't have fresh water on them.*

CAPTAIN'S LOG

Happy New Year! Dehydration now slowly setting in as the rationing hits 3rd day, as is hunger. But banter is on a high as there is no rowing during the day so nothing to do other than sit on deck and shoot the proverbial. Lots of talk about food, with imaginations running wild . . .

Position: *17°45'N 42°12'W*
Distance covered: *56nm in past 24 hours*
To Barbados: *1,041nm*

Day 29: 2nd January

The night-time-only rowing shifts allowed the crew to spend time talking on deck during the day. Invariably food dominated conversation, although there was also plenty of time for reflection. Will and Ed discussed Will's hopes of one day owning a butcher's shop down the road from his beloved Gloucester Rugby Club while Ed and Alex discussed their own futures in business and what they might look to change when they got home. But almost always, the conversations reverted back to food. The 'mystery meal' game became a favourite way of passing the time.

Carl: *We'd take turns to talk the others through our 'mystery meal' and how we'd go about it. My absolute favourite was turkey stir-fry for main course. I'd start off by walking round the supermarket, explaining which aisles I'd walk along, how I'd pay for it – cash or card? Then I'd talk through driving home, going through the front door and unpacking the shopping bags. You'd include every little detail. Chop the turkey up into fine long strips and empty into your wok. Put your key ingredients in. Red pepper sliced. Garlic, two cloves finely chopped. Onion. Mange tout with the ends nipped off – nice and fresh. Ten mushrooms, nicely chopped. Ginger. Red and green chillies, remembering to take the seeds out, diced into very small pieces. Into the bowl. Oil in the pan, maybe sesame oil for extra flavour. Add that all in with the turkey, get it browned off. Add the veg. A glug of soy sauce to steam through and add an essence of flavour. Chilli powder, more ginger and a little cumin. You've got your pak choi as well. Cook all that up, noodles into boiling water at the side. That's four minutes. Cook them off, drain them and then into your wok. Add some chow mein sauce, two sachets. Stir it all up, mix your noodles and then into your bowl and away you go.*

We could make these mystery meals last up to two hours by going into every little detail of how we would make them. What cutlery we'd use, the lot. It was a kind of torture in a way because we were all so hungry but it filled the time and was good fun.

Alex: *Rory and I were probably the main players in this. Carl's were not that imaginative. One of his fantasy meals was a mashed potato* *sandwich! We did summer and winter menus and my favourite meal of all was the seven-course breakfast served by Helena Christiansen in her underwear.*

But despite their creative imaginations, the crew were becoming increasingly listless and lethargic due to the lack of food and water. Will also found more sores emerging on the back of his stump as he could no longer adequately clean his prosthetic socket. Ed and Neil continued to row sporadically during the day, much to Rory's frustration as the medic, but the others found they needed to rest to preserve their energy for the night-time rowing.

CAPTAIN'S LOG

Testing to see if we can row during the day as well as at night without dramatically impacting our bodies and attempts at keeping hydrated.

Will's prosthetic causing issues = stump sock won't disengage from socket due to salt build-up. Now sorted. Broke the '1,000 miles to go' milestone . . .

Position: 17°22'N 43°12'W

Distance covered: 61nm in past 24 hours

To Barbados: *980nm*

Day 30: 3rd January

The crew's frustration was eased slightly by a satellite phone call from Alex to the London support team, when he learned that their plight was generating a huge amount of media coverage in the UK. Several newspapers, including *The Times, Daily Mail, Sunday Telegraph* and *Sunday Mirror* ran page-lead stories while Radio 4, Radio 5 Live and ITV News all requested interviews. *The Sunday Telegraph* devoted its page three to the story under the headline, 'War Heroes Adrift and Thirsty in Atlantic Race'. While the crew would have swapped every single column inch for a speedier resupply, they at least took some comfort from delivering on one part of their mission: to raise awareness of the plight of injured soldiers. It was also reassuring to hear that as the media coverage continued, the money was still pouring into the website at a rate of more than £1,000 per day.

Alex: *I spent a lot of time and effort sending all the images and video footage back. I was happy because we were getting a lot of great coverage but delivering it meant sitting in the cabin, rolling around, with the laptop on my knees, editing footage. Every time I sent stuff back it was a two- to three-hour job. Load, edit, upload, send, complete sending. It was never something I looked forward to doing but it was my big job. I just did it when it was required. Sam would call and say, 'We need this extra bit of footage and we need it by a certain time', and I would just get on with it while Carl slept next to me.*

The crew even managed to achieve a broadcast first. In a further testimony to the quality of the on-board communications equipment provided by Marine Camera Solutions, Alex was able to deliver a live camera link-up into the ITV News studio, broadcast on the 6 o'clock news, from the middle of the Atlantic Ocean.

CAPTAIN'S LOG

Day 5 of rationing and now getting v hungry. The water situation is manageable – we are all very dehydrated but still able to row at night and a little by day without the onset of heat exhaustion – yet . . .

Apparently this is causing a media storm back home but it is hard to understand what that really means back here in our little world of shifts, discomforts and little pleasures (chocolate bar . . . beef jerky . . .). Large pod of dolphins joined us for a few minutes – made our day.

Endless talk of what we will do, what we will eat, what we will change when we get back!

Dinner tonight is pepperami and a bag of sweets. I could murder a burger.

Position: 16°53'N 44°12'W
Distance covered: 65nm in past 24 hours
To Barbados: *918nm*

Day 31: 4th January

Despite significantly reducing their rowing time, the Row2Recovery crew were still making reasonably good progress by steering on the currents and utilising the tailwinds that continued to blow them towards their destination. It was far from speedy progress, and they were steadily dropping back in the race, but it was important for morale.

Ed: *One of the things you do on an ocean rowing boat is to use the wind angles. You want the weather to be not exactly behind you but at a slight angle of 10 degrees off the boat because then the wind hits the side of a boat which acts a bit like a sail and gives you an extra little bit of speed. That was on our minds all the time when we were steering, looking at wind angles and always trying to understand where the weather was coming from.*

Will's constant refrain of 'Morale is high' jarred with some sections of the media who implied that cracks were appearing in team unity. But the reality was that, despite their misfortune, the team was tight and focused on the bigger mission: getting across.

CAPTAIN'S LOG

Good day, good banter and some morale as we get to the ²/₃ mark. Double ration of chocolate is welcome as hunger has really set in now. Lads are dehydrated but no sign of heat exhaustion yet.
Position: 16°30'N 45°07'W
Distance covered: 58nm in past 24 hours
To Barbados: *862nm*

Day 32: 5th January

The crew were by now all experiencing dramatic weight loss and were only passing urine once a day, at most. Their urine had turned brackish and dark brown in colour, and they were warned by the doctors whose advice they'd sought that they were putting themselves at risk of long-term kidney damage.

Will: *I really struggled with the lack of water and felt like I needed a drink all the time. Being one of the fatter members of the crew meant the hunger wasn't such an issue because I had plenty in reserve but I sweat a lot, especially since the injury. I think your nervous system takes a while to get used to what's happened and you have less surface area to sweat from.*

Neil: *I would drink most of my water through the night so I'd normally pass urine first thing in the morning. My wee was a horrible brown colour. I was producing very small amounts. I used to really skimp on water during the day so that I would have enough for the rowing spells at night.*

Carl: *I had a dilemma. Did I put water on my balls and arse or did I drink it? I probably took on less fluid than the others because I was using around half of it to try to clean the salt off my body to reduce the soreness and stinging. I was only actually drinking about a litre of water a day for several days and very little food. We all started to lose weight quite rapidly. I became very skinny.*

CAPTAIN'S LOG

Delay to arrival of Aurora. We were expecting her on 8th but now 10th. Hopes of increasing our ration significantly die away, although we have increased our ration to 2.5L pppd [per person, per day]. This will allow for everyone to have an evening meal which is much needed.

Hungry and thirsty all the time . . . v hot today. Prob 35°C.

Position: 16°15'N 46°03'W
Distance covered: 56nm in past 24 hours
To Barbados: *806nm*

Day 33: 6th January

Unbeknown to the crew, while they soldiered on towards Barbados other boats in the fleet were also encountering serious difficulties. Persistently high winds and seas had made this year's conditions the toughest the organisers had ever known, with several crews being forced to withdraw after suffering capsize or kit failure. All the boats in the fleet were taking a vicious pounding. At the same time the Row2Recovery's water-maker had broken, another boat in the fleet, the aptly named 'Patience' crewed by actor Bertie Portal and personal trainer James Cash, had snapped all their oars and was floundering dangerously without any means of propulsion. Another boat, 'Dream it, Do it', was having severe problems with its rudder.

The knock-on effect was that the Aurora, the race's only support vessel, had to be diverted from its mission to resupply the Row2Recovery crew in order to deal with these more imminently life-threatening situations for their fellow competitors.

Will: *We were constantly running through different scenarios, breaking down how much water we needed and how many days that would last. How much of an extra cushion we needed.*

It didn't take a genius to work out that if the safety vessel didn't get to us quickly enough then we'd be in the shit. Initially we were told it would take eight days, but it soon became apparent that wasn't going to be the case. It just kept on being pushed back so we had to keep on rationing down, which was difficult.

Initially we said, 'Okay, eight days, then let's make sure we have enough for 12'. Then when it looked like it was going to be 10 days we said, 'Okay, let's make it 14 days'. It just kept on going up.

The crew spent some time swimming, attached to the boat by a safety harness, and discovered the terrifying yet exhilarating effect of putting a face mask on and staring down into the abyss below.

Alex: *It was an incredibly strange feeling to be able stare down into the crystal clear waters knowing there were several thousand feet of ocean between you and the sea floor.*

Spirits were also boosted when Will and Ed phoned the support team at a pre-arranged time only to be greeted by the sound of 'Three cheers for Row2Recovery' at the other end of the line. Ed's parents had generously invited family and friends of all the crew members to their central London flat for a drinks and buffet reception. The crew smiled when they heard their loved ones together, enjoying themselves, although there was no shortage of tears back in the Janvrin's living room as they listened to Ed and Will on speaker phone.

CAPTAIN'S LOG

Saw a blue marlin today that circled the boat for 10 mins.
   Quiet day with winds down to F3 so cleaned the boat – most of us got in. Great experience having 2000m of water under you! The ration of 2.5L is allowing most of us to have a meal in the day which is doing wonders for energy levels. We did a call back to the families tonight who were all gathered at 'chez Janvrin' for drinks and nibbles. Good to see them bonding well as well . . .
Position: 16°02'N 46°53'W
Distance covered: 50nm in past 24 hours
To Barbados: *756nm*

Day 34: 7th January

The crew continued to monitor each other for signs of

dehydration, heatstroke, and general physical deterioration. After overcoming his own medical issues over Christmas, Rory was now acutely aware that the rest of the crew's health was, to a large extent, his responsibility.

Rory: *I was conscious that I was now doing my job and I needed to deliver. I was a little concerned about Ed and Neil because they were still rowing which meant they were exerting themselves when they shouldn't have been. They seemed to be functioning okay, but I kept a close eye on them. I checked the guys' urine to see how much they were producing and what colour it was. I felt like it was my time to step up.*

The former company medic made a video diary which was sent back to ITV in which he expressed concern at Ed and Neil's unwillingness to stop rowing.

Rory: *Ed and Neil were bored and had rested and didn't have to take on board as much water as the others. They were in decent nick. But I was thinking, 'It's 40 degrees centigrade, we're on two-and-a half litres of water in 24 hours, they're topless with a warm wind drying off their skin. This just goes against everything we should be doing'. It was concerning.*

CAPTAIN'S LOG

Admin today – reorganised food and supplies in the various hatches on board. Ditched 7 days of rations. Have 3 weeks left. Guys finding it hard to stay hydrated during the day – still no rowing between 12pm and 5pm.

Position: 15°51'N 47°38'W

Distance covered: 45nm in past 24 hours

To Barbados: *712nm*

Day 35: 8th January

The crew were informed that the likely date for the resupply was now the 12th, four days time. If they carried on consuming water at their current rate they would be cutting it very fine. Ed and Will continued to carefully monitor water levels on board.

CAPTAIN'S LOG

Water resupply now due on 12th. This will be tight. Water usage has been as follows:

30 Dec: 2L each = 12L from ballast
31 Dec: 2L
1 Jan: 2L
2 Jan: 2L
3 Jan: 2L
4 Jan: 2L
5 Jan: 2.5L each = 15L from ballast
6 Jan: 2.5L
7 Jan: 2.5L
8 Jan: 2.5L

We therefore have 80L left. On 2L each this will take us to 15th. It's tight!

Position: 15°29'N 47°38'W
Distance covered: 57nm in past 24 hours
To Barbados: *656nm*

Day 36: 9th January

With the risk of running out of water now a very real possibility, the crew began to discuss alternative options to waiting for the Aurora to arrive.

Carl: *We could have sent a 'Mayday' distress signal but it would have meant the nearest vessel being legally bound to pick us up and we wouldn't then be able to complete the crossing. Being resupplied at* *sea by a large commercial vessel was also a possibility but it was such a dangerous option that we were only ever going to consider it if we were on the brink of chronic dehydration and there was a risk to life. We'd also heard that one of the other crew's rudders had been broken by the support vessel itself so there was no way we could risk a tanker or anything of that size. We could be crushed.*

Putting a 'Pan Pan' distress call out was another option. A Pan Pan was a level below a Mayday call, meaning the sender urgently required assistance, but was not in immediate danger of death. Sea-faring etiquette dictated that most vessels would respond to a Pan Pan, although they were not legally bound to do so, while the risks of damaging the boat remained high.

After much discussion, the decision was made to sit tight and wait for the Aurora.

CAPTAIN'S LOG

Now looks like resupply will be on 13th Jan. Rory sought professional advice on minimum survival water rations in this environment from 3 sources: mountain rescue medics, Special Forces doctor and senior doctor at Headley Court. The consensus is that 2.5L per person per day is the minimum we should be taking in – beyond that and we are risking damaging our bodies (eg kidney damage). This makes the decision to drop to 2Lpppd all the more difficult, but it may be necessary.

We are looking after each other. Looking for signs of heat injury – headaches, piss quantity (750ml/per day is min), etc . . .

Our options, which are not mutually exclusive, are as follows:

1. Aurora resupplies us on time – no change

2. We slow ourselves down, potentially w/para anchor, to allow Aurora to catch up

3. We reduce our water ration to last longer

4. We look to initiate an interim resupply from a passing vessel

5. We initiate a 'Pan Pan' and get the nearest vessel to come to our aid

The weather is due to get stronger on 13th, adding to the already significant risks of the resupply itself.

Position: 15°14'N 49°27'W

Distance covered: 54nm in past 24 hours

To Barbados: *602nm*

Day 37: 10th January

To add to everyone's sense of frustration, just when they needed it most, the wind dropped to around five knots, further slowing Aurora's progress. As her estimated time of arrival continued to slip as she struggled to cope with the demands of resupplying three stricken boats spread out over an area as big as England in unhelpful weather conditions, the media interest showed no sign of abating. Ed did a piece to camera which was aired on ITV's News at Ten in which he looked painfully emaciated and occasionally slurred his words. His appearance concerned his family, who made their feelings known to the support team in London. As a result, the crew decided they should each put in a satellite phone call home to try to allay any fears about their health. Will couldn't help but draw parallels with the phone call he'd made home the day after he'd lost his leg.

Will: *I knew the whole experience of having me away and not being able to do anything to protect me would just bring things home to Mum and would conjure unwanted memories. I've not been the luckiest person so she would have expected the worst. I totally understood that. I wanted to be the one to tell Mum when the delays began to happen. I knew I could put it across in a way that would minimise worry. I encouraged the rest of the crew to do the same.*

Alex: *We were talking about the bad luck we'd had during the crossing and Will looked around at the other injured blokes on board and joked that we'd hardly picked the luckiest blokes in the world to go away with!*

DARK DAYS

I had a chat with Mum. She was keeping a close eye on us through the news, the website and via our support team. She said, 'I've spent all weekend crying' which I didn't feel great about. She's normally pretty resilient but it was distressing for the families.

Despite managing to maintain morale on board, there was growing unease as to whether or not the promised resupply would now be achieved before the water ran out. Will and Ed spent hours working out equations and options, looking at possible arrival times versus the level of the water supplies. Whatever happened from now, it was going to be a close-run thing.

The crew made a series of increasingly frantic phone calls to the charity's patron, General Sir David Richards. Having the Chief of the Defence Staff's office number was definitely an advantage, but it transpired that no Royal Naval vessel was in the vicinity. Alex also called his McKinney Rogers colleagues in Barbados, many of whom had strong military ties, while long-term supporter Paddy Nichol, who was also in Barbados, tried to establish if a light aircraft could fly out to resupply them, or if he could source a high-speed boat. No option was ruled in or out.

The idea of putting down the parachute anchor to allow Aurora to catch up faster was also raised again.

CAPTAIN'S LOG

Spoke to Aurora today and did the maths on when she would join us. She is 655nm away and currently in a weather dead spot so only doing 7kn. From tomorrow weather should build till Sunday Force 6. The upshot is that we now expect resupply on 15th, not 13th. Disappointed, another moment of low morale as our water will run out then. Decision taken today, to be reviewed tomorrow. We will not go on para anchor, we will reduce water consumption from 2L to 1.5L. We will look to initiate an interim resup by all means.

In the last few hours we have been speaking to contacts in Barbados + CDS's (Chief of Defence Staff) and to anyone with alternative options. Sadly nothing is really viable at the mo. All's well that ends well . . .

Position: 14°57'N 50°18'W

Distance covered: 51.4nm in past 24 hours

To Barbados: *551nm*

Day 38: 11th January

The option of stopping rowing altogether and deploying the para anchor was strongly favoured by the race organisers, the crew of the Aurora as well as the Row2Recovery support team in the UK. Deploying the anchor would prevent the boat drifting on the currents and enable the support vessel to reach them faster. But it would not come without risks. The crew had already experienced the pounding the ocean gave them when they'd briefly gone on the anchor two weeks earlier, resulting in Ed having to jump in at night to untangle the retrieval lines. If they sat stationary on the anchor they knew they would be in for a bumpy, uncomfortable few days. Any hope of a 'fast' crossing under 50 days would also be lost. With Barbados barely 500 miles away, their final destination seemed so near yet so far. Neil, Will and Rory strongly believed they should take a chance and continue rowing, while Ed was more cautious. No one on board found the prospect of sitting static on the ocean appealing.

Neil: *When the idea of going onto the para anchor was first raised I was definitely against it. I wanted to press on. We did the maths and worked out that if we went on the para anchor the support boat would get to us maybe a day earlier. I thought, 'Let's just keep going'. I wanted to stick with the routine we were in, just going at night. I wanted to trust the Aurora would get to us before the water ran out. I wanted to risk it.*

Alex: *The cabin doors were open and we had a long conversation. Everyone was involved. Ed was very patient. It wasn't necessarily that* anyone was right or wrong but everyone had the opportunity to put their opinions on the table and feel part of the plan. Rory, Will and Neil were quite strongly against going on the para anchor and my starting position was that I would rather keep rowing if possible. But we had to understand what was going to enable us to complete the mission. That's what turned Will around I think, because he hadn't completed his Afghan tour.

We did speak to a Greek fishing vessel nearby and asked if they would come and resupply us and they said they could only address a 'Mayday' call-out. Their owners would not permit them to redirect course because it would cost a lot of money. They said: 'If this is a Mayday you need to send it, but if it's not I'm afraid we can't do anything.'

Reluctantly, but with the overall mission at the forefront of his mind, the decision was taken by Ed to deploy the para anchor and sit tight in the hope the Aurora could get to them in time. When they deployed the anchor they had just 44 litres of water left between the six of them, with Aurora still more than 500 miles away.

Neil: *The decision was taken and that was it. It was very military in that way in that we all got to have our say and then it was, 'This is what we're doing'. That suited all of us. You don't want indecision.*

Will: *Ed and Neil were the ones who physically took the para anchor out and deployed it. It was a deflating moment. We had to keep the shift system going because of the limited cabin space, so we had to get into the routine of going out on deck but not rowing. That was just crap, really crap. Just seeing no progress at all on the GPS was awful. All of us were suffering the effects of dehydration and the salt sores were becoming intolerable. The mood on board was pretty bleak.*

CAPTAIN'S LOG

Today we took the difficult decision to go on para anchor and let Aurora catch up. Yesterday she caught us up by 130 miles (she was doing 7kn, we were averaging 2-2.5kn) – she is now 530 odd miles away.

The reasoning for going on para anchor was:

1. *It gives us a little margin for error so is the cautious way*
2. *It ensures we still have water on 15th/16th if Aurora does not speed up, against expectations*
3. *Conditions for resupply are likely to be better on 13th/14th than 14th/15th*
4. *It follows the professional advice of the race organisation and Aurora's skipper*
5. *We can always up the water rations and start rowing to make up for lost ground if Aurora speeds up*

This decision will be reviewed daily.

Position: 14°40'N 50°49'W

Distance covered: 32nm in past 24 hours

To Barbados: *519nm*

Day 39: 12th January

With the para anchor deployed, the crew had to make the best of their circumstances and keep out of the way of the increasingly prevalent flying fish which seemed to take particular pleasure in dive-bombing the boat as it bobbed about on the anchor. Often up to 40 fish would 'beach' themselves on board overnight, apparently attracted by the navigational lights in the same way moths are attracted to light bulbs.

Watching the website back in the UK it was heartbreaking for all the crew's supporters to see the worm-like line depicting their progress on the map of the Atlantic on the website stuck in one place after weeks of near continual progress.

Having attracted more than 5,000 Facebook and Twitter

followers, the campaign's support team were also working overtime to keep supporters up to date with the latest news about the crew. And the good news was that people were responding, with more than £43,000 raised since the start of the crossing, taking the overall campaign total to almost £700,000.

Alex: *Waiting on the para anchor was an uncertain time. It was impossible to relax. I thought, 'Until we get to that finish line I can't even draw breath'.*

While we were stopped there would be times when I would go on deck in my full waterproofs and just curl up and sleep in the rain – we took all the seats off and stowed them so we had a flattish deck. It was ludicrous. I was using a dry bag full of spare food as my pillow.

Neil: *When we put the para anchor down we really got pounded and thrown about by the waves. It was very different to when we were just drifting along on the current. Everyone was trying to catch up on sleep.*

We had a couple of dips in the sea and came up with some stupid games. 'Who Dares Swims' was the best one. The original game that we discussed, but never actually played, was, 'See who can swim furthest away from the boat without a rope attached'. Thankfully that evolved into, 'How far will you slide yourself down the para line towards the para anchor?' Alex was probably the ballsiest. I reckon he made it 20 feet down that line before getting the fear.

CAPTAIN'S LOG

Stayed on para anchor and will do so until Aurora is 12-24hrs away.

As at 2pm today Aurora was 380nm away – this is much slower progress than anticipated. We are being told her ETA is now 14th evening. Mostly we are bored, hungry and catching up on sleep.

Position: 14°45'N 50°51'W
Distance covered: 3nm in past 24 hours
To Barbados: *517nm*

Day 40: 13th January

Carl: *We just had to chill out and wait. I listened to Shackleton's adventures on an audio book. Part of his adventure saw him cross the Southern Ocean on an open rowing boat which he'd converted into a sailing boat to get across the worst sea in the whole world. His crew were rowing at night, getting ice on the oars and ice on the sails. They were getting hit by waves all the time and suffering from frostbite. Absolutely horrendous. But they kept going. I comforted myself with the fact we were in a warm climate and we knew we weren't going to die.*

CAPTAIN'S LOG

Still on para anchor. Moved to a new time zone – now 3hrs behind GMT. Aurora was 210nm away at 1400HRS GMT today so she should be with us tomorrow evening. Winds have increased to F4/5.

Position: 14°42'N 50°53'W

Distance covered: 3.9nm in past 24 hours

To Barbados: *513.1nm*

Day 41: 14th January

Finally the wind began to pick up and Aurora was able to increase her speed after several days of unfavourable conditions. But stronger winds meant bigger seas and before long the crew and the boat were suffering from increasingly large waves crashing down on their static position.

Will: *You could see the guide rope straining on the para anchor as we started taking a bashing from the waves. It got so bad that there was a real possibility we would have to retrieve the anchor and just run with the weather.*

Ed: You *definitely don't want to be on para anchor if the wind gets above 30 knots. That's about a force seven. I judged it to be just under that, but it wasn't far off. The power of the sea never ceased to amaze us. The waves were just smashing over us and it crossed my mind more than once that there was every chance the boat could be ripped apart. It was pretty scary. Exhilarating, but scary.*

At 10.05pm there was a crackling over the VHF radio.

'Row2Recovery this is Aurora, do you copy, over?'

Alex grabbed the radio's handset.

'Aurora, this is Row2Recovery, yes we copy, over.'

'Roger. If you look to your starboard side you should see a light about 100 metres away. We come bearing gifts!'

Aurora had arrived, and with it the desperately needed supplies of drinking water.

PRESS RELEASE ISSUED BY ROW2RECOVERY SUPPORT TEAM 2300hrs 14.01.12

Ed reported back that at 10.05pm UK time tonight (Saturday) the support boat Aurora reached the Row2Recovery in order to resupply the six-man crew with urgently needed drinking water.

An ecstatic Row2Recovery crew, who had been on two-litre water rations per man for the past 16 days since their desalinator broke, celebrated with an extra half-litre ration each in order to enjoy their first hot meal in over a week.

The boys also enjoyed an extra chocolate ration as morale on board the boat soared.

'It's fantastic news,' Ed said in a satellite call back to the Row2Recovery support team.

'We're in contact with Aurora, we are definitely going to get resupplied and we are very relieved.'

With a high sea state and darkness beginning to close in as Aurora arrived, the decision was taken to carry out the water resupply at first light on Sunday morning.

CAPTAIN'S LOG *(WRITTEN AT 1900HRS):*
*Another day on para anchor. Conditions overnight were very
rough. Up to Force 6, possibly even 7. We decided to stay on
para anchor although we could have chosen to run with the
weather because beyond that it gets dangerous.*

*We can't see Aurora but we know she is very close now. We
are entering our 17th day on water rationing.*
Position: 14°41'N 50°55'W
Distance covered: *2nm in past 24 hours*
To Barbados: *513nm*

Day 42: 15th January

But the crew's joy at Aurora's arrival was soon tempered. Not long
after the press release was issued, Ed heard a banging noise on the
outside of the cabin. He listened with Will before peering out of
the rear hatch to see what was going on. The rudder had snapped
almost in two. It was yet another crushing blow to the crew, who
had momentarily allowed themselves to believe their problems
might almost be over when the Aurora had arrived. They should
have known better. When Ed relayed the news to the rest of the
crew there was an audible groan.

'Fuck me, this boat's like Apollo 13,' Alex quipped. 'There's
nothing left to break.'

The fact that they would soon be resupplied with 350 litres of
drinking water failed to lift anyone's mood, as the realisation
dawned they now had yet another potentially critical equipment
failure on their hands.

Their hopes were pinned on a combination of their own
ingenuity and the technical expertise of Graham Walters on board
the Aurora. A four-time Atlantic rower himself, Graham was known
as the 'Mr Fixit' of the seas and his understanding of the boat's
set-up would be critical.

At first light, and in high seas, Graham and another Aurora crew member loaded a tiny rubber dinghy, powered by an outboard motor, with 175 litres of bottled water before making their way to the stricken Row2Recovery boat. It was a nerve jangling time, as everyone present knew the dangers involved. If the 60ft yacht got too close, she could smash Row2Recovery to pieces, but she needed to get close enough to allow Graham to make it safely across.

Rory: *I was on medical standby for the resupply. It was discussed before we started. The medical kit was out on deck and everyone was prepped. We were in some seriously choppy water and anything could have happened. A serious head injury was the big concern, but there was also a risk of broken bones, fingers especially, as well as drowning obviously.*

With the Row2Recovery crew on high alert, the resupply was carried out without mishap. The first drink of icy-cool water tasted like nectar to the parched team, diluting the disappointment of being disqualified from the race.

Rory: *When we got water on board it became a dash to stow it away, get it counted and numbered. It was a hell of a luxury just being able to wash the salt off our clothes and face. It was a fantastic feeling. But at the same time it was like, 'Wow, we take water for granted'. When you are handed a two-litre bottle of water and told, 'That's your water for the day', it does hit home. Then when you are handed two two-litre bottles of water it is like, 'Oh my God what am I going to do with all of this?' Four litres was amazing. We could have two hydrated meals if we wanted, we could wash stuff, wash ourselves. I'm sure some people use four litres of water brushing their teeth. I realised then and there not to take water for granted ever again.*

But the joy was tempered with the knowledge that no matter how much water they had, without a rudder they were going nowhere.

Will: *There was this really hollow feeling on board. It was great to have all the water we needed but I felt empty, distraught. All the way through the water resupply there was this constant concern about the rudder. What should have been an amazing moment wasn't.*

Getting water on board was great because it meant we could all have a big swig of water. Although we had to stay very disciplined because we were aware that we had to increase our water intake gradually because it had gone down so low it would have been dangerous to increase it too quickly. We agreed to increase it by half a litre per day.

But water was no longer our biggest concern. It was a question of whether we would be able to repair the rudder sufficiently and then whether we could reattach it in such high seas.

The entire campaign was hanging by a thread. After the water resupply had been completed, Graham and his team took the rudder back to the Aurora and set to work in the workshop below deck. Part of the steering mechanism at the top of the rudder had snapped off completely, and there was an alarming-looking crack running down the centre of the rudder itself. No one was in any doubt that if a solution was not found, the crossing was over.

The rudder was returned from Aurora in the early afternoon but it was soon apparent that the first attempt to fix it had been unsuccessful as the centre board began to buckle alarmingly in the process of reattaching it.

Neil: *That was a long day. We tried a few alternatives in case we couldn't fix the rudder. We had other emergency storm equipment called drogues which we could hang out behind us to slow us down in really rough conditions. We had an idea that we could have two lines with drogues out behind us and that by pulling them in and out we would be able to steer the boat. But it wasn't effective. There was also talk of pulling up the keel and turning that into a makeshift rudder, but that would have left us far too unstable and was quickly dismissed.*

DARK DAYS

The crew were on edge but no one got over-excited. Everyone remained calm, although some nervous looks were exchanged as each attempt to reattach the rudder ended in failure.

Neil: *We'd all been in hyper-stressful situations so many times and learned to act reasonably and think things through rather than just fly off the handle.*

Carl spent more than three hours in the water desperately trying to align the rudder to the four pins attaching it to the boat. It was a hugely stressful job in difficult, rough seas.

Carl: *I was always attached to the boat but it did get a bit hairy. The danger was that the boat would slap back down after rising on a wave. I had to be careful but I was much happier being in the water and feeling like I was contributing in some way towards the effort.*

When I first got in the water was quite warm. I moved along to the stern of the boat where we were trying to fix the rudder back on. There was a big metal rod with a metal pin and a screw at the top. But because the sea was so high and the rudder was so light and buoyant it proved incredibly difficult to push it down far enough to get the pin through and fix it into position. It was bouncing around everywhere. There were four pins to get in and the danger was if we got the first pin in and not the others the rest would buckle under the pressure and cause even more damage.

Our first attempt took close to four hours and we didn't have any joy. Eventually we decided to have another go the following day.

The rudder was taken back on the dinghy to Aurora, where Graham and his team worked through the night in one final desperate bid to find a solution.

Will: *I had unfinished business in the Army and here I was now facing the prospect of leaving more business unfinished out in the Atlantic. I* *was pretty depressed at points within myself. I just could not envisage it finishing this way. We kept it to ourselves but we shared looks here and there that spoke volumes about what we were all thinking.*

The idea of finishing as a plucky failure again did not bear thinking about. I didn't want the pats on the on the back with people saying, 'Hard luck, great effort' when ultimately we had failed. All the work we'd done and all the supporters and people who'd donated money would have been let down. We'd had so many good things written and said about us and we'd bullishly said, 'Whatever happens, we'll get there, even if we have to swim', and we'd be made to eat those words. I was dreading it. It was eating me up.

CAPTAIN'S LOG

Aurora joined us late last night and held off until first light this am. 350L of water transferred without a hitch despite difficult sea conditions (Force 6).

Long day in the water trying to reattach rudder. Initial signs promising but the rudder board was so badly damaged that it threatened to snap in half so Aurora has taken it back to see if they can reinforce it.

We are not out of the woods yet.

Position: 14°39'N 50°59'W

Distance covered: 4.4nm in past 24 hours

To Barbados: *509nm*

Day 43: 16th January

The uncertainty over the rudder was playing on everyone's minds. No one slept well that night.

Carl: *That night was bad. For the first time I think a lot of us felt completely helpless. There really was nothing we could do other than wait and pray that Graham could come up with a workable solution. Our fate was in his hands. We had another night on the deck getting wet. It was pretty grim. I didn't sleep well at all.*

DARK DAYS

The next morning Graham and another Aurora crew member returned at first light, around 32 hours since first spotting Row2Recovery. The painstaking process began again. Everybody knew the next few hours would decide the fate of the entire campaign.

Carl: *Our first attempt failed again. The pins just wouldn't go in. So the six of us and Graham sat around on deck and talked about our options. We had a few different ideas. One idea was to take an oar and use that as a kind of stand-up rudder like a gondolier steers a gondola. But it was all pie in the sky. The reality was it was the rudder or nothing.*

Then, Alex had the idea of detaching one of the two pinnacles – circular metal attachments fixed to the stern of the boat – from the boat itself and then somehow threading the pin through the rudder and then reattaching it to the boat so the top was still attached. It would take the other four pins which were causing all the problems out of the equation.

Alex's novel idea proved decisive.

Alex: *The top of the rudder had a T-bar steering section which had snapped off, so I suggested they drill as far back as possible to maximise leverage and then tie the steering lines straight on to the back of the rudder. Our biggest problem after that was going to be reattaching it to the boat in the rough conditions. The rudder was designed so that if it came off it would float, but as long as it was attached you would still be able to retrieve it so what's the point? A buoyant rudder is fine to attach on land but when you are trying to align four pins in huge rolling seas it's something else altogether. It made life incredibly difficult.*

The plan involved Ed leaning out of the rear-cabin hatch and removing the back plate which held onto the pinnacle at the top of the rudder. Carl was again in the water, while Graham directed proceedings from the relative safety of the dinghy. The metal looped pinnacle was taken off so there were two holes there. Will and Alex then took the screws out and put a rope through the two holes and around the pinnacle itself. They were then able to put the pin in and pull very tight so it locked in place to the stern of the boat. With Carl in the water and Ed poking his head out of the stern hatch, the rudder could be held in place and pushed down.

Carl: *The timing had to be perfect to avoid the waves forcing it out of position so as soon as Ed and Graham forced it down I put some rope around the bottom to lock it in place. We had to work quite fast. It probably took a maximum of a minute. Once the rope was through the holes we put a screw through either side to bolster it. Bingo!*

Alex: *We knew it was make or break. Carl and Ed were the rudder SWAT team. Ed was inside the boat hanging out of the back hatch, leaning over the top of the rudder. Graham was in the resupply dinghy. Carlos had his life jacket on in the water. There were several attempts to do it and then a big cry of 'Yessss!'*

Will: *Finally something worked and the rudder clicked into place. We all knew it was the pivotal moment of the whole crossing but it wasn't a high-five moment. It was more a case of, 'Breathe, thank God for that, let's get rowing'. We were still so nervous because it was only working at 70 per cent, it wasn't as responsive and we didn't know how long it would last. It wasn't the most robust rudder, it was a workable solution. So we just nervously cracked on.*

Alex: *We treated ourselves to a bag of pork scratchings to celebrate.*

With the rudder now back in position, Ed was understandably keen for Aurora to stay close by for as long as possible in case anything else went wrong. With the Row2Recovery crew eager to get back to rowing, Aurora stayed with the crew and observed the rudder's performance. Although the steering was much heavier, the early signs appeared promising, and after three hours of observation Aurora was able to leave the Row2Recovery behind to check on other crews in the area just before nightfall.

Neil: *The Aurora crew were fantastic but it was actually good to see them off. It was us against the ocean again. We had a lot of pent-up energy because we'd been eating for a couple of days since the water had arrived and we were ready to get going. Barbados was now back on the agenda.*

CAPTAIN'S LOG

Very emotional day today trying to fix the rudder to the boat. The rudder was reinforced overnight which was critical, but useless if we couldn't fix it to the boat. We tried a number of options for the latter, all failing dismally. In the end we had a light bulb moment which worked out, so we are now rowing again which is great. We are absolutely delighted to get off the para anchor, but are already bracing ourselves for the next failure . . . Darkest 48 hours so far.

Position: 14°36'N 51°09'W

Distance covered: 11.2nm in past 24 hours

To Barbados: *499nm*

My Story:
Alex Mackenzie

Age: 33
Regiment: The Parachute Regiment (Third Battalion)
Army career span: 2001–2007
Rank: Captain
Combat experience: Iraq (2002), Afghanistan (2006)
Physical injury: none
Honours: Mentioned in Dispatches for leadership

My regiment, The Parachute Regiment (Third Battalion), better known as '3 PARA', was the first British unit into Helmand Province in June 2006. I remember the defence secretary at the time, John Reid, being widely misquoted in the media as saying he expected us to come back 'without a shot being fired'. Even then I knew enough about the way some sections of the media operate not to take too much notice of what they were telling us.

All the information we were getting, and all the briefings we were having at the time, strongly indicated that we were about to enter a world where brutal, unremitting and extreme violence would be a part of daily life. We prepared with the mindset that we were going to encounter things none of us had ever encountered before.

One incident, fairly early on in our tour, highlighted the immense difficulty of our job in Afghanistan, and the personal challenges we would face on a day-to-day basis. A combined patrol including elements of C Company 3 PARA and a contingent from a small patrol led by a young officer from the Royal Irish Regiment was due to go out to a village called Zumbelay on a hearts-and-minds mission to try to win over the local population. It was the major reason we were there – to convince the local population that they were better off with us than with the Taliban. My Fire Support Group, 12 men from 3 PARA, was there to provide depth and fire support to ensure the patrol could get in and get out.

When I heard the brief I had some reservations. It felt like we were looking for trouble, for no real purpose. Gereshk, our base for the past few weeks, had been quiet and I wondered whether people were just getting twitchy.

I carried out some research on the target area. We had a US Special Forces unit with us in our camp and their intelligence operator had already been in the region for some time so I went to pick his brains. His summary was unequivocal: 'You guys better have a good reason to go up there. Every patrol we have sent there has ended up in a two-hour firefight at best. Why do you want to go there?'

I relayed this to the Royal Irish officer who told me bluntly that he didn't care. Having given him the option to make an informed choice of his own he chose not to take it, so I said, 'Fine, I'll put it to my commanding officer and he can make the final decision'. He was an experienced bloke who went on to win a Military Cross and I anticipated he would see things the way I did.

He didn't.

He said that we were going to conduct the patrol anyway although he accepted the difficult terrain would make it difficult to withdraw if anything went wrong. He did agree to reduce the area of ground we would cover by two kilometres. This may not sound like much, but when there are six-feet-deep drainage ditches between you and a safe route out, then 100 metres is a long way. There is no doubt in my mind that this decision saved lives.

Despite the concession, I left the meeting incandescent. We were about to attempt a hearts-and-minds operation in the middle of a

My Story: **Alex Mackenzie**

known ambush killing zone. I didn't feel that we had a really clear sense of what this plan was going to achieve.

If my face showed my discontent the blokes didn't acknowledge it. Most paratroopers just want to be on a mission and to get into the action. They were imagining the deep thud of the .50 calibre heavy machine gun and grinning with excitement. This was what they had all signed up for.

When we left on that patrol there were about 50 of us in total. Our commanding officer was with us, as was Sergeant Major Mick Bolton, plus drivers and a whole host of hangers on – mechanics, cooks and the like – who had been cobbled together to conduct the patrol.

Also in the group was a reporter, Christina Lamb, the *Sunday Times* foreign correspondent who had been embedded with us for a couple of days, along with a photographer, Justin Sutcliffe. Christina is the leading Western journalist on Afghanistan and extremely well-connected in the region – she knew the brother of Afghan President Hamid Karzai personally and she was subsequently on the same bus as former Pakistan Prime Minister Benazir Bhutto when Bhutto was assassinated. She'd been around the camp for a few days and spoken to a lot of people. It wasn't a close relationship, we just knew her and who she was.

I think the idea of taking them on patrol that day was that it would be a good opportunity to get them out there to see some of the hearts-and-minds stuff with the local communities. It didn't quite pan out that way.

The patrol crossed the Helmand River before part of it separated out into a foot patrol. The Fire Support Group which I was commanding moved into a position where we could provide cover and protection for both the foot patrol and the troop-carrying vehicles.

By the time we got close to the village of Zumbelay it was around 2pm and the temperature was well over 50 degrees centigrade. It was an environment which made you rethink the rules. Drivers and gunners often had to wear gloves because pistol grips and steering wheels were too hot to touch.

THE ROW TO RECOVERY

We dropped off the foot patrol and maintained radio contact with them. Christina and Justin also got out of the vehicles to enter the town on foot. They were integrated into the patrol and kept well protected. You can move an arm's length away from someone in that kind of environment and it can be fatal. Taliban fighters will snatch you in an instant.

Meanwhile, the vehicle group which I commanded had been in position for over an hour, and probably for longer than it should have been. I should have kept moving positions regularly in order to mitigate the chances of the enemy mounting an opportunistic attack and disabling the vehicles.

Then we received a radio message from the platoon sergeant of the Royal Irish saying, 'I've seen a suspicious group of young males to the south of our position, can you investigate?'.

I said, 'Leave it with me', and went to brief the Fire Support Group (FSG) team.

I was in the process of getting the vehicles together when suddenly we started taking heavy incoming fire. Paul 'Spud' McMellon, my Platoon Sergeant, was already in action engaging the firing position with his commander's machine gun while his gunner had the .50 Cal in action too. We quickly got our four FSG vehicles into action and unleashed a rapid rate of fire on to the building. As I was sending my contact report I heard the foot patrol being engaged at the same time. It was a double ambush.

Shit.

With two ambushes taking place simultaneously, it was just about the worst-case scenario. We needed to act decisively or we were sure to take heavy casualties.

I eyeballed a couple of the lead-vehicle drivers who stared at me as if to say, 'What the fuck do we do now?' These guys had been roped in to make up the numbers and some were clearly overwhelmed. They were in shock and we had to get them focused. I shouted and gesticulated and somehow managed to get the message across and get them in their vehicles.

I told them to move south out of range of the contact and Spud and I covered the withdrawal. We were taking incoming mortar fire and machine gun fire. Thankfully it wasn't accurate enough, although we had mortars landing less than 100 metres from us, with some landing and not going off.

Having extracted the troop-carrying vehicles we had another problem to deal with. Paddy and the rest of the foot patrol – along with the two *Sunday Times* journalists – were in immediate danger of being overwhelmed. Taliban fighters were engaging them from all sides in a 360-degree ambush. It defied logic because it meant they risked killing their own side in the crossfire. Conventional wisdom suggests that if you have two friendly forces with an enemy in the middle it is madness to fire across them because you stand every chance of killing your own people. The Taliban fighters were doing exactly that. It was completely insane. I began to think fatalities were inevitable.

In moments like that, everything is in technicolour. There's a feeling of intense focus, of determination and of consequences. Real and immediate consequences. Adrenaline and a sense of urgency takes over. It's exciting and unnerving at the same time; it's where you burn through every fibre of mental and physical energy without even knowing it. We were also burning through our options and, of course, ammunition.

Having extracted ourselves we made the decision to head straight back in to provide covering fire to get the other foot patrol out. They were pinned down in deep drainage trenches. We couldn't see them. It was like something out of World War II. It turned out Christina and Justin were pinned down, along with Sergeant Major Bolton and several others. It must have been terrifying to be in that position.

Mitch, one of the FSG vehicle commanders, told me that he had seen a group of 12 to 15 Taliban moving into the low ground between our position and the rest of the patrol. He wanted us to advance and destroy them. Leading the patrol of four FSG vehicles forward we advanced up towards the threat. It was the key decision of the day.

As we drove over the crest of the hill an RPG fizzed passed my gunner's head. It missed him by no more than two metres. I could smell the propellant. The RPG was accompanied by a wall of incoming machine gun fire. The Taliban were no more than 200 metres in front of us. Incredibly, they all missed.

We didn't give them a second chance.

We returned fire with everything we had. Four vehicles. Four .50 Cal machine guns. Four commanders' machine guns. It was our first contact of the tour and some of the guys were getting very excited. At one point my driver dismounted and took his SA80 rifle from the vehicle rack and started to fire as well. This was a bad call, but we were all in a heightened state of exhilaration and in a strange way I was thankful for his aggression.

I was aware that Christina and Justin had managed to get out along with Mick Bolton because of our actions.

Mick said afterwards, 'When you guys opened up it was like *Star Wars*'. Every time I've seen him since he's bought me a beer. Christina wrote a front-page piece about the incident a couple of days later. But her presence made no difference to the decisions we took that day. You could say we saved her life, but the fact is that we were simply doing what needed to be done and ensuring her safety happened to be part of that.

But we'd all had a lucky escape. We didn't sustain a single injury. It was a miracle.

After that contact, my overriding emotion was relief. To make the decisions we had made, take the risks and be successful was great, but we still had a long time to go on the tour.

People have asked me since what it was like to kill someone. It's not a great question, but the fact is that it was the easiest decision I've ever made. Failure to act would have been fatal. I didn't take pleasure from pulling the trigger. I didn't hate the people who were trying to kill me. I did it because it was the logical thing to do to protect my life and the lives of my colleagues. I didn't feel good that I'd done it and I didn't feel bad. I just felt it was a decision I had to make.

My Story: **Alex Mackenzie**

A family acquaintance recently asked my mum whether I'd killed anyone and her response was: 'What a stupid question to ask. Why on earth would you ask a question like that?' People ask questions like that because they don't understand the gravity of those decisions.

People watch films and somehow think it might be cool. Well it's not. There is context to it. You wouldn't casually ask someone about their wife's death or a miscarriage, so why would you ask about killing someone? It's not exactly dinner-party conversation is it?

One of the first stories I'd heard before deploying to Afghanistan was about a Canadian officer who had been conducting a meeting with local elders – known as a 'shura' – when, without warning, someone just walked up behind him and chopped his head off with an axe. He'd been commanding an isolated location sitting high above the Sangin valley known as 'Forward Operating Base Wolf' (which later became 'Forward Operating Base Robinson'). I didn't think much of it at the time. Little did I know that one day I'd end up commanding it myself.

The base that was in the headlines on our tour was a few kilometres away, at the District Centre in Sangin. Like FOB Robinson, when your patrol left the compound gate you knew with absolute certainty that you were about to get into a firefight. You wouldn't know when and you wouldn't know where from, but at some point you were going to be shot at. There was a risk of casualties and fatalities on every single patrol. The tempo was so high that we were often involved in four or more contacts a day. In Afghanistan the enemy will fight for days, weeks, months on end. They keep coming at you. If I'd been told that in training at Sandhurst I would have thought, 'There is no environment like that in the world'. Well there was: Sangin.

The environment was extreme, but somehow you just got used to the idea that the scale and intensity of these places was the norm. The local elders wore the conflict all over their faces. Their eyes were sunk deep in their heads and they looked a hundred years old at the age of 40. Wizened frames were cloaked in dark, flowing dish dash robes. Their skin was like the surface of a walnut and they walked with a steady, metronomic pace that suggested that the chaos around them no longer meant anything or moved them. That was life in Helmand Province – they might not have liked it but they were numb to its impact. Sometimes we were too.

Private Damien Jackson was killed on the helipad only a few days after I got to Sangin Disctrict Centre. We were being resupplied almost exclusively by air at that stage and that was the vulnerable point. The Taliban could shoot a helicopter down. Damien was among a group that went out to secure the helipad which came under contact and he was shot and died from his wounds. He had his body armour on but the round went through a vulnerable point at the side. It was a terrible blow. I didn't know Damien personally, and I didn't witness the incident in which he was killed, but I knew a lot of the guys who'd been working closely with him at the time. Seeing the real hard men of the battalion at their lowest ebb brought it home. Strong, bright, resilient guys, the bedrock of 3 PARA, seemed broken in that moment. They recovered and got on with it. We all did. But you had to wonder how people would reconcile these experiences when the fighting stopped and they had time to reflect again.

We didn't have a lot of time to reflect because the District Centre, like FOB Robinson on the outskirts, was a prime target for the Taliban so we had a daily and nightly succession of contacts of increasing severity and complexity. The early days were often quite unsophisticated, but the Taliban were learning fast.

We were able to purify water from a nearby river, but as time went on we started running out of food. The intensity of the fighting multiplied, as did its frequency. The air support we needed was a scarce resource and when the RAF turned up to do an air drop they missed the target.

Then there was the sheer volume of fighting we were engaged in – not just patrols that left the camp, which were helping to keep us

My Story: **Alex Mackenzie**

safe and enabling us to operate. But even within the camp itself, because it wasn't in a great tactical position and, with the built-up walls around it, it was hard to defend. When I first arrived the guys showed me around and they had gaffer-taped claymore anti-personnel mines into trees. They had been really ingenious in how they'd built defences. They needed to be. We had Taliban crawl up to five metres away from the camp to throw a grenade in. It was a very vulnerable position.

It's six years now since that Afghanistan tour, but it will always be part of who I am. There are strange moments that take me back there. Recently, I felt a strong but unexpected sense of déjà vu when I watched a documentary about the Air France plane disaster. It was a Sunday night, I was sitting with my girlfriend eating a stir fry in my flat and we were watching the programme document the story of the Sao Paulo-to-Paris flight that crashed in the Atlantic in 2009. As I watched this story unfold I started not only to understand what happened, but to feel it, to experience it, to live it. It became more than a programme – it was about real people in real fear for their lives. Hearing the genuine fear in those pilots' voices made me feel connected to it. I remembered that sensation and it was unsettling. The black box voice recordings were real people in the last moments of their lives. I could feel my breathing and that adrenaline flowing back. It was action stations again.

I found it compelling but it also reminded me of the toughest days on tour. The hardest part of those operations for me was the waiting, the thinking time. When you were in the firefight or the ambush you simply had to pull it off. The dangerous bit was in-between patrols, when your mind and imagination could wander wherever it wanted.

Even when I came home on mid-tour leave, I couldn't switch off. Subconsciously I was still on alert because I knew I had unfinished business. It was only when I finished the tour and was back for good that I felt the fatigue kick in. I also started to reflect on things.

We invested everything we had on those tours and physically and mentally I felt exhausted when I got back. My ex-girlfriend had a picture of me from my mid-tour leave and people asked, 'Had you lost weight?', but I hadn't. What that photo showed was the culmination of time living under sustained physical and mental pressure. You can see such hollow cheeks and sunken eyes in the faces of many soldiers who return from the battlefield. You may have the most commanding physical presence, but you will still wear that experience on your face.

The intensity of these tours left people deeply affected. Personally, I didn't sleep brilliantly when I got back, but I had my support network around me which was incredibly important. Journalists and aid workers don't always have that kind of support. Nor do the families of soldiers in many cases. Being an individual and not having anyone to share your experience with is dangerous, and that's why the Army do everything they can to factor in decompression time before you head out on post-tour leave. For individuals who leave tour early or are wounded, an experienced support network is vital.

Like Ed, I was the oldest of four children so I was used to taking responsibility and having to be the leader. The stiff upper lip attitude was pretty ingrained in me by the time I joined the Army, where it was only reinforced. I finished my tours physically intact and I had no right to do anything other than be thankful for the good luck and great comrades who meant that we made it back alive.

I don't feel like I have the right to make a single complaint, but the fact is that you cannot go into an environment like that without it having some impact. It is more worrying when people brush it off. I just know that however sizeable the challenge has been for me, I have plenty of friends who have found it harder.

Many ex-soldiers are the same. We focus on getting on with life just as we used to approach an Army mission. There is no time for emotion or weakness. I have probably been on my own mission since the moment I finished Afghanistan; I don't think that has ever really relented. It would have been hard to complete the tours or indeed the row if we were all having emotional meltdowns left, right and centre. Nonetheless, having the maturity to talk about the experiences we had and to share them was something I noticed we

My Story: **Alex Mackenzie**

did very carefully as a crew when we were at sea. We often talked when it was just two of us together, but as a team we went back to putting personal interests in second place.

What's it like to be in combat? Well you have to do it to truly understand it. You can only tell people facts. It doesn't mean you can convey the full range of emotions and feelings you go through. I've heard of journalists who've suffered from PTSD after being embedded with regiments and I can completely understand why.

But I actually enjoyed my experience of the tour. It's not a complicated lifestyle. You're not thinking about your mortgage, your gas bill, your car tax, when you're going to do the shopping. You don't have time to. You don't need to. You just have to do your job, eat, sleep, patrol, write your orders, brief your guys, do your after-action review, load up your ammunition, go test-firing, go to the range, go to a briefing, eat. A lot of the things you have to do are hard, but fundamentally it's a straightforward existence.

I didn't see my blokes get injured or anyone on my side get seriously hurt. That side wasn't tangible for me, which makes a fundamental difference. It's easy for me to look at it as a positive experience. For guys who've had psychological and emotional challenges about what they've experienced afterwards, it comes down to two factors. One, what you saw, because however resilient you are some things you can't just pass off. The second thing is your background. If you've come from a broken home or had a difficult childhood or uncertainty in your life then processing those experiences can be a lot tougher.

I think the psychological burden of what Ed went through on his tour is considerably greater than mine. He was in a tiny team working almost exclusively with Afghans. A very, very difficult job. So I think I was lucky.

On the other hand, while you can tell how the visible wounds are healing, mental scars can take longer to surface. And, if you are physically wounded you are perhaps more likely to talk about the psychological impact too. When I got back I felt I had nothing to prove. I thought, 'I've done this now, I don't need to shout about it', but in myself I know I've faced certain things that most other people will never face and I've come out on top. The tour transformed my self-confidence. It also gave me a lot of perspective. I definitely felt I could achieve more than the majority of the population believe is possible. Ed is an even more polarised example of that. Because of the very difficult circumstances he faced and got through I think he genuinely believes there are no boundaries. He can do anything.

'Are you running your life or is your life running you.'

That was the question that I was asked at my first session of Cognitive Behavioural Therapy (CBT) in February 2011. What the hell was I doing in therapy? It's for complete wimps, isn't it? There was nothing wrong with me, all my arms and legs were attached so what was I doing there?

I had been out of the Army for about three years by that point, but January of that same year I had begun to crack under the pressure of a self-induced and overwhelming workload. My travel schedule at work was demanding, but manageable in its own right. But holding personal relationships together on top of my job and organising the row meant there wasn't a spare second to breathe.

My girlfriend at the time was absolutely wonderful and had supported me despite my frantic and erratic lifestyle, but I knew deep down that I could not make the commitment to her that she deserved so I broke it off.

As soon as I left her house I called Ed and we went to a pub in Marylebone and drank quite a lot, which is the usual, and habitually unsuccessful, way in which many of us Army types tend to try to deal with our shittiest relationship problems. But what a good bloke Ed was to do that; he dropped everything at a second's notice and trekked across London to meet me. That's the kind of thing my best mates from the Army do for each other regularly and instinctively.

By this point I just needed to step back and I told my bosses I needed some time out and I didn't really want to talk about why I needed it. They gave me the support without question and I headed off to Heathrow, where my old drinking buddy Jim, who now worked for an airline, had booked me a first class return out to the Middle East. I escaped for a few days, met up with some old mates and tried to draw breath. The reality was that I could not really leave the discomfort behind so by the time I got back I was straight back in the therapist's chair trying to work out how I had reached this point. All-in-all I had around eight sessions of CBT and I did find them helpful. I was able to clear space in my mind and address some of the patterns of behaviour which were causing me to lead this relentless lifestyle.

The fact is that my experience in Afghanistan was a positive one – things had worked out. I don't have PTSD or any trauma from the tour. But I did have a thirst for a challenge which seemed to have become unrelenting. I had entered a pattern which had led me to take on more than I could ever sustain. Who else would be stupid enough to fly back from China straight into a 24-hour rowing session? It seems obvious now when I look back at decisions like that. Slowly I began to programme rest and 'non-mission critical' things back into my diary and life started to become manageable again.

Lots of people have said to me, 'It must have been terrible going to Afghanistan, and doing and seeing the things that you did'. Well, not really. It was a very positive experience to face the kind challenges that environment threw up and emerge successful. I lived for the challenge but the best challenge was yet to come. The Row2Recovery campaign would change all of our lives. Again.

CHAPTER 6
PORT ST CHARLES:
'THE BEST BEER EVER'

Day 44: 17th January

There had been no wild celebration when the rudder was reattached. Relief was about as much as anyone dared allow themself to feel. A temporary solution might have been found but no one was taking anything for granted. With almost 499 nautical miles still to row there was much that could still go wrong before they reached Port St Charles on the north-west coast of Barbados.

Alex: *We were in a permanent state of permanent collective paranoia.*

After four days on the parachute anchor waiting for Aurora's arrival, the Row2Recovery crew had at least been able to catch up on some sleep, while the water resupply had enabled them to begin the process of rehydrating and putting some of the weight they'd lost over the previous 17 days on reduced rations back on. The return to rowing also meant a return to the relentless physical routine. Despite improved energy levels, it still took time to settle back into a rhythm.

Rory: *There was a lot of pent-up energy on board after so many days of reduced activity. We were all desperate to row as hard as we could but that meant getting back into that hard routine we'd been on before the desalinator broke. In some ways it felt as if we were starting all over again and I could feel the difficulties I'd had at the very start of the row resurfacing. It was, like, 'Here we go again, this is hardcore again'. It was really difficult to readjust.*

The nervous crew – Ed especially – felt the need to constantly check the rudder. The boat's steering had been affected but the strengthening work that had been carried out by Graham seemed to be doing the trick, while Alex's ingenious reattachment solution was also holding firm.

Alex: *I was more cautious with the steering and much more aware of it. If I needed to steer hard then so be it, but the steering was far less responsive from that point onwards. I could steer all the way over to one side, but the boat would take an age to respond. By the time we got going again we just wanted to get to the end. We were all sick of being on that boat.*

CAPTAIN'S LOG

On the move again – feels absolutely great. Rudder is playing the game. Distance not great today due to calmish conditions (F3) but we'll take anything.

Estimate as follows on ETA in Barbados:

Avg 50nm/day: 26th approx 1600 hrs

Avg 55nm/day: 25th approx 2200hrs

Avg 60nm/day: 25th approx 0400hrs

Position: 14°32'N 51°54'W
Distance covered: 44nm in past 24 hours
To Barbados: *455nm*

Day 45: 18th January

Forty-eight hours after resuming rowing, and with the rudder still functioning adequately, the crew's anxiety began to ease slightly, but only slightly. The heavy weather that had helped Aurora's progress in the days immediately prior to the resupply had dropped off and they were once again reliant on the strength of their rowing rather than the strength of the tailwind. While the more sedate conditions slowed the boat's speed, they were also less likely to cause damage to the rudder. Cautiously, the crew began to count down the miles to Barbados.

Will: *We rowed really hard from the moment the rudder was fixed but we didn't dare relax. I checked the rudder pretty much every time I came on shift and I know the others were doing the same.*

We started upping the calorie intake again too. We had three good meals a day which was a real luxury. It got to the point where we actually started casting off rations, opening the dried meal packets and pouring them into the sea in an effort to make us go quicker.

While the return to the hard rowing routine was generally welcomed, the reduction in sleep brought with it a return of a problem they'd all encountered before: hallucinations and vivid dreams.

Rory: *I think we all hallucinated. Not through lack of water, but through lack of sleep. I had a few hallucinations throughout the row. Even after the rudder was fixed I hallucinated. I was very, very tired.*

There was one time when I was convinced that there was lovely rolling, green countryside all around us and we were rowing through it. There were massive redwood trees and I remember looking up and thinking, 'Wow, trees', and then coming to, realising it was impossible and just carrying on rowing.

Another time, I hallucinated that Alex had grown his hair all the way down to his arse. I was rowing along and looking at Alex's back and seeing this amazing hair. I pulled my oars in and touched him on the back, trying to feel this incredible mullet. He turned around and said, 'You alright mate?', and I was like, 'Yeah I'm fine'. The mullet had gone.

But that wasn't the weirdest one. We had our life jackets taped to the spare oars on the right hand side of the boat, and they looked like little waistcoats. I was rowing along one day, listening to my iPod, when I looked down and there was a little boy lying on the deck with his chin resting on his hands. His little legs were kicking and he was just watching me, kicking his feet. I stopped rowing and reached over to him, came to, and realised it was my life jacket.

We all had vivid dreams as well. It's strange because when I dream I always have both my legs. In the dream I'll realise I only have one leg in reality and tell myself, 'This isn't real, but enjoy the dream'. I'm conscious within my subconscious that I have one leg. I will always stop myself in the dream and go, 'Yeah Rory, you wish', but then let the dream carry on so I can enjoy it.

CAPTAIN'S LOG

Good day on the oars – just desperate to get to Barbados now. Weather is F3-4 so reasonably slow. If it picks up it won't go amiss.

Position: 14°30'N 52°53'W

Distance covered: 57nm in past 25 hours

To Barbados: *399nm*

Day 46: 19th January

Part of the reason for Neil arguing against going on the para anchor, even if only subconsciously, was the nagging concern he had over his ability to walk again once they reached dry land. His stumps had lost almost all the muscle he had worked so hard to build up since his injury and he was certain the sockets which had troubled him in La Gomera would continue to cause him problems in Barbados. Every day at sea was an extra day of deterioration for his stumps. He was also missing his children, Callum and Mia.

Neil: *I'd tried to maintain the exercise regime I'd been prescribed but the boat was so cramped, with so many awkward surfaces, that it proved incredibly difficult to keep up. I was keeping my fingers crossed that getting back on my prosthetics would be like riding a bike but it was always on my mind that I might really struggle with walking. I'd heard stories of able-bodied rowers who'd collapsed the moment they set foot on land so I was definitely wondering what would happen to a bloke with no legs at all. No one like me had ever done this so there was no manual!*

But even though the crew were all feeling the strain, there was some relief when they received a visit from another British vessel, the spectacular tall ship 'Tenacious'. At 54 metres in length and with a keel to masthead height of more than 44 metres, the magnificent vessel could hardly have contrasted more starkly in appearance to the weather-beaten Row2Recovery boat. But with a crew also made up predominantly of men and women with varying degrees of physical impediment, the two boats in fact had much in common. Days earlier Tenacious, already in the vicinity, had generously offered her assistance while the Row2Recovery was experiencing rudder and water problems. But with the rowing boat patched up, the crew of the Jubilee Sailing Trust-owned ship simply wanted to express their admiration with a sail past.

A message posted on the Jubilee Sailing Trust's Facebook page later that evening read: *Tenacious has met up in the Atlantic with Row2Recovery, a UK team of Transatlantic rowers including four disabled ex-Servicemen. They passed close by and greeted them with a Mexican wave and a rousing cheer. It was wonderful that two craft* with a common interest in mixed-ability sailing should meet up in this way in mid-Atlantic. After an exchange of greetings on the VHF, Tenacious left them to continue on their way to Barbados and turned northward for Dominica now only a few days away.

As Tenacious turned north towards Dominica, Row2Recovery maintained its course for Barbados.

CAPTAIN'S LOG

Tall ship Tenacious came to visit. Just plugging away at the distance. Boat v stern heavy despite all the resupply water being in the bow. Not sure why.

Position: 14°22'N 53°46'W

Distance covered: 52nm in past 24 hours

To Barbados: *347nm*

Day 47: 20th January

As the miles began to tick down the crew on board Row2Recovery allowed themselves to tentatively start thinking about arriving at Port St Charles. Back home in the UK anxious parents and loved ones had delayed booking their flights out to Barbados while the uncertainty over the rudder remained. Now, with the equipment holding firm, many of them took the plunge and confirmed their travel plans.

Will: *I phoned Mia and she was at my brother's house with her suitcase packed and waiting to catch a taxi to the airport. It felt very surreal. On the one hand I was constantly nervous about the rudder but then, on the other hand, the realisation that my family would soon be flying, almost literally overhead, made the finish line feel very close. From that point on I would stare up into the sky every time a plane went overhead and wonder if my family was on board.*

Carl: *We began quizzing Alex about what was going to happen on our arrival, trying to picture what Barbados would be like and the places* *we'd be staying in. We talked about how good it would be when we finished and what our first meal would be. We fantasised about the things you take for granted in day-to-day life. Things like having a shower or clean sheets on our beds. We were so desperate to get the row finished and get off the boat.*

With winds freshening helpfully, the steady progress also provided more time for contemplation and reflection.

Carl: *I thought a lot about my girlfriend, Tori, and moving house with her when I got back. I was 27 years old and it was time for me to start growing up a little bit. Take the next step. I spoke to her once a week. She cried once or twice on those phone calls, but she coped really well. She found it hard before I left the UK but she's very independent and had the support of her family around her so I knew she'd be fine. She was also looking forward to a holiday in the Caribbean. That was a bit of a trade-off for what I was doing.*

Alex: *As the finish line got closer, all I could think about was comfort. Things like being able to go to the loo sitting down, having a shower and clean sheets . . . not seeing Carl's arse every time I woke up.*

CAPTAIN'S LOG
Revised ETAs
50nm/day: Thurs 26th 1600hrs local
53nm/day: Thurs 0700 hrs local
55nm/day: Thurs 0200 hrs local
58nm/day: Weds 25th 1900hrs local
Plugging away. Morale high but fragile if something else goes wrong. Weather favourable. F4/5 easterly pushing us along nicely.
Position: 14°14'N 54°51'W
Distance covered: 64nm in past 24 hours
To Barbados: *283nm*

Day 48: 21st January

Back in London, Helen Janvrin was helping the support team coordinate the families' flights while a team of McKinney Rogers employees and their friends were putting the finishing touches to the Barbados arrival plan and hospitality for the families and crew. While the Dixons had flown out a day earlier, the rest of the families gathered expectantly at Heathrow, equipped with prosthetic legs, fresh clothes, clean razors and bags of nervous energy.

Nearly 3,000 miles away, 200 miles off the Barbados coast, the crew also received a surprise call on their VHF radio from a passing cruise liner.

Alex: *There was one remarkable night a couple of nights out when Will spoke to a cruise ship. He heard back over the radio, 'Is that Will Dixon?' and Will was a bit confused.*

'Yes'.

'Hello Will Dixon, this is Jack Martin'.

It was his old flatmate from university, just randomly crewing a cruise ship out in the Caribbean.

The 21st January was also a significant date for Rory, as it marked five years to the day since he'd lost his leg. His mother Shealagh, an avid supporter who'd been following the crossing from her home in South Africa on Facebook, posted a heartfelt message on the site. It read: *Happy rebirthday my sonshine! Five years ago your life was blown apart and you landed up in Selly Oak swollen and yellow from massive blood transfusions and in danger of losing your right hip due to infection. Then the progression to Headley Court and learning to walk again. A bleak time. Five years later and you are rowing 3,000 miles in a gruelling race. You are the epitome of 'Beyond injury, achieving the extraordinary'.*

I am so proud of you.

Will, Neil and Carl have gone through the same valley of death and

*emerged triumphant. What an incredible crew on the Row2Recovery –
all six of you with hearts as big as the ocean you are on. Come home
safely Row2Recovery.*

CAPTAIN'S LOG

*Boat very stern-heavy still but not much we can do about it
other than hope for the best. Families flying to Barbados today
and tomorrow: arrival begins to feel real.*

*Today was Rory's 'rebirthday'. 5 years ago today he was
injured.*

Position: 14°04'N 55°56'W

Distance covered: 65nm in past 24 hours

To Barbados: *219nm*

Day 49: 22nd January

As Barbados drew ever nearer, talk on board turned more and more
to the arrival. The crew had been advised that from a media point
of view a morning arrival would be ideal as it would coincide with
early-evening prime-time TV news time back in the UK. Four of the
other crews had already arrived – with race winners Toby Iles and
Nick Moore in 'Box Number Eight' pipping solo rower Andrew Brown
to the finish line just 40 days after departing La Gomera – but the
word was that the crews who had arrived in the middle of the night
had received low-key welcomes and limited media attention. With
the overall mission of the campaign never far from his mind, Ed
began to consider the unthinkable: Going back on the para anchor.

Ed: *All the way across I had been working out estimated times of
arrival in Barbados, which I constantly updated and reviewed. Part of
our mission was to raise awareness and to tell our story and we'd
actively sought media attention as a means to achieve that. We'd
been strongly advised by Graham Walters on board Aurora to avoid
going back on the para anchor if at all possible because of the risk of
further damage to the rudder. But we had to consider the campaign.*

We needed to time our run to try and arrive in the middle of the morning to maximise media exposure. To an extent we were at the mercy of the elements but if getting our timing right meant going back on the para anchor it was a risk I was ready to consider.

The London-based support team, and the race sponsors, were all in agreement that the timing of the arrival was vital to the overall success of the mission. But the prospect of going back on the para anchor – the very cause of the rudder failure – was not well received by the rest of the crew. With their final destination so close they could almost taste the rum punches. The idea of risking everything for the sake of media attention did not go down well.

Neil: *I couldn't believe it was even being considered. Being on the para anchor was what had broken the rudder in the first place. If we'd just gone with the weather it wouldn't have been a problem. I said, 'So the one thing we were told to definitely avoid doing, we are going to do?!' But Ed was pretty adamant that if we did arrive early we were going to put the para anchor down. I thought, 'If we can see Barbados and break the rudder again that really will be devastating'. I was of the view that if we got there in the middle of the night then so be it. We could control our rowing but we did not want to be putting the para anchor out unless we really had too. To risk everything for media attention seemed crazy to me.*

With the wind strengthening all the time, the miles continued to tick down.

CAPTAIN'S LOG

Great progress. Weather state F5/6. Planning final approach.
Position: 13°45'N 57°06'W
Distance covered: 70nm in past 24 hours
To Barbados: *150nm*

Day 50: 23rd January

Once the 100-nautical-mile mark was crossed, even Will allowed himself a wry grin at the impending prospect of their arrival.

'We could swim it from here,' he joked.

The crew were becoming increasingly excited about seeing their loved ones again, while having a hot shower and sleeping in a clean bed were also high on everyone's list of things to do. However Ed knew it was important to maintain focus and discipline on the shifts to avoid any last-minute mistakes which could still cost them dearly.

Ed and Alex were steering for a point around a mile north of Barbados where the race 'finish line' was, although no one on board Row2Recovery would consider their mission complete until they were on dry land at Port St Charles some four miles further south.

A satellite phone call was arranged from the boat to Headley Court, where Carl and Will talked to staff and patients alike about their experiences at sea.

Carl: *I made the call to Kelly, one of the remedial instructors, and one of the occupational therapists. There were some other patients there as well and they had the phone on loudspeaker. They said they were really proud of us and that it was an amazing achievement and thanked us for what we were doing. Someone asked me what was next? Maybe an Ironman? 'Maybe,' I replied.*

I definitely didn't want lots of gushing praise from the blokes at Headley Court though. I was actually a bit worried they'd think we were showboaters with all the media attention we were getting. I'm pretty sure that's what I'd have thought if I'd been a patient at the time. I certainly didn't want to be tagged a hero either. I didn't think we were heroes for doing it. We were doing it for our own personal reasons as much as the charity side of it. We needed to achieve something for ourselves as much as to raise money and awareness. I just hoped all the guys who'd been recently wounded could see what it was still possible to achieve with pretty severe injuries.

Much to Neil's relief, it also became clear that the para anchor would not be required again as the crew found that by easing off their rowing pace when appropriate they were approaching Barbados right on cue.

CAPTAIN'S LOG

Just celebrated less than 100nm to Barbados!
Position: 13°30'N 57°58'W
Distance covered: 53.1nm in past 24 hours
To Barbados: *97nm*

Day 51: 24th January

The closer Barbados came the more signs of life were spotted by the crew. They had started noticing more and more recreational sailing boats in their vicinity over the past couple of days, while a local Bajan fishing boat also approached them and offered some refreshments.

Rory: *They wanted to throw us bottles of Coca-Cola. That iconic image of a Coke bottle with icy water dripping off it. I was like, 'Yeah, yeah, yeah', and the fisherman was just about to throw them across when Will said, 'No thank you, we will not take cola'. I couldn't believe it. It was very honourable I'm sure to try to limit the amount of support we had, but Neil and I were like, 'We've just taken 350 litres of water and had our rudder fixed and we can't even have a bottle of Coke!'*

The first sight of land ensured any lingering irritation passed almost immediately, just as it had with every other minor spat that had occurred over the previous 51 days.

Rory: *I really wanted to be the first to spot land. I was actually quite selfish about it. I made sure I was constantly looking over my shoulder; every third stroke for a day I was looking. I wanted to spot* the land. I mean, how many people on earth have been able to say, 'Land ahoy' for real after 51 days of being out at sea in a rowing boat?

I was doing a cooking shift. It was one of the only times I was actually very happy doing the cooking. I was facing in the direction of land because I'd turned my seat around and was listening to music. It was dusk. The sun was going down and there was a cloud on the horizon with what looked like another jagged cloud below it. I thought to myself, 'No'. All of a sudden I heard myself shouting, 'Land ahoy!'. I could just see the outline of an island. There was a big cloud behind it, but I could definitely make out the dark outline of the island. It was around 7.30pm.

Everyone stopped rowing and turned around. Will surfaced from the cabin and said, 'No way. Are you serious? Are you serious?' I said, 'Yes'. I don't think Neil could see it, but everyone else saw it. It was an amazing feeling. Our first sight of Barbados.

Carl: You could see the silhouette against the sky. I thought, 'That is awesome'. It made it real. We'd crossed the Atlantic Ocean. The more we rowed the clearer the lights got and the bigger the island became. It was a great feeling.

Will: When Rory gave it the big 'Land ahoy' I could barely see land and it seemed to take forever to get any bigger. From that point on we were all fixated on it. We'd go out on shift, do a bit of rowing for two hours, and then go back in to the cabin. The great thing was when you came out two hours later it would be far more visible. It got bigger and bigger and gradually the lights got brighter and brighter at night. When we saw cars and could make out individual trees it really became real.

CAPTAIN'S LOG

So close. It's starting to feel real now. Small aircraft flew over to take shots. V low passes. V good for morale again . . .

ETA is 0700hrs tomorrow at finish line, and 1000hrs at Port St Charles. Aurora should be joining us to see us in at 0200hrs.

1830hrs – land sighted. Lucky. Humbled. Relieved.

Position: 13°24'N 59°01'W
Distance covered: 62nm in past 24 hours
To Barbados: *36nm*

DAY 52: 25th January
The end was, at last, in sight.

**Rory's Blog (posted on the Row2Recovery website as the crew
pulled the final strokes on their epic 2,590 mile Atlantic crossing):**
*On 21st January, 2007, I lost my leg when the vehicle I was travelling
in was blown up by a roadside bomb. In the days and months that
followed I wondered if my life was worth living.*

*In the dark days that followed, and believe me there were many, I
developed a pretty unhelpful habit of counting up all the things I
would never be able to do again.*

*Never again would I be able to ride a horse, play rugby, go for a
run, ride a bike.*

*I spent the first two years after being blown up requiring extensive
psychological counselling and even spent a month in the Priory
psychiatric unit.*

Today, I feel like I can take on the world!

*Today, my band of brothers in this boat will complete our mission
to row across the Atlantic. Today I feel alive like I have never felt alive
before. It is the most awesome feeling.*

*Don't get me wrong, I can't wait to get off this wretched boat and
fall in to the arms of my beloved girlfriend, Lara, who has travelled all
the way to Barbados to meet us.*

*But I would not have swapped the last 51 days for anything. It has
been the most incredible thing I have ever achieved in my life and it
just goes to show that there is life after serious injury.*

*Five years ago I thought my life was as good as over and I was
embarrassed about the way I looked. Today, I have never been
prouder.*

Don't get me wrong, I'd rather have a few extra inches of stump to make it easier to fit my prosthetic. But overall, my life now is pretty lush.

I learned to accept what had happened to me about two-and-a-half years after I was injured. I only wished it had been sooner. Because I can honestly say that since losing my leg my life is so much richer.

I have learned that anything is possible if only you put your heart and soul into it. Well, apart from cattle grids that is. I don't think I'll ever get the hang of those!

But I'll swap cattle grids for rowing the Atlantic. That's right, rowing the Atlantic! It really is hard to believe that we have completed this mission.

All the technical issues we encountered on the row were tough to take, but we always had perspective to fall back on. We were able to put the issues we faced, like the desalinator breaking or the rudder snapping, into context. Yes, we desperately wanted to complete our mission, but we had all been in worse spots before.

We pulled together and found solutions because that is what we do. As soldiers, you find answers, and we managed that throughout this row.

It's going to be so amazing to see all our friends and family when we get alongside in Port St Charles, as well as all the other crews who have completed this incredible challenge of physical and mental endurance.

The next few days are going to be an opportunity to say 'thank you' to everyone who has supported us and made this row possible.

Hopefully it will also be a chance to hit our target of £1 million for service charities.

We have all been on an amazing journey that will stay with us forever. Just like the physical injuries that, in some people's eyes, define who we are.

But mind will always win over matter, and we have shown that where there is a will to succeed, there is a way.

People have asked me what I have left to achieve. What more can I do after achieving this? The answer? Get married and start a family. I can't imagine anything could possibly top that.

But right now, five years after my lowest point, it is time to enjoy the moment. Right now, without any shadow of a doubt, it is time for a beer. I think we've earned it.

Much love, Rory.

As the crew excitedly rowed their way around the northern most tip of Barbados before heading south to Port St Charles, a large crowd was beginning to gather at the exclusive resort where they'd be welcomed ashore.

Friends, family and members of the Row2Recovery support team were joined by hundreds of well-wishers, fellow transatlantic rowers, local dignitaries and dozens of members of the local, national and international media, all eager to witness the climax of this truly extraordinary crossing. The presence of several employees and friends of the Barbados Council for the Disabled was a telling sign of the impact the crew's row had made.

The night before, the crew's immediate family and friends had gathered at the former plantation house home of Damian Mckinney, Alex's boss, where the mixture of nervous excitement and sheer joy at the prospect of seeing their son, husband, boyfriend or dad was overwhelming.

Among those gathered was Carl's dad, Chris, and his wife, Emma. Chris told Emma off when she cried at a video montage of the crossing being played on a big screen in the living room. The families had lived every moment of the crossing via the internet, through the media, and in their own minds. It had been an emotional journey for them all.

'Don't be soft,' Chris had said, before wiping the tear from Emma's cheek.

No one slept easily that night, not least Ed's mum, Isabelle, or Alex's mum, Ginnie, who had seen their sons work tirelessly on the project for the past two years. They knew precisely how much this meant to them.

The next morning the families were by the quayside bright and early, many of them by 6am, and were gradually joined throughout the morning by a growing throng of well-wishers.

A small advance party of family members were taken out by boat to see the boat cross the race finish line to the north of the island, although the crew remained adamant they would not consider their mission complete until they reached Port St Charles.

Carl: *First we saw the Aurora, it was good to see her again, and then our friend Paddy Nichol came out with beers for all of us. They didn't last long. Our wives and girlfriends came out on a support boat as we crossed the official race finish line. It was great to see them, but for us the real finish line was always going to be when we physically reached dry land. That was still a couple of hours away.*

Will: *We were stupidly excited about seeing our loved ones and getting off that boat!*

Aurora came out and then a few other boats. Mia was the first person I saw when the advance party came out to meet us. It wasn't quite right because we were separated by water. Everyone was there so we couldn't really say personal things. We just asked if each other was okay. It was very British. 'Hello, how are you?' I just felt really awkward. I think all the guys felt the same because we just couldn't have the full-on conversations we craved.

Rory: *It was weird seeing the girls. I saw Lara and I said to myself, 'Say something'. Just saying 'hello' to anyone other than the crew members was bizarre. We'd built up such a rugged, survival layer, to see someone you loved right there was so surreal. It's hard to imagine what it is like to be at sea for 51 days and then all of a sudden there are your loved ones in a boat next to you off the coast of Barbados. It was weird.*

Will: *Time seemed to slow down. Those last two or three hours felt like an eternity. Once we'd changed our course from the east and headed south down towards Port St Charles we had all the pleasure boats coming out to see us and people wishing us well and shouting* *their support and words of encouragement. It was just brilliant. Geraint was there with his same old white shirt. The first question he asked was, 'How was it?' and everyone replied 'Easy!' without prompting. It took him about five minutes to get a serious answer out of us. You could see he was amused to start with but after a while he started to get tired of it and said, 'Come on guys, you've got to give me something I can use here'.*

As the crew made their way south towards Port St Charles, one particularly significant message was received, from Her Majesty the Queen. The message read: *Please convey my warm thanks to all the members of the Row2Recovery team on the occasion of them reaching the end of their row across the Atlantic, in aid of injured soldiers and their families.*

I heard of the trials and tribulations on your journey and, in return, I send my good wishes to you all for the successful completion of the challenge.

Back at Port St Charles, Neil's wheelchair had been placed by the side of the dock, ready for him to use upon arrival.

Sam, Diana and James from the support team ensured a table was laid out with hamburgers, chips and ice-cold beers as the increasingly excited crowd, among them local resident Sir Cliff Richard, craned over the harbour wall to catch first sight of the crew.

Suddenly, a flare went up. 'There they are, I can see them!' someone shouted. Slowly, surely, a guttural roar began to build as the cheers, whistles and applause rang out. Union Jacks were plastered across the harbour wall and the crew were applauded and cheered all the way in to port. Sir Cliff led the applause.

Rory: *I sat on top of the cabin and I looked across to the rocky outcrop. We weren't sure exactly where we were going, and there were hundreds of people along the sea wall. I couldn't believe it. There were so many people that it looked like they were part of the rocks.*

PORT ST CHARLES: 'THE BEST BEER EVER'

We were all absolutely buzzing. It was such a great sense of elation. The atmosphere on the boat was electric. We'd done it.

The tears flowed on dry land as proud parents, wives, girlfriends, brothers and sisters cheered the boys in. A section by the jetty where the crew would be coming alongside had been cordoned off for immediate friends and family to greet their loved ones. Every person present on that jetty had their own story to tell of how catastrophic injury had changed their lives too. Will's parents, Jilly and Rob, embraced Will's girlfriend, Mia, older brother, Tom, and his wife, Marigold, as the boat drew around the harbour wall and into the Port St Charles marina.

Will: *Ever since the day I'd phoned home to tell them I was injured I'd been desperate to be able to give my family a really proud, positive moment. This was it. We'd become even closer since my injury and seeing them at the end was amazing. Hugging them for the first time was an awesome feeling.*

Chris Anstey, an electrician from Nottinghamshire who had worked tirelessly behind the scenes to put on a fundraising party in his home village of Gotham that raised close to £9,000, almost burst with pride when the boat pulled alongside.

As Cliff Richard joined the crowd in spraying champagne over the boat, Ed let out a primeval roar and thumped his chest at the realisation that the dream he'd first discussed with Alex on that bike ride in the Surrey hills had been realised. Truly the crew had gone beyond injury and achieved something extraordinary.

'How does the beer taste?' Geraint asked Ed as the boat pulled alongside the dock and the assorted media surged forward to take photos or grab a quote. 'That is the best beer I've had in my entire life,' the sun-beaten skipper replied.

Everyone involved in the arrival had been determined Neil should be granted the dignity he deserved but, with the marina wall several feet above the water line, a shaky pontoon was the only way to safely bring the boat alongside. As the crowd cheered and the cameras flashed, Neil was safely hoisted by his crew-mates into the wheelchair waiting alongside. Within seconds his children, Mia and Callum, had run over to embrace him.

'Don't do that again,' Mia said with a frown on her face.

'Don't worry, I won't. I promise,' Neil assured her.

Neil: *Seeing the kids had been at the very forefront of my mind for days. Mia told me off for leaving her. It was amazing to be able to give them a big hug. So many people came up and said, 'I just want to shake your hand, we're so proud of you'. That's kind of nice when people you've never met say those things. It made it a bit bigger than just us going across. We had an idea people had seen it but to meet some of the people who'd been following us was great.*

Once I'd got alongside and sat down and pondered things it really started to hit home what we'd achieved. We'd finished, we'd made it across. All the things that went wrong made it the journey it was.

Ian Heritage: *The kids ran to Neil, I couldn't get near him. When I finally got to him I just held him. It was so good to have him back with us. It was wonderful. I was enormously proud of him.*

Tears streamed down Chris Anstey's face as Carl clambered out of the boat. Carl embraced his girlfriend, Tori, and told her he loved her as the applause continued.

'I'm so proud of you son,' Chris said before engulfing the former sniper in an enormous bear hug.

'Thanks, Dad.'

'Three cheers for Row2Recovery,' Chris roared. 'Hip hip . . . Hooray!'

Carl: *I had absolutely no idea what to expect. I thought there would probably be a support boat and then some family and friends to greet us. Maybe 50 or so people. That would have been great.*

But the reception we did get was astonishing. When we saw the harbour wall, Ed said, 'What's all that movement along the harbour', and someone said, 'It's people'. It took a while to take in how many people had come out to cheer us in.

It was very humbling. Seeing our family and friends waiting for us on the dockside was amazing and seeing the table laid out for us with all the food was almost as good. When I'd spoken to Ben Fogle on Christmas Day he'd told me there was no better feeling than that first step onto dry land. He was right. There was an overwhelming sense of relief mixed with satisfaction at what we'd achieved. We'd proved people wrong who didn't believe we could do it and worked incredibly hard to overcome the odds.

I'd started something and finished it which was also incredibly important to me personally. It was great.

For Ed and Alex, it was the culmination of two years of relentless hard work, planning and dedication.

Alex: *That was the best day of my life. We could never have contemplated the sort of reception we received. Ed was rowing and as we came up to the dock he said, 'The whole dock is lined with people'. We looked around and all we could see was people. It was incredible. All the Union Jacks. Amazing. You are almost meant to feel uncomfortable sometimes about being patriotic so to actually feel proud to be British was amazing. To see Cliff Richard was utterly surreal, but to see the dinner table laid out on the harbour side was even better.*

We just said 'Thank you' a lot.

My Story:
Carl Anstey

Age: 27
Regiment: The Rifles (Sniper Platoon)
Rank: Lance Corporal
Army career span: 2007–present day
Combat experience: Afghanistan, Helmand Province (2008, 2009).
Injury: Severed sciatic nerve, shattered femur and multiple trauma to lower limbs

A bearded face rose from behind the fractured ruin. I wondered for a brief moment what the hell this Taliban fighter was thinking. Was he nervous or just plain stupid? Slowly moving my rifle so I was in line with him, I glared through the Schmidt & Bender scope and began the routine of split-second contemplation and double-checking myself. I could make out the distinct shape of a rifle barrel in his hands. I started adjusting the dials on the scope.

He was closer than I had anticipated. Twenty-two clicks for the elevation and 12 clicks left to compensate for the fresh breeze that was blowing the barren, gold-stained fields in front of me. There was no silence as people may imagine, no sweet sense of calm you may see in the movies. The adrenaline was pumping through my body, but my mind was concentrated. As I adjusted the zoom on my rifle sight I was confronted by the man's face. Slowly I aligned the cross-hairs, took a deep inward breath and gently squeezed the trigger. At lightning speed the head smashed back and there was stillness as the figure slumped and disappeared behind a low mud wall. Springing back to life with the customary crack and thump of rounds speeding past my position, I exhaled and began to relax.

I never felt any guilt when I fired my rifle. A kill-or-be-killed philosophy had been ingrained in my mind long before I had deployed. Now, with the reality of taking someone's life confronting me, it gripped me and clung to my subconscious, preventing me from feeling anything but satisfaction. Killing someone before they have the chance to kill you, or the man next to you, is one of the most basic traits of human nature. In Afghanistan, it was all that mattered.

There is a long history of military service in my family. My great, great grandfather fought in the First World War and my uncle was in the Parachute Regiment and served for 15 years in the SAS. When I was growing up I would always dress up in Army kit he had acquired for me. I would paint my face with camouflage cream and run around the garden chasing my brothers, making machine gun noises. I knew I was going to join the Army from a young age. Two weeks after I turned 21, I passed recruit selection and signed on the dotted line.

The night before I was due to get the train to Catterick Garrison to begin my basic training I had a phone call from my uncle. 'When it comes to the Army,' he said, 'always be the grey man'. What he meant by that was simple; 'Don't get in trouble, don't try too hard to impress people, just work hard and you'll be fine'.

Basic training began in March 2007 and I loved every minute. I joined The Rifles in September 2007 and was soon placed on the highly demanding sniper course, passing it six months later. Passing this course was pretty unusual for someone just out of basic training and a few of the more experienced guys thought it had come to me too soon, but I didn't care. I had reached the pinnacle of what being an infantryman was all about and I was determined to make the most of it.

My Story: **Carl Anstey**

We were due to go on tour to Afghanistan in a couple of months and, despite hearing stories of sections being ambushed and of brave men being killed, I didn't have any reservations about going there. I was in the prime of my life, serving my country in a career I had always dreamt of. The only thing missing was the acid test. I had to prove I was capable of performing when it mattered – when my own and other people's lives were on the line, on the battlefield of a country 3,500 miles away.

On arrival in Afghanistan in September 2008, the primary role of my battalion was to mentor Afghan National Army (ANA) soldiers. My role as a sniper was to engage Taliban positions and enemy snipers on the ground, put enemy vehicles out of service and kill enemy commanders and high-ranking officials.

One of our first missions was to the town of Nad-e Ali which was a Taliban stronghold. Our aim was simple: we were to advance to contact and drive the enemy from the area. We were looking to provoke a fight. An estimated 300 enemy fighters were in the area and they had dug rat runs, escape tunnels and peppered the roads with IEDs. We left the main base in Lashkar Gar a few hours before first light and travelled in convoy with our ANA counterparts towards Nad-e Ali.

On arrival, we seized a compound from a local farmer. The vehicles were parked up and it was time to get kitted up. Osprey body armour, rifle, copious amounts of ammunition, high explosive grenades, phosphorous grenades, smoke grenades, Sig Sauer 9mm hand gun with spare rounds, bayonet, medical equipment, two full water bottles, spare radio batteries and food. The entire kit weighed well over 100lbs.

Each section deployed separately and in different directions. The north and south of the town were both covered by a section of British and ANA soldiers. As we left the relative safety of the compound the noise of sections in contact rattled over the radios. Gunfire and the sound of RPG explosions echoed to our south. Adrenaline began to flood my veins. The midday sun meant the temperature was a searing 40 degrees and sweat seeped from every pore in my body. We arrived at a crossroads which signalled the entrance to central Nad-e Ali. There were poppy fields to our right and the road going to the left seemed to have no end. My Sergeant in charge began to use a Vallon mine detecter to sweep across the centre of the crossroads and I provided cover as he inched towards the middle of the road.

Suddenly an RPG fizzed over our heads and exploded in mid-air above the poppy fields while bullets cracked and thumped all around us. We jumped for cover as rounds ripped up dust beneath our feet and we sporadically returned fire towards a compound 300 metres to our north. As we took cover behind a high compound wall the rounds continued to rain in over our heads. To the far north of Nad-e Ali, two ANA soldiers had been killed in a contact with the enemy and the boss was taking no chances. An air strike was called in on the enemy compound and within a matter of minutes the contact was over. As I wiped the sweat and dirt off my face and continued on towards the centre of Nad-e Ali, I realised I was enjoying myself.

After five weeks at Patrol Base South West I was sent south to Musa Qala to the United States Patrol base. A kilometre south of the Patrol Base (PB) there was a maze of a village called Yatimchay and the Taliban had been swarming in and out of there, attacking patrols, intimidating locals and setting IEDs. Every man in the PB agreed they needed to be smoked out.

Lying on top of a compound roof a few days later on the edge of Yatimchay, I had just been winded and temporarily deafened by an RPG fired by an ANA soldier. He had fired at a window from which we were receiving sporadic fire, and he had not seen that I was lying right next to him. I regained my breath and grabbed his helmet, screaming at him to watch what he was doing. Yatimchay had suddenly erupted and the Taliban had mounted a counter-attack. RPGs were screeching through the air and thumping into the compound wall directly below my position and rounds were screaming over our heads. All around me men were engaging doorways and windows, searching with bullets for the ever-elusive enemy. The ANA soldier who had just put me on my arse was laughing as he reloaded and fired again.

Mortars had been called in and were dropping onto compounds directly in front of me, smashing into the earth and leaving a trail of smoke. Apache helicopter gunships were spraying the whole area with .50 calibre machine gun rounds, and an occasional sidewinder missile shot out like a firework, curving as it flew until it celebrated in an explosion, destroying its target. My heart was pounding as I fired 7.62mm rounds from my sniper rifle into possible enemy positions. By now they were on the retreat, crawling back into their nests via escape tunnels and rat runs and I began to smile as the firefight had once again been won.

Two ANA soldiers had been injured in the course of the battle. One had a clean wound through the upper right arm, while the other had been shot in the head. Despite the best efforts of his ANA colleagues he wasn't moving. They were both patched up and loaded onto Warrior vehicles that had arrived late for the offensive.

Time to withdraw. There was a 300-metre stretch of open ground to cover before we were in the relative safety of a ditch. As my turn to run came, I sprinted in zig-zag fashion through the boggy fields, almost tripping as my boots became weighed down with mud. I was halfway across when a burst of machine gun fire bounced at my feet, making me dance like a character in a western film. Running faster than ever, I almost dived as I reached the safety of the ditch, letting out an array of expletives as I landed. The machine gun position was quickly engaged by an Apache and we managed to extract and move out to the patrol base. Walking through the gate of the PB, my kit felt heavy as the adrenaline abandoned me as quickly as it had arrived. I removed my body armour and sat on a small wall, drenching myself with water and quenching my thirst. I smiled as I recalled the firefight and then realised everyone in the team was smiling. This addiction to being shot at had gripped me and I was well and truly hooked.

THE ROW TO RECOVERY

On 17th January, 2009, Corporal Richard 'Robbo' Robinson was killed in Gereshk. He was hit by an RPG during an ambush and suffered devastating injuries. I knew him well and it was a shock to the system. He was one of the first guys on my sniper cadre and whereas some people had been against me joining the platoon, Robbo had supported me and guided me through some tough days.

The guys who knew Robbo in the PB talked about how he was the best of the best. A flask of whisky was passed around and the mood was sombre. We would still be patrolling the next day as if nothing had happened. We had no choice. If Robbo's death was to mean something we had to continue to dominate the ground and contain the enemy. You take whatever sadness, anger and frustration you have and you either bury it deep within yourself or you channel it towards the enemy. For me, focusing on the task ahead and channelling my emotions was the best way to deal with the loss.

Corporal Danny Nield was 31-years-old and the Forward Air Controller (FAC) attached to my section. He had come along for an operation in order to call in close air support if needed during the following day's events. It was a couple of days after Robbo was killed. He had grabbed the hammock space next to mine and as the evening drew in we talked about life outside Helmand. He had a Canadian girlfriend and was looking forward to returning home to see his beloved Gloucester Rugby Club play at home. After shooting the shit for a few more hours and hearing his trademark saying – 'Guns for show, jets for a pro' – far too many times for my liking, we called it a night.

I awoke in pitch black to a C130 Gunship deploying illumination flares to the south-east of the Patrol Base. It was a diversionary tactic signalling the start of our planned counter-offensive against the enemy and also time to get out of bed. The operation had us heading 5km north until we were deep within the shadow of 'Mount Doom'. Mount Doom was a prominent mountain that was always used as a point of reference on maps of Musa Qala. It was officially called Mount Musa Qala but had been unofficially renamed after the mountain in *The Lord of the Rings*. We were heading into Taliban-controlled territory and the operation was designed to destroy a recently discovered ammo cache and pinpoint the location of the enemy command points.

We left just before first light. My section of eight men was accompanied by 40 men from 205 ANA Kandak and a handful of Afghan National Police (ANP). A similar mix of men headed north-west, chaperoned by a section of British soldiers from PB North. We stuck to the low ground, cutting through compound walls and down narrow passageways, finally arriving at a low mud wall. As the morning sun began to beat down on the dry Afghan dirt we checked in on the radio and looked at our position on the map. We were in the right place and, so far, we were unnoticed.

Seeking higher ground in order to gain a good view of the Taliban village in front of us, I climbed onto a compound roof. I was immediately joined by my Sergeant, Danny Nield and Captain Rupert Stranks who was in charge of calling in artillery support. I looked through my binoculars for any sign of the enemy. An hour passed and I saw nothing.

At around 10am a cloud of smoke filled the sky to our west as one of our units blew up the weapons cache. Even if the enemy hadn't seen us yet, they now at least knew we were close by. Through my binoculars I spotted an ICOMs radio antenna. ICOMs were used by both the enemy and ourselves, but with a very important difference. We could hear them but they couldn't hear us. Following the antenna down, a fat, bearded face confronted me and I straightaway knew he was enemy. 'Taliban 400 metres to the front, fat guy in a dish-dash holding the ICOMs radio, engage'. We had been given clearance to engage all enemy and with an ICOMs scanner being the only proof we needed, this man was surely going down.

Suddenly a burst of gunfire sounded. The section to our west had spotted this bearded foe too and had been quick to the trigger. But their rounds fell well short and the man ducked behind a compound wall, quickly raising the alarm. Machine gun fire then blared out and through a hole in a compound wall to my front, a muzzle flash indicated its origin. We returned fire and I quickly yelled at a young ANA soldier to climb up onto the roof to engage the enemy with RPGs. Dave Maclean, a riflemen in our team, jumped up too and crawled onto the roof, slotting in between myself and my Sergeant. He was quick to the trigger and began suppressing the enemy machine gunner with great effect.

The first round boomed as the RPG flew from its barrel and everyone on the rooftop took cover. It was quickly followed by a second and then a third. Boom... Boom. Machine gun fire still blared out from the tiny hole in the compound wall as the RPGs landed around it. 'Keep firing, keep firing,' I told the soldier. 'Keep bloody firing until you hit the bastard!'

The young soldier reloaded the RPG and fixed a new rocket in place. I shouted, 'Back blast!' and again we all took cover. I turned to my left, facing away from the RPG gunner and began to count down. '5...4...3...2...1' The RPG didn't fire. I had just started to count again when... Boom!!!

A searing pain ripped through my right leg and then it went numb as I found myself sprawled out and lying on top of Dave Maclean's right foot.

'My foot!' he screamed, 'You're on my fucking foot!'

I managed to roll off Dave's foot when I heard my Sergeant shout, 'Four casualties, we've got four casualties!'

I went into immediate shock. I reached down and touched my right leg and was horrified when I realised my hand was stained with blood.

'Fuck, fuck, where's my leg? Has it gone? Tell me where it is, tell me where it is!'

I didn't know it at the time but my sciatic nerve had been lacerated, my right femur shattered and my femoral artery missed by milimetres. Dave Maclean had been taken off the roof and was receiving treatment to deep wounds to his right thigh and foot. I was next to be dragged off the wall, and I immediately noticed Danny Nield leaning on his radio against the curved compound wall roof.

My Story: **Carl Anstey**

'Danny get off the fucking roof, what are doing, get off the roof!'

In the seconds it took for me to be dragged off the roof the thought struck me that he was probably dead. I landed hard on the mud floor and took in my surroundings. I had realised straightaway that the RPG launcher had misfired. The young ANA soldier who had fired the rocket lay dead with a missing right arm and a contortion of twisted flesh where his face had once been. I checked my bollocks with my left hand and was relieved when my hand came back clean.

Danny Nield had been taken off the roof and was unconscious. He was being given CPR and all I could hear was Rupert repeatedly shouting, 'Come on Danny, come on!' There was no pulse but no one was giving up. They tried and then retried as I reached for my field dressing. I rolled onto my side as one of the guys stuffed it into the biggest of the wounds in my thigh. The pain was excruciating as it was pushed hard against the muscle and soft tissue that was entangled in my leg. I held it in place as the bandage was wrapped around, gripping my skin as it reached the end. When it was tied off, two more were applied to the back of my right knee and calf.

Adrenaline was pumping through my body and I began to scream, half in pain and half in frustration. Scrambling in the pocket of my webbing I grabbed a morphine auto jet and slammed it into my left thigh but it didn't work. I grabbed my second and, after feeling a sharp stab, I leaned back and stared up at the sky. I felt thirsty, sick and confused. In my mind I questioned the events unfolding before me. 'How could this have happened, how the hell had this happened?'

Dave Maclean and the dead Afghan soldier had been loaded onto an ANA pick-up truck that was first to get to us and a Vector armoured vehicle had arrived to transport the rest of the injured to the casualty extraction point. I was loaded into the back of the vehicle with Rupert and we sat back to back leaning against each other.

'How's Danny?' I asked.

Rupert looked saddened. 'I don't know,' he said, 'I don't know.'

THE ROW TO RECOVERY

Casualties have what's known as a 'golden hour' when their chances of survival are dramatically improved if they're treated inside that time. I was flown to Camp Bastion well inside that window. The medical emergency response team had patched me up during the flight and passed me into the capable hands of one of the ambulance crews waiting on the runway. My clothes had been cut away and I was exposed, naked, and slightly embarrassed. As I apologised profusely to the ground crew loading me into the ambulance, I realised the morphine I had self-administered on the ground had started to wear off. The pain had returned to my leg and my foot was throbbing.

I was given a shot of ketamine by an American medic and a haze of confusion hit me as the horse tranquiliser flowed through my bloodstream. The lights went out and for a split-second I was alone, in a quiet place. There was no pain, with only the occasional feeling of someone prodding my legs to disturb my solitude. I thought about exploring the darkness all around me and reached out with my hands. They were pushed down and I was confused as my leg was prodded once again. I thought about reaching out again but no sooner had the thought crossed my mind than I woke up.

I was lying on a hard surface and after blurrily reading 'MRI' on the sign above me I guessed I was in radiology. Someone showed me a scan of my leg. It was a shadow with prominent white shapes dotted along it.

'That's frag', a British voice said. 'Your femur's broken but has been placed in traction. Don't worry you're going to be... '

I blacked out.

I awoke high up on a hospital bed. Oxygen flowed from a mask fixed by an elastic cord over my nose and mouth and the ceiling above me seemed abnormally close. As I tried to take in my surroundings I realised I couldn't feel my legs. I tried to shout out to somebody, to anybody to tell me what the hell was going on. I ripped off the oxygen mask and was about to try and sit up when a nurse arrived.

'It's okay Carl, it's okay,' she said. 'You're in Bastion hospital.'

'Why are my legs numb,' I murmured. 'What's going on?'

My Story: **Carl Anstey**

She explained that I had been given a nerve block in theatre and that it was to stay in place until I was back in the UK.

In a bed to my right Dave Maclean was being prepared for surgery and to my left Rupert was awake staring back at me.

'Danny?' I said.

'He's dead, mate,' Rupert replied.

Tears began to blur my vision, but I wiped them and turned away. I wasn't embarrassed about showing emotion but I didn't feel now was the time to grieve. I knew there would be plenty of time for that once I was back in the UK. Inside, I was gutted.

There was a television in the corner of the room and the news came on as Rupert was wheeled off to surgery. 'A British soldier from the 1st Battalion the Rifles was killed in Afghanistan yesterday.'

I phoned home. 'Dad, don't worry but I'm in hospital,' I said as I waited for the delay on the line. I told him I'd been involved in an explosion and that my right leg had been hit, but that was all. At the time it was all I really knew and I knew the battalion welfare team would be driving to see him as we spoke.

'I'll be home in a few days, Dad . . . Don't worry . . . Bye, mate . . . Bye.'

I handed the phone across to the nurse to see if she could tell him more about my injuries. As the phone was placed down on the receiver it all became real. I began to feel bad about leaving the rest of the guys behind. I felt guilty they were staying in Afghanistan and I felt guilty about being able to go home.

As the engines of the C130 Hercules aircraft roared, myself and Dave Maclean were wheeled on our stretchers across the runway. The plane was full of military personnel taking the short flight from Camp Bastion to Kandahar and the atmosphere seemed to be cheerful as we were placed down on to the cabin floor and strapped down tightly. Almost as soon as we were secured I realised the mood had changed. As the plane took off, eyes glanced back and forward at the two casualties lying before them.

THE ROW TO RECOVERY

The oxygen pouring from my mask had dried my mouth and I couldn't get any moisture to wet my lips. I began to panic as I struggled to breathe but was quickly reassured by a nurse who was making the journey home with us. After an ingestion of oral morphine, I relaxed and looked across to Dave. He looked in a lot of pain and after smiling and waving my hand, I began to wonder if I looked as bad. As the plane touched down on Kandahar airfield, I was excited at the prospect of having only one more flight before I'd be back in glorious England.

S4 was the military ward at Selly Oak hospital in which all casualties were treated by an expert team of both military and civilian staff. Once I had been wheeled in to my bay, I was briefly introduced to the military welfare officer. He had lost a leg serving in Iraq and I felt reassured as he went through the plan of action. I was to be meeting the senior medical team in a short while and they would be-able to explain to me in more detail about the treatment I required.

My family had all converged in the hospital waiting room and as they poured in to my bay, an overwhelming sense of happiness engulfed me. It's a memory that will stay with me for the rest of my life. They were surprised by how well I looked. My hair was sun-dyed and I looked tanned and healthy. It must have been hard for them to see me lying in a hospital bed, with my exact injuries not fully understood. It is something that I look back on and try to imagine from their perspective. They too had to deal with the reality of a life-changing injury.

Later that evening my twin brother Adam, my best friend, tried to sum up the situation. 'How I see it, mate,' he said, 'it's like you're mowing the lawn and all of a sudden the lawnmower blows up. It's no one's fault. You were just in the wrong place at the wrong time.'

I said it was nothing like a bloody lawnmower accident! But he was putting things into perspective. He wanted me to know it wasn't my fault.

As he left for the night and the ward lights went out, I looked ahead to the operation that was to follow the next morning. I was down for an exploration of my sciatic nerve to see how badly it was damaged and to see if it could be repaired. I was excited at the prospect of taking the first step to recovery.

After five days in Selly Oak I learned the full extent of my injuries. My right femur had been shattered and required reinforcing with a metal plate attached to the bone by eight tiny screws. My sciatic nerve had been completely lacerated and had been repaired by taking sections from a nerve in my lower left leg. The pieces of nerve were then grafted on to my injured nerve in the hope it would eventually grow and return function to my lower right leg. Fragmentation from the explosion had blown a seven centimetre hole through the bottom of my right foot and the surgeons had luckily managed to close the wound without the need for a skin graft. The nerve block had been removed a day earlier, but I was unable to move my right leg. The surgery was pioneering and although I was in a lot of pain, I knew I was being well taken care of.

Danny Nield's body had been repatriated a week earlier and his funeral was fast approaching. Time seemed to have stood still since the explosion and reality had become a mixture of family visits and bed baths by the nurses. I desperately wanted to attend Danny's funeral and pay my respects but it was out of the question. Making the journey to the cemetery in Cheltenham would be far too dangerous, despite how strong I felt. I had open wounds and my immune system was working overtime. Deeply saddened to be missing his funeral, I decided to write a letter to his parents. My mother was there at the time visiting and after scribbling on some lined paper, it was obvious my handwriting was not up to scratch. She offered to rewrite the letter and once sealed I handed it across to Dave Maclean who was stable enough to make the trip. Despite my frustrations, I felt reassured that Danny's parents would receive my letter.

'Your recovery will be long and, with the nerve damage you have sustained, it will be at least two years until you can walk again.'

THE ROW TO RECOVERY

The doctor had ambushed me during breakfast a few days after I arrived at Selly Oak and I had been totally unprepared for the news. Two years seemed like a hell of a long time. My heart sank, but at the same time I promised myself I would never let my injury defeat me. Just an hour later a nurse approached my bed and told me I'd picked up an infection through the dust being sucked into my body as the metal fragments ripped through my skin and into my soft tissue. Gram negative bacteria had invaded my wounds and an infection known as *Acinetobacter baumannii* was threatening not only my health but the health of others around me. If it was allowed to travel freely around my body it would lead to extreme wound healing complications and if allowed to strengthen enough to enter my bloodstream it could migrate to my major organs and cause my death. I was extremely concerned by this new development but remained confident the amazing team on ward S4 would take care of me.

I was immediately moved to an isolation bay, a single room in which people entering had to wear face masks and protective clothing. A nurse attached a bag of antibiotics to the drip stand next to my bed and, after attaching it to the canula in my arm, left me to it. The next four weeks in isolation involved near constant visits from my family, medical staff and members of the welfare team. Every Tuesday morning there would be a walk round by the doctors who would decide my fate for the following week.

When the day finally came to go home it was the end of March and I'd been in hospital for eight weeks. The *Acinetobacter* infection was under control and, with a bag full of antibiotics, painkillers and dressings, I said my goodbyes and was taken home to Nottingham.

The first time I attended Headley Court I was there for just two days. An abscess had formed on the inside of one of my newly closed wounds and a soft bubble appeared on the outside of my right hip. I was sent straight back to Selly Oak. A screw had sheared off the metal plate stabilising the shattered femur and a pocket of infection had formed. I was in hospital for another six weeks during which time it became clear the metal plate in my leg wasn't strong enough and needed replacing with an intra-medullary nail. It was to be the first of five operations to change the metalwork in my leg.

Another ten weeks passed before I was back at the five-star rehabilitation complex of Headley Court. By the time I was treated there it was an amazing place full of state-of-the-art equipment and dynamic-thinking staff who want you to succeed. I spent my first year of rehabilitation on crutches and then gradually transferred on to two walking sticks, and then one. The rehab was interwoven with hospital appointments and ultimately surgery which meant me returning to crutches in the middle of 2010. The process then began all over again. Once I was able to rehab again after the surgery I was back at Headley Court regaining fitness and mobility.

During the Row2Recovery campaign I was the fittest I have been since my injury and was able to enjoy a gap year from surgery to achieve something truly special. But I am now once again back on crutches following surgery to lengthen my right femur in an effort to improve my mobility further. I am due to leave the British Army in March 2013 and if all goes well, by the end of 2013 – almost five years after my injury – I will be walking without the need for any mobility aids.

CHAPTER 7
REFLECTIONS
By Sam Peters

I came across a poem while I was researching this book. It was written on a specially adapted computer by a young soldier named Stephen Vause who, at the age of 19, was left wheelchair-bound and unable to speak or swallow after a mortar attack in Basra, Iraq, in 2007 left him paralysed. Stephen's injuries were so severe that he was not expected to survive. But survive he did. Today, Stephen has left the Army but requires 24-hour medical care. His treatment programme is no longer the responsibility of the Ministry of Defence, it is in the hands of the National Health Service. Stephen's mother, Jessica Cheesman, has kindly given her permission for us to print Stephen's poem here.

As I See It
by Rifleman Stephen Vause

When I was just a little kid
I liked to fool around
I often played some footie
On grass or solid ground

I'd love to play a friendly match
As yet I cannot start
Cos when we fought the war on terror
They blew my world apart

I worry for my comrades
As they are still out there
I'd like them to come home to us
But life just isn't fair

Sam she was my girlfriend
So beautiful and bright
But now that we have parted
I think it's pretty shite

My mum, she has a new dog
Milo is his name
I cannot bring him here with me
And that's a crying shame

SOOOOOO

I'd really like to speak again
To tell you how I feel
I'd really like to eat again
To have a decent meal

To help me mend with greater speed
The hand of friendship's all I need
To all my friends I love so much
I'm glad that you all keep in touch

REFLECTIONS

Stephen is one of many former servicemen and women severely wounded in the line of duty, who will require long-term care for decades to come.

During the past two years it has been an honour and privilege to be a part of the Row2Recovery campaign. Getting to know the crew members, their families, the charity's supporters and volunteers has been an enormously rewarding, humbling and sometimes emotional experience. If there is one lesson I will take from the whole experience it is that life-changing injuries do not only change the lives of those who suffer them, but also the families and loved ones who face the consequences on a daily basis.

As an 18-year-old I spent a year between school and university commissioned as a second lieutenant into the Royal Regiment of Fusiliers as part of the now defunct Short Service Limited Commission scheme. Three bouts of rugby-related shoulder surgery at university subsequently put paid to my hopes of becoming more than the 'civvy in uniform' I'd been during my brief spell with the Regiment's second battalion in Celle, Germany, in 1996/97.

In October 2010 I agreed to get involved with Alex and Ed's inspirational mission to raise £1 million because I fundamentally believe men and women who are prepared to make the ultimate sacrifice for their country must, if injured in the line of duty, be provided the ultimate medical care in return. And the families who support those soldiers should in turn be supported themselves. It's the same reason the likes of Steve King, Diana Rose, Tom Rose, James Grant, Jon Hodge, Paddy Nichol, Dan Chapman, Will Pollen, Bobby Thatcher, Oli Jedrej, Christina Boyle, Liza Mitchell, Tim Kelly, my wife Debs, and countless others – you know who you are and thank you – have given so much of their time to the Row2Recovery campaign and asked for nothing in return. It's the same reason so many brilliant service charities are able to deliver critical care, often on a shoestring budget through a nationwide network of volunteers. It's because, like so many people in Britain today, we care about the welfare of the young men and women who go to war in our name.

Since getting involved with Row2Recovery I have again looked on in awe at the determination, focus and professionalism of the average British soldier, wounded or not. The courage and stoicism of our wounded servicemen, women and their families is something our country should be proud of. They are the backbone of Britain, and should be treated as such. 'Inspiring a generation' has become an almost hackneyed phrase since the Olympics, but as inspirational role models go, we need look no further than our military. Men like Neil Heritage.

It never crossed my mind when I first got involved that it would result in me writing a book. But as I stood on the jetty as the crew pulled in to Port St Charles marina to the acclaim of hundreds present, and thousands watching remotely, it was clear this was a story that needed to be told in its entirety. For me, the story was always as much about each crew member's individual journey from the battlefield, as it was the epic collective journey across the Atlantic. I dearly hope that sentiment has been reflected in these pages.

It was so right that the crossing had a happy ending. There were times when we all doubted it would. But through Ed's calm leadership, and the courage, determination and sheer ingenuity of the crew, they were able to deliver an astonishingly positive story of triumph over adversity. Seeing their arrival at Port St Charles was a moment that will live with all of us who were lucky enough to have been present. In a media landscape so often dominated by doom and gloom, it provided a welcome beacon of light. For that, every single person who has contributed to the campaign should take enormous credit.

But while the end of the row was rightly greeted with a wonderful outpouring of joy, the fight goes on for our crew and their families, just as it does for so many young men and women like Stephen Vause in this country right now. For Neil, Rory, Carl and Will, the battle to return to full physical fitness will never be won completely but, as each man has demonstrated on countless occasions, they will always strive to be the best they can be. That is the strongest message they can possibly send to those young men and women who have only recently been injured or indeed those, like Stephen, who will require care for the rest of their lives. That care will come at a significant economic cost to Britain but as the Row2Recovery campaign has demonstrated, how can you quantify inspiration?

Ed and Alex, while not physically wounded, also face their own challenges in coming to terms with their experiences on the battlefield. Mental and emotional trauma is hard to quantify and is not something people find easy to discuss. For the families of the wounded, too, the scars of war may not be physically obvious, but they also run deep. It is hard to comprehend the mental anguish that spending every waking hour dreading that 'knock on the door' must bring, let alone having to confront the reality of the situation when the knock does happen.

'I still get upset by Will's injury,' says Will's mum Jilly. 'He won't like me for saying that. It's easy to forget when he's wearing long trousers and then I'll see him in a pair of shorts and see his leg and I don't feel comfortable with it even now. I look at photos of him before he went out to Afghanistan and there he is looking whole and perfect. Now he isn't. It's very hard to see your child mutilated.'

Both Alex and Ed were made acutely aware of the families experience by what happened to their friend Tony Harris and his wife Liz. Alex hardly needed any reminding.

'Going to war and seeing combat makes you think about life fundamentally,' he says. 'Life is in the balance there. I never thought, 'Shit, if I die here it will be terrible'. I wasn't worried about that. What I was worried about was, 'If I die here what is the impact on my family? What's the impact on my parents?' That's what concerned me.

'Ultimately, we could have been blown up or injured but it's the families who have to deal with it and they are invisible from a lot of this dialogue. They are the ones who take the hit. I would rather go on tour to Afghanistan than be the person who is left behind for six months.

'We talked about it a lot on the row. Guys were saying, "Seeing stuff like this when I was wounded would have been great for me and for my family". If I had just been wounded and seen wounded guys doing this it would be a really powerful message that it's possible to do it.'

Neil's dad, Ian, understands better than most the impact life-changing injuries can have on a family. 'When your child gets wounded in this way it's all you ever think about,' Ian says. 'It consumes your whole life. People only ever ask about your son, no one ever asks me about my daughter. I couldn't give her the time she needed when it happened. She was mortified. We all were. I'd never considered it would end like it did. Neil had been to Bosnia and two tours of Northern Ireland and come back unscathed. He'd been to Iraq before. We'd had years of him being in war zones.'

Some people have questioned why so many millions of pounds from the charity, private and public sectors, have been spent upgrading facilities at places like Headley Court, Selly Oak Hospital and the Help for Heroes-funded Tedworth House Recovery Centre in Wiltshire. The answer is simple: To provide care and opportunities in the long-term, not just for tomorrow.

The youngest of the wounded are just 18-years-old. Under different circumstances they would be finishing their A-Levels. Instead, they are in Headley Court or Selly Oak, missing multiple limbs and quite possibly their genitals. Society owes these young men a duty of care.

According to a survey carried out by *The New York Times* in 2011, the percentage of injured troops who died from their wounds in Afghanistan and Iraq in 2010 was 7.9 per cent. That was compared to 19.8 per cent in 2005, the year after Neil was injured. During World War II, between 30 and 50 per cent of injured soldiers died from their wounds. That dramatic improvement to a wounded soldier's chances of getting off the battlefield alive can be attributed to a number of factors; from better medical training and lessons learned by soldiers on the ground, to greater availability of better equipped helicopters, to improved practices by more experienced trauma surgeons.

The outcome has been, and will continue to be, more severely wounded servicemen and women living with previously 'unsurvivable' injuries. Further medical advances in the future will only serve to see that trend grow as medical lessons learned on the battlefield are transferred into civilian hospitals.

One of the most rewarding experiences I had while researching the book was putting Will Dixon back in touch with the trauma surgeon who amputated his leg at Camp Bastion Field Hospital in 2009. Major Tom Konig is a specialist registrar in general, vascular and trauma surgery, who has been on multiple tours of Iraq and Afghanistan. Tom's insight into the work of the trauma team at Bastion was utterly compelling, while his calm manner and good humour marked him out as a man the soldiers could trust with their lives. In many ways those doctors and nurses are the unsung heroes, working around the clock carrying out some of the most complex surgery known to mankind. By the end of Tom's last tour he had operated on every single part of the human anatomy and witnessed almost unimaginable horror while maintaining the highest professional standards at all times.

It is so important that medical lessons learned this time around are passed on to future generations. There are certain to be further developments in the future, with the idea of injecting a coolant liquid into injury survivors in order to bring down their core body temperature to keep them in stasis – therefore buying them vital minutes – before being 're-heated' in the operating theatre, just one example of the incredible steps being taken to keep blast victims alive.

But with greater numbers of survivors comes even greater responsibility upon society to care and provide support for veterans returning from the front line. The government may have seen fit to announce that by the end of 2014 all allied combat troops will be withdrawn from Afghanistan, but for thousands of wounded servicemen, women and their families, the battle has only just begun. Once the media spotlight has moved away, the charities face an enormous challenge to keep the wounded soldier narrative in the public consciousness. If they are unable do so, the funds will soon dry up.

When soldiers are discharged from the Army today they are technically no longer the Ministry of Defence's responsibility. Where the line is drawn between MOD care and the NHS remains contentious. There is an argument that the most severely wounded should stay under the MOD's umbrella, in order to prevent them being lost in the NHS system without a voice. The excellence of the care provided 'on the inside' is far from guaranteed upon discharge and uncertainty surrounding the level of prosthetic care 'on the outside' is stopping many wounded servicemen from leaving the Army. With cuts to public services being made across the board in these difficult economic times, charities will be required to plug the gap between decreased supply and increased demand.

Bryn Parry was inspired by men like Neil Heritage, Rory Mackenzie and recent Paralympian Derek Derenalagi to found the wonderful Help for Heroes charity in 2007. Since then it has raised more than £140 million to provide support and long-term care for wounded veterans. Help for Heroes, along with SSAFA, The Soldiers' Charity and all the other splendid service charities, will play a vital role in the coming decades in ensuring those British men and women wounded on the battlefields of Afghanistan and Iraq are not allowed to slip through the care net.

'When you see a 22-year-old who gets his leg blown off, everybody is thinking about him today,' Bryn says. 'But when he's 40, when he's 60, or when he's 80, are we still going to be there for him? We have to be.'

Analysis by the Charities Aid Foundation showed that giving to Armed Forces charities rose by 26.2 per cent in real terms between

2008 and 2010, while donations to all other large charities dropped by an aggregate of 4.3 per cent over the same period. It demonstrates the huge depth of goodwill among the British public for our Armed Forces, but also poses the question, 'Is enough being done by the state to care for their wounded?'

There is much good being done, and the partnership between the MOD and Help for Heroes at Tedworth House, along with the three other personal recovery centres at Catterick, Colchester and Plymouth, is a model for the future. To see so many service charities all operating under one roof also gives hope that more focused and individually tailored support can be delivered in the long-term.

The public has clearly demonstrated an understanding that the Armed Forces do not dictate government policy, they only implement it.

For those wounded and traumatised by the conflicts in Afghanistan and Iraq, and their families, the support they will receive will come in the main from the public purse, although the private sector is beginning to recognise the commercial value in associating with such impressive individuals and projects. Increasingly, big business is aligning itself with the injured soldier's story. It is recognition of their growing status as role models in society. Let's hope the result is even better care for the wounded, and not just commercial opportunism. The early signs at least are promising.

One of the biggest challenges will be managing the expectations of young men used to living outdoor, active lifestyles, who see no reason that should stop just because they have been injured. Prosthetic limb technology has improved so much over the past decade, not least because the demand is so much greater, but as the technology progresses, so often do the costs. Even top-of-the-range prosthetic knee joints can wear out every five years, so if Neil lives until he is 90 he may need another 24 knee-replacement joints at a cost of £15,000 each in his lifetime. That burden will fall on the NHS. With several hundred wounded currently being treated within the Army, we have only seen the very beginning of this process of transition. The early signs are not encouraging.

'The National Health Service is struggling to provide Neil's legs,' says Ian Heritage. 'The private sector can do them no trouble if the funding is there. It would actually save the country money to use the private sector more because the guys would get back into work so much faster. The NHS are forever throwing poorly made sockets and other things away. They are wasting money by trying to do what they cannot do. It should be left with the private sector.'

Stephen Vause's mother Jessica is similarly unconvinced about the NHS's ability to cope with demand in the future. 'At first Stephen's care was brilliant but as time has gone on the quality of the care has deteriorated. The opportunity to access medicines has become a bit of an issue. It seems just as much of a battle now to maintain the quality of care and for Stephen to make progress as it was when he first arrived back in the UK.'

Places such as the Recovery Centres at Tedworth House and elsewhere will provide a haven for both serving and former soldiers to access vital skills training as well as physical, psychological and emotional support. Headley Court will also continue to provide rehabilitation care in the short-term, although its future is less clear. It should, in my view, become a designated 'one-stop shop' for wounded veterans to be able access appropriate prosthetics care because the concern is that the NHS is not equipped with the resources or the knowledge base to deliver on such a large scale.

Neil Heritage, who along with his friend Mick Brennan was the first British soldier of modern times to survive a double traumatic amputation of his legs, still has so far to travel on his own personal journey. But his selflessness and inherent sense of service embodies everything good about our Armed Forces. Neil was cautious about discussing the lack of compensation he received after his injuries in this book. He told me he 'didn't want to come across as a whinger'. It was typical of the man. His reason for getting involved with Row2Recovery had nothing to do with gaining attention, but everything to do with saying 'thank you' to the charities who stepped into the breach when he needed them.

Neil would never make a fuss of his situation because it is not his style, but imagine going through what he has been through, only to be told he was not entitled to a lump sum payment because of the timing of his injury. While he was rehabilitating in Headley Court, he saw fellow soldiers, sometimes with less severe injuries, receiving compensation cheques that would enable them to pay off their mortgages and make them financially secure in order to concentrate on recovering from their injuries. While much good work has been done by the MOD to adequately recompense wounded servicemen, and the Armed Forces Compensation scheme should be broadly welcomed, it seems to me simply wrong not to backdate it to include veterans such as Neil and Mick who were injured before 6th April, 2005.

I recently made an application via the Freedom of Information Act asking the MOD to publish the number of wounded veterans who would be eligible for compensation if the Armed Forces Compensation Scheme was backdated to the start of the War on Terror. They belatedly replied, telling me my question was 'hypothetical' and refusing to publish the apparently innocuous information I'd requested. It is my understanding that the number eligible for the maximum pay out would be in single figures.

It is not my intention to denigrate the MOD, where an enormous amount of work is being done in constrained financial times to ensure the wounded are cared for, but I would urge them to look at this issue again. Neil, typically, considers himself fortunate to have escaped with the injuries he has.

'I'm one of the lucky ones,' he says. 'There are people at Headley Court right now who are going to need nursing care for the rest of their lives. I can pretty much do whatever I want but that's definitely not the case with some of those guys. The really severe brain injuries are the hardest thing to deal with. The physical stuff can be adapted in most ways but you can't really repair a brain. That's really hard for the individuals and for their families. Those are the guys I did the row for. They are the ones who will need support for the rest of their lives.'

Few of those wounded want pity, they just want a chance to live their lives to their fullest potential and not to have to rely on hand-outs. For the majority, like Will and Carl, there is a deep-seated desire not to be defined by their injuries. It is right that they are provided the opportunities to achieve that.

'When you come back from Afghanistan, especially if you're injured, people just think you're a run-of-the-mill guy,' says Carl. 'Sometimes I feel like saying, 'Actually I got injured doing something pretty significant'. When I'm in the gym and I have a brace on my legs people ask me what I've done and you have to explain it. By rowing the Atlantic everyone knew what we'd done.

'I do more now than I've done before. When I'm in the gym I still have the mind-set that I'm fitter than anyone else there.'

It is not just about providing the very best prosthetic technology either. A statistic known only too well in the military community is that more veterans of the Falklands conflict have committed suicide in the intervening 30 years than those killed in the conflict itself (255). Neil's dad, Ian, sums up the concerns many parents of veterans hold.

'I do have fears for Neil's future,' he says. 'By the time he's in his seventies he'll definitely be wheelchair-bound. His heart is a big concern because it takes twice as much energy for him to walk with artificial limbs meaning there's far more pressure on his heart. Having said that, the medical world moves on so you don't know, do you?

'But what worries me most is that more than 250 soldiers died in the Falklands but since then more than that number have committed suicide. That figure worries me. While I don't think he's suffered any terrible short-term mental illness I do worry long term.'

The spectre of PTSD looms for many veterans and can strike years after the event. The Trauma Risk Management process initiated on the battlefield for those involved in high-stress incidents enables soldiers to share their feelings at the time, but it seems upon returning home those not physically injured are provided with few opportunities to talk about what they have been through. As Ed explains so eloquently, often people are afraid to ask difficult questions for fear of causing even more upset or trauma. The provision of more easily accessible confidential counselling services for veterans to talk with other veterans or share their experiences would be an important step forward. It is also clear to me from meeting so many wounded veterans' families that many of them have themselves suffered the effects of PTSD.

As the Paralympic Games demonstrated so joyously, sport can play an enormously important role in providing rehabilitation for men and women who have been brutalised, psychologically or physically, by war. Eight members of the GB Paralympic team had served in the Armed Forces. Expect there to be many, many more in Rio in 2016. Rory Mackenzie learnt to ski as part of Help for Heroes Battle Back programme and has gone on to row the Atlantic, play the lead role in the Paralympic Games closing ceremony and who knows what else in the future? His future, at least, is bright.

'When you get blown up you go from being at the absolute peak of physical fitness, and two seconds later you are in essence regressed to an infant learning to walk again,' Rory says. 'What that does to your mind is sometimes more difficult to deal with than the physical impact.

'I've never done something physical to prove something to anyone, I have done it for psychological rehabilitation. Realising I am still capable of doing things and still able to live a good and active life is so important.

'I missed the wind on my face and I realised sport was the key for me to a healthy mind. For me, learning to ski, having a go on a hand bike, learning to walk, all those sort of things, are about approaching the fact I have one leg. No other reason. All the adrenaline stuff I do now — like wing-walking, Row2Recovery, skiing — is therapy for me. I need to do these things for my own peace of mind. It's about aggressively confronting PTSD before it strikes.'

So let us celebrate the glorious achievements of the Row2Recovery crew and all those they represent. For Carl Anstey, the impact of throwing his heart and soul into the campaign has been dramatic:

'There were three reasons I wanted to do the row,' he says. 'One, to show I could do all the training and complete something and demonstrate my injury wasn't going to hold me back. Two, to raise money for some of the charities who helped me. And, three, to prove to people that with the right support, training, dedication and teamwork it is possible to achieve things that most people would consider impossible.

'Hopefully we were able to show people that with the right attitude and determination there is life beyond injury. Just try different things, don't give up, keep working hard. Hopefully the guys who were recently injured can see that there is a future and that once they've healed up there are opportunities out there.

'When I was injured, lying in the isolation ward staring at the maps on the wall, I knew I wanted to do something, but I didn't know how to go about it. With all the support team around Row2Recovery it was amazing because all the injured guys needed to do was take part in the row. Now I have an idea about what it takes to put a campaign like this together. All the planning, the marketing, the PR and media, the fundraising. I could definitely see myself doing something like this in the future. I'd love to.'

A central part of the Row2Recovery philosophy involved empowering the wounded crew members not just to feel as if they were part of the team, but to actually be part of the team. For Will the satisfaction came from finishing his mission.

'The row has had a huge impact on my life,' he says. 'The time away was incredibly useful for looking at what is important in life and the bigger picture. But my self-esteem and self-confidence have also definitely been boosted. I wasn't lacking confidence before but it was such a positive thing for me to do after my injury. I don't know if closure is the right word because I will live with the consequences of losing my leg for the rest of my life. But

REFLECTIONS

I needed to do it. I have completed this mission and I can hang my hat on that. I am genuinely proud of myself for doing it, in the best possible way I think. I'm just chuffed with myself for doing it.'

Neil, too modest to even consider that he might be an inspiration to others, suffered many dark days in his sometimes tortuous recovery and rehabilitation process.

'The row has made me feel like my old self again, like I did before I got injured,' he says. 'I feel like that bloke again. I changed a fair bit because of my injuries – I became more reserved, shy, I lost a lot of confidence. That's come back since the row. I feel back to normal now. It's been more than seven years since I felt like this.

'You go on a journey and I expected it to feel like an achievement, but for the effects to go far beyond that was completely unexpected. Beyond the physical rehabilitation, the emotional rehabilitation of being able to achieve something like this has been massive. Doing something that not many people have done is a big confidence booster. Especially when it's a challenge that is so physically demanding.

'The message is that life is different but it can still be pretty good. It takes a little while to get there, but things can get back to normal. It's about adapting from what was normal and accepting there's a new normal. That becomes your life and there are a lot of opportunities for us now, things we wouldn't have had if we hadn't been injured. It's about taking the rough with the smooth.'

His dad, Ian, who works as an area manager with South West Trains based out of Poole Station in Dorset, has also had to adjust to a new kind of normal. For him, seven years after seeing Neil hovering on a metaphorical precipice between life and death, his son achieves the extraordinary every single day.

'When Neil first got injured I never thought he'd live a fulfilling life,' he recalls. 'I always thought there'd be something missing. But the last three or four years he's really come on. He plays golf now . . . he's rowed the Atlantic for goodness sake! But it's silly things that really bring it home. Last summer he had a wasps nest in his garage. I had about three goes at getting it out and he got fed up waiting for me, got up on the ladder and pulled the wasps nest down. You can't get more normal than that.

'He came into Poole Station recently on his way up to London. He just walked into the station, bag over his shoulder, bought a ticket to get on the train and walked on like anybody else. I didn't think I'd ever see that. Of all the things he's done, just seeing him do that was so special. It was so normal. He was just like anybody else.'

From the seed of an idea in Ed's head grew a magnificent two-year campaign which has inspired thousands already and, hopefully, through this book, will continue to do so for years to come. Barely a week before this book went to print the original £1 million fundraising total was reached. That money will be needed for many years.

'Never in my wildest dreams did I expect it to get as big as it did,' says Ed. 'It has been absolutely overwhelming. We are just ordinary people, none of us were necessarily outstanding in our fields, in the Army or at home. The point is: Anyone can do this.'

For once Ed is wrong. Everybody involved in Row2Recovery, and everybody the charity was set up for, is extraordinary. Beyond injury, achieving the extraordinary.

THE ROW TO RECOVERY ROLL OF SUPPORTERS

Hazel R. Abendschein
Ian Adam
Ralph & Lynn Ainsworth
The Alcock Family, Staffs
Vince Alongi
Adam William Anstey
Chris & Emma Anstey
Stephen Anstey
Derek & Marjorie Anstey
Donna Arbuthnott
Atlantic Campaigns SL
Oliver & Victoria Back
Alan Bailey
Miss Jayne E Baker
Sgt Jay Baldwin 1PWRR (Tigers)
Barbados Council for the Disabled
Paul Barnes
Lee Bartley
Baz
Nicholas Beazley
Catherine Bedford
James Bedford
Willa Bedford
Andy Bexley
Steve Bodger
Adam Boon
Aly Boswell
Jes C. Boyle-Moller
BP plc

Pamela Brider
Glen Brodie
Fraser & Emmeline Brown
Dave Burgess
Sharon Anne Canning
Captive Minds Communications
Cayenne Asset Management Ltd
Jo Chadderton
Hannah Chambers
Stephanie Clark
Stephen Clark TD Trustee ABF
Jane and John Clifford OBE
Clifton College Prep School
Oli Cochrane & Jess Houlgrave
James Compston, TD
Iain Conn
Ben Conway
Anne-Louise Creasey
Nicola Dadswell
Margrethe Dantzer
Mr & Mrs John Davies
Leigh Davies
Tyron Dawkins (Oakley UK)
Patrick de Pelet
Samuel E. Deards
Isabella Dixon
Jilly Dixon
Robert Dixon
Sean Doherty

THE ROW TO RECOVERY

Rowena Doodson
James Duffy
Ian Duffy
Rachel Eden Moore
Stuart Edgar
Lee Ellaway
Mary Elliott
John Emery ex 143 Plant Sqdn RE (v)
Debbie Emmett
Rodney Fleming
Alan Fotheringham
John & Helen Franklin
Sarah Franklin
Lionel and Ann French
Stevie G and Lou Wilson
Len Gayler
Rita Gayler
Kat Gayler
Georgie Gayler
Rosella Gilbert
Gill (R2R Clothing Sponsor)
Mary and Malcolm Glenister
Chrissy & Nigel Golding
Stephen Goodenough
Karen Goodyer
Sara & Jamie Grant
Edward F.W.A Grant
Sue Grant-Marshall
Alex Gray Muir
Jane A Gregory Tighe (Carl's mum)
Edward Griffiths
Sarah Hale
Matt Hamilton
Sally-Ann Hatcliffe
James Hayward
Elly Hayward
Freddie Hayward
Thomas Hayward
Gerry Hayward
Jill Hayward

Ian Frank Heritage
Mathew Heritage
Annabel Hickox
Faye & Mike Hornby
Kelly Howarth
Tom Howe
Jenny Hunter
Capt Gregg Hutchison
Sharon Inch FCIPD – Oliver Valves Ltd
Elton & Debbie James
Kris Jane
Robin and Isabelle Janvrin
Helen and Louis Janvrin
Alice Janvrin
Felix Janvrin
Philip and Lotte Jarvis
The Joel family from Chesterfield
Tiarnan and Emilie Keenan
Dr Tom Konig
Jon-Michael Lindsey
Catherine Lindstrom
Frank & Ann Lomax
Corporal Daniel Lowrie 1 Mercian
Fred and Emma Mackenzie
Andrew Mackenzie
Ginnie Mackenzie
Taylor Manning
Pamela J Marchant
Marine Camera Solutions
Kirstie Martin
Chris Martin
Peter Mather
Nick May
Mr David Merrie
Mr Trevor Merrie
Mr Keith Merrie MBE
Dave Methuen
Andy Mihalop
Liza Mitchell and Michael Mitchell

THE ROW TO RECOVERY ROLL OF SUPPORTERS

Cecilia Morgan
Julia Morgan
Juliet Mosney
Jenny Mumford
Rachel, Josh and Chloe Myhill
Captain Paddy Nicoll
D.L & D.G Nomad Medical
   Solutions
Matthew Nunan
Mike & Julie Orme
Nikki Park (Chichacoca)
Edward Parker
Steve Parker – Reg. Coord. H4H
Jenny and Roy Peters
Tom & Kavita Peters
Alex & Hilary Petrie
Olivia Plunkett
Gary Pursell
Alexis Rawlinson
Sara Reeves
Chris Reid
Jen Reid
Ken Reid
Jayne Reynolds
Alistair Rich
Alma Rippon
Henry Roberts
Vince & Heulwen Roberts
Michael Robinson
James Rolfe
Tom and Diana Rose
John & Caroline Rowland
Pamela Salter
Hayley Saunders-Somerville

The Setchell Family – Cambs
Mike Shepperd
Michael and Julien Sheridan
Belinda Sims
James Skipwith
Hilary Smith
Michael & Valerie Spencer
Mary Stephens
JJ Stirling
Tiger Team
Tony Tighe (Carl's step dad)
Jenny & Francis Tilsley
Arnold Torch
Alan Towle
Rosamund Trembath
Rose Vivaciou
Liam Conway Wakeman
Nick Wall
Ruth D Warden
Christine Warren
Clare Watson
Miles Webb (Major retd)
Sally & Ken Webb IMOf Dan Read
Janet Welch & Family
Russ Welburn, York
Adrian Welsh
Phil Williams
James M Willoughby
Anna Wilson
Miss Alexandra Wood
Graham Woodley
Daniel Wright
The Young Family, Crowthorne

The Row2Recovery would like to thank Talisker for their support during the campaign

EST^D 1830

TALISKER™

SINGLE MALT
SCOTCH WHISKY